I Kings
TORN IN TWO

Yeshivat Har Etzion ישיבת הר עציון

MAGGID

Alex Israel

I Kings
Torn in Two

מלכים א׳

Maggid Books
Yeshivat Har Etzion

1 Kings:
Torn in Two

First Edition, 2013
Second Printing, 2020

Maggid Books
An imprint of Koren Publishers Jerusalem Ltd.

POB 8531, New Milford, CT 06776-8531, USA
& POB 4044, Jerusalem 91040, Israel
www.korenpub.com

Cover Design: Yehudit Cohen

The publication of this book was made possible
through the generous support of *Torah Education in Israel.*

ISBN 978-1-61329-004-0, *hardcover*

A CIP catalogue record for this title is
available from the British Library.

Printed and bound in the United States

Dedicated to my dear parents,
Frances and Henry Israel

Contents

Introduction and Acknowledgments

I witness the magic of Bible study on a regular basis. My students sit in the *beit midrash* and embark upon a study of *Nevi'im Rishonim* (the Former Prophets). They study in pairs – the traditional *ḥavruta* study format – reading one chapter at a time, wrestling with the text and its commentaries, encountering timeless biblical characters, rejoicing with the triumphs and feeling disappointment at the failures of Jewish history. We convene in class to place the narrative in its historical and geographical context, examining the language, structure, and message of the chapter at hand. As we progress, the biblical figures become living, complex personalities, and we begin to absorb the powerful spiritual lessons of the prophetic books. Ideally, we supplement our textual study by stepping outside the classroom to visit the sites at which the ancient events transpired: Shiloh, for example, in the footsteps of King Saul, or the City of David, engaging with the persona of King David. At these moments, I see the light shine in my students' eyes as they begin to synchronize with the contours of the text, as the biblical text comes alive with new vibrancy and relevance.

My hope is that some of this wonder can be transmitted through this book. It is addressed to a *ḥavruta* in a yeshiva or seminary, to a mother and daughter studying a chapter of *Navi* each Shabbat afternoon, to a teacher preparing a class, or to university students in an evening study group. This book is not an academic work or a close commentary on every phrase in Kings. It seeks to supplement the study of the Bible itself, offering a context, a wider perspective, and a deeper focus upon Kings' structure and central themes. Kings can be impenetrable for many readers due to its complicated timeline and wealth of details. I hope this book will serve as a companion volume, weaving the various threads of Kings into a meaningful tapestry. It will thus be best read alongside a reading of Kings itself.

I have called the book *1 Kings: Torn in Two*. This title partially reflects a key feature of 1 Kings – namely, the division of the kingdom. However, it is also a paraphrase of an expression in chapter 18: "How long will you waver between two opinions?" With this celebrated phrase, Elijah criticizes the wavering, the indecision, the two-mindedness of Israel as it struggles between its commitment to God and the idolatry of Baal. To my mind, this challenge encapsulates much of the inner drama of Kings. The nation as a whole is caught between monotheism and idol worship. The heroes of Kings too, are entangled in conflicting extremes. King Solomon is torn between his imperial wealth and influence on the one hand, and adherence to God on the other. Jeroboam clings to power but must decide whether to replace the Temple and Jerusalem. Ahab wavers between God and Baal, and between two influential personalities pulling in opposite directions – Jezebel and Elijah. Kings is full of this-worldly religious dilemmas and clashing cultural forces.

In this regard, Kings bears a deep relevance to contemporary times, as we too find ourselves pulled – between tradition and modernity, between universalism and particularism, between our duty to God's law and our own desires, between Judaism and other pursuits. Many of the struggles depicted in Kings are our dilemmas, and through the study of these chapters we can learn lessons about our own personal and national conflicts and seek enlightenment from the words of the prophet, gaining from the experience of our forebears.

This book could not have been created without my studies at Yeshivat Har Etzion, an institution that was a formative influence upon my learning and my religious worldview. From its inception, the yeshiva pioneered Bible study as a central component of the curriculum, innovatively combining a traditional approach – loyalty to the masoretic text and veneration for Ḥazal and traditional commentaries – with a *peshat* reading of the biblical narrative.

From my first classes with Rabbi Menachem Leibtag, and later with Rabbi Yoel Bin-Nun, my eyes were opened to the big picture of the Bible – not a verse-by-verse reading with commentaries, but broad structures spanning entire books. Over the years, I was exposed to literary techniques such as patterning, parallelism, intertextuality, chiastic structures, and leading words. These are methods employed by Midrash and traditional commentators, although more systematically developed by modern scholarship. Beyond the text itself, the perception of the Bible's historical, political, and geographical context also brings biblical stories into clearer focus. The infusion of these techniques into the *beit midrash* continues to unveil new avenues of reading and understanding the Bible. This textual and contextual approach is the toolbox I have employed in my studies, and it is the method we shall follow in this book. However, I should add that just as we place one eye upon the raw biblical text, our other eye looks toward Ḥazal, our rabbinic interpreters. As will be evident throughout this work, rabbinic readings play a focal role in critically reading and understanding the Bible. Throughout this book, we shall mediate a dynamic dialogue between the text itself and the views of our sages.

I am indebted to my teachers – first and foremost, Rabbi Leibtag, who introduced me to Bible study and continues to be a role model, a mentor, and a dear friend. Studying with master teachers and scholars of Bible such as Rabbis David Nativ, Yoel Bin-Nun, Yaakov Medan, Mordechai Sabato, and Elchanan Samet has been a formative experience, shaping my understanding, knowledge, and approach to Bible study; I am indebted to them. In addition, I thank my dear and revered *rashei yeshiva*, Rabbi Yehuda Amital, *z"l*, and Rabbi Aharon Lichtenstein, *shlit"a*, whose religious personalities and philosophies have shaped and guided my vision of Judaism and the path of my life.

This book is a direct result of almost twenty years of teaching Bible in wonderful Torah institutions. I would like to thank my students and the administrations of Midreshet Harova, Midreshet Lindenbaum,

Orot, Emuna VeOmanut, the Pardes Institute, and Yeshivat Eretz HaTzvi for providing me with an opportunity to bring Torah alive, introducing new students each year to the wonders of Bible study. I want to thank in particular my class of 5771 at Eretz HaTzvi for its overwhelming enthusiasm and encouragement regarding this book, and my students at Pardes for assisting me in clarifying several chapters.

The initial manuscript was written as an online series for the Israel Koschitzky Virtual Beit Midrash (VBM) of Yeshivat Har Etzion. The VBM is one of the prime resources available for Bible study worldwide, and I am proud to be part of its team. The VBM's weekly deadlines and the structure it gave me were the framework that created this book. Thank you to Rabbi Reuven Ziegler, Debra Berkowitz, and Rabbi Ezra Bick for giving me this opportunity.

Thanks also to Koren Publishers, and in particular to Matthew Miller for his instantaneous enthusiasm in publishing this book. Thanks to Gila Fine, Rabbi Reuven Ziegler, and the entire Maggid team for professionally chaperoning the process from the moment I delivered the manuscript to the printing of this book.

Thanks to my friends and colleagues who read sections or chapters of the book in various stages of its creation: Rabbi Shalom Berger, Rabbi Zvi Grumet, Rabbi Gideon Sylvester, and Rivky Krestt. A particular thank you is due to Rabbi Yitzchak Blau, a dear friend, who encouraged and pressured me to embark upon this journey of authoring a book and never ceased to inquire about it over the past three years.

It would have been impossible to write this book outside of Israel. For me, the entire Bible is interwoven with our national existence, flowing out of the text and into the hills and valleys of our beloved land, through the battlefields and the corridors of government, and to our collective life as a nation-state. Our national return to *Eretz Yisrael* and God's gift of the State of Israel have reconnected us with our national drama in a sense that previous, less privileged generations were unable to grasp. It is not incidental that our return to the land and to Jewish sovereignty has generated a reawakening of Tanakh study. I thank God for the overwhelming privilege of living in our sweet land, in an astonishing era of Jewish pride, independence, and hope. The very fact that

I can teach the pages of the Bible daily in the holy city of Jerusalem is nothing short of a miracle of Jewish history.

Upon leaving the study hall, the Talmud records an ancient prayer that thanks God for "placing my lot among those who sit in the *beit midrash*" (*Berakhot* 28b). I echo these sentiments as I thank God for my good fortune at being able to make my career in the field of Jewish education, filling my days with Torah study and having the privilege of infusing others with a love of Torah. This daily experience is not taken for granted, and is a deep source of fulfillment and joy.

This book is dedicated to my wonderful parents. From them I absorbed the ethos of Torah and *derekh eretz*, love of Israel, learning, communal service and leadership, Jewish education, and the *joie de vivre* of Judaism. All that I have achieved is built upon the foundation they gave me. May they continue to thrive in good health, surrounded by their family here in *Eretz Yisrael*.

Aḥaron aḥaron ḥaviv – to my dear family, my pride and joy. To my children, Avinoam, Maayan, Hillel, and Yehuda, and to my wife, Aliza, I thank you for all your support, love, and inspiration. A special thank you to Aliza for putting up with my long hours at the computer, and for her extensive assistance and endless patience and encouragement with this book. My prayer is aptly expressed in the traditional words that mark the conclusion of Torah study: "that the Torah never depart from us or from our descendants."

Alex Israel
Elul 5772
Alon Shvut

Background
to the Book of Kings

WHO WROTE THE BOOK OF KINGS?

The book of Kings documents a retrospective of the four hundred years of history from Solomon to the exile, from the advent of the Temple to its destruction. Whereas we can never be certain of the precise authorship of biblical books, Ḥazal and academic sources concur that Kings was composed from the vantage point of the Temple's demise and the nation's exile.[1] The Talmud asserts that the author was none other than the prophet Jeremiah:

> Jeremiah wrote his book [the book of Jeremiah], Kings, and Lamentations. (*Bava Batra* 14b–15a)[2]

---

1. Academic opinion is divided regarding the date of Kings' composition; for a good summary, see *The Biblical Encyclopedia* (Jerusalem: Bialik Institute, 1962), vol. 4, s.v. "book of Kings," cols. 1141–43 [Hebrew]. Because the book speaks at length about the Temple's destruction but fails to mention Cyrus and the permission to return to Jerusalem, most Bible scholars support an authorship after the destruction of the Temple in 586 BCE and before the Cyrus declaration in 538. The basis of this claim is Kings' closing statement, thirty-seven years after the exile of Jehoiachin (in 561–560 BCE), some scholars maintain that the book was composed in Babylon. Others claim that the fact that there is no depiction of the exiles in Babylonia points to authorship in Eretz Yisrael, possibly closer to the destruction.
2. The introduction to the *Da'at Mikra* commentary on Kings gathers significant internal literary evidence that Jeremiah in fact authored the book. See Yehuda Kiel, *Da'at*

1

For an entire generation, Jeremiah campaigned desperately to avert the catastrophe of the Temple's destruction. He failed – the great prophet was forced to endure the painful tragedy of the destruction and Israel's subsequent exile. In the aftermath of any disaster, people respond by posing the question: What went wrong? The book of Kings seeks to survey and examine the First Temple period in response to that very question, hoping to learn the lessons of the past and avoid its recurrence. From a prophetic perspective, this book is an investigation and spiritual evaluation of an era.

The book of Kings targets the leadership in particular, evaluating – king by king – which leaders accelerated the path to destruction and who reversed the momentum, turning instead to God. Every king, from construction to destruction, is surveyed in order to understand his part in the national collapse.

But Kings goes further, identifying one specific area of deviance as the core of the problem – the sin of idolatry. Hence, when a king is described as "doing that which is right in the eyes of the Lord" or "doing evil in the eyes of the Lord," it is always a function of the purity of his worship of God or, conversely, his attraction to and involvement in idolatry. This is a focused book, pinpointing idol worship and its associated practices as the key criterion for national ruin.[3]

THE STRUCTURE OF THE BOOK OF KINGS

Nowadays, the book of Kings is divided into two sections – I and II – but that is not its original form. The Talmud speaks of Kings as a single book, as does Josephus. The separation into two segments, instigated by the Greek Septuagint, is not inherent to the book and did not feature in Hebrew versions until the Venice printing of the Bible in 1517. The dividing point between I and II is rather awkward, interrupting the reign of

---

Mikra, 1 Kings (Jerusalem: Mossad Harav Kook, 1989), 202–08 [Hebrew].

3.   Other crimes feature as well – for example, murder and misappropriation of property in the story of Ahab and the vineyard of Naboth (1 Kings 21). But the critical factor of whether a king is assessed as "good" or "bad" is certainly a product of the idolatry issue. Moreover, a comparison with parallel books – such as Chronicles and Amos – demonstrates that whereas they address a wider range of religious values, Kings focuses almost exclusively on idolatry.

kings Jehoshaphat and Ahaziah and the stories of Elijah. When we try to understand the structure of Kings, we will perceive it as an organic whole.

That structure is difficult to discern. On the one hand, scholars have noted three sections:

1. United monarchy   I Kings 1–11
2. Divided kingdom   I Kings 12–II Kings 17
3. United monarchy   II Kings 18–25

Others have identified a more sophisticated, chiastic structure:[4]

A1	Solomon: United monarchy	I Kings 1–11
B1	Jeroboam: Rise of northern kingdom	I Kings 12–13
C1	Kings of Judah/Israel	I Kings 14–16
D1	House of Omri: Elijah and Elisha	I Kings 16–II Kings 11
C2	Kings of Judah/Israel	II Kings 12–16
B2	Fall and exile of northern kingdom	II Kings 17
A2	Kingdom of Judah	II Kings 18–25

This outline charts the entire book in a rise-and-fall motion, a trajectory of ascent and decline. Segment A1 represents the rise of the nation to its imperial height; A2 charts its slow fall, through the crushing Assyrian invasion in the time of Hezekiah to its final demise at the hands of the Babylonians. Similarly, segment B1 presents us with the rise of Jeroboam, mandated by God to establish the northern kingdom. Yet that kingdom sets up images of golden calves, almost immediately violating God's command; B2 charts its fall. The central stage (D1) charts the rise of Baal worship in the northern kingdom during the reigns of Omri and his son, Ahab, narrating the continued domination of idolatry in the kingdom and the terrible aftermath, as Israel reels from Aramean military incursion. This stage ends with the demise of the ruling house of Omri by God's command in the form of Jehu's bloody revolt.

---

4. See George Savran, "1 and 2 *Kings*," in Robert Alter and Frank Kermode, eds., *The Literary Guide to the Bible* (Cambridge: Harvard University Press, 1987), 146–64.

Significantly, this section highlights the central role of the prophet in guiding the nation, depicting Elijah's determined battle against Baal, followed by the story of his student, Elisha. This symmetrical understanding of the book reveals its unity and form.[5]

LITERARY STYLE

Notwithstanding the neat structural framework we have suggested, Kings' texture is uneven. The book comprises several luxuriously long narrative segments – the reigns of Solomon and Jeroboam, the Elijah and Elisha stories, the reigns of Hezekiah and Josiah – but these sections are linked by a series of brief, formulaic accounts of kings.

Nonetheless, we can identify a stylistic unity and rhythmic consistency to Kings, particularly in the manner in which each and every king is depicted according to a fixed formula. This standardized language provides a regulated structure, a backbone or outline to the book. In general, the account of each king contains the following elements:[6]

1. the year the king ascends the throne;
2. the length of his reign;
3. for the kings of Judah, the king's age upon ascent to the throne,[7] and the name of his mother;[8]
4. a religious assessment of whether he "did that which was right in the eyes of the Lord,"[9] or "he did evil in the eyes of the Lord."[10]

---

5. The vertex or pivot of this entire structure is Elijah's ascent to heaven. Indeed, one ongoing theme of Kings is the power of prophecy and its role in guiding the king to a leadership that is faithful to God.

6. This style and these specific formulations apply to all the kings recorded in the book of Kings, but there are sections in which we read a sequence of terse formulaic summaries. For example, see I Kings 15–16 and II Kings 13–15.

7. The two exceptions to this rule are the kings Abijam and his son Asa (I Kings 15:1, 9).

8. The king's mother, or at times grandmother, seems to have held an elevated status in the palace. She was known as *gevira* (often translated as queen). For more information, see ahead, I Kings 15 – Civil War n. 9. Only two kings' mothers are not recorded altogether: those of Jehoram son of Jehoshaphat (II Kings 8:16) and Ahaz (II Kings 16).

9. For example, I Kings 15:1; II Kings 12:3, 14, 3; 15:3, 34; 18:3; 22:2.

10. For example, I Kings 11:1; 15:26, 34; 16:25, 30; II Kings 8:37; 13:2; 14:24; 15:9; 21:2, 20.

One of the most interesting instances of these standard-ized religious evaluations regards King Zimri. He ruled for only seven days, yet Kings tells us that "he did evil in the eyes of God, walking in the path of Jeroboam and the sins he had committed and caused Israel to commit" (16:20). Did he really do all that in a week? Rather, this is a code, a standard assessment format applied by the author of Kings to every king, good or bad.

Beyond these basic appraisals, supplementary phrases are used in evaluating the kings. Regarding religiously loyal kings of Judah, we read: "But the high places did not cease to function; the people still sacrificed and offered at the high places" (22:44).[11] In the northern kingdom, the phrase usually relates to Jeroboam as a baseline: "And he walked in the path of Jeroboam and his sins" (15:34).[12] There are also references to King David: "He continued in all the sins his father had committed; he was not wholehearted with the Lord...like his father David" (15:3), or he "did what was right in God's eyes, like his father David" (15:10).

5. Milestones of his reign: Following the aforementioned introduc-tory information, we may hear of wars, victories, or invasions, events that concern the Temple and its treasuries, or impressive construction and civil achievements – or of assassinations and conspiracies.

6. Concluding elements: The account of the king closes with his death and burial, frequently mentioning his successor. At times, a reference will be made to other historical sources – "the Book of Chronicles of the Kings of Judah" or its counterpart, "the Book of Chronicles of the Kings of Israel" – which provide more details about the king.

7. Correlation and synchronization: The book of Kings synchro-nizes the kingdoms of Judah and Israel, ensuring that as we progress with the one, we never lose hold of the other; the stories of both kingdoms are told in tandem. This feature makes an unequivocal statement that the Jewish people is a single unit.

---

11. See also I Kings 3:2, 15:14; II Kings 12:4; 14:4; 15:4, 35.
12. See also I Kings 15:26; 16:7, 19, 26, 31; 22:53; II Kings 3:3; 10:29–31; 13:2, 11; 15:18, 24.

The kingdoms of Israel and Judah each constitute equal and legitimate organs of the Jewish nation, both bearing the blame for its destruction.

THE SOURCES OF THE BOOK OF KINGS AND THE NATURE OF PROPHECY

Some people mistake the book of Kings for a royal archive of sorts, listing the technical statistics of ancient Israelite kings. Nothing could be further from the truth.

Royal archives clearly existed during the period in which Kings was written; chapter 11 refers us to "the Book of the Words of Solomon" (11:41), and other references are made to the chronicles of the kings of Judah or Israel.[13] These books, the royal annals that recorded and publicized the king's victories and achievements, were lost over the course of time. From his mention of these parallel works, we see that the author of Kings used the historical works at his disposal, and this comes as no surprise – one would hardly expect the prophet to know how many years a king reigned on the basis of prophecy. Thus, given that historical information was accessible, we can assume that any stylistic brevity in Kings is deliberate. It is not a product of insufficient source material, but rather a means of distilling the data and focusing on the religious lessons of the book.

Kings is not a history book. Although the prophet grafted his prophetic perspective onto a historical frame, it has an overtly religious agenda. In contrast to royal-sponsored histories, 1 Kings is exceedingly critical of monarchs and, more often than not, records their shortcomings and failures. This is one of the surest proofs that this book did not emerge from royal sources. Prophetic works are highly subversive readings of history; no royal-sponsored work would ever record the flaws and sins of a monarch in the manner of the book of Kings. The king would never allow a litany of this sort to be published! Rather, Kings transmits

---

13. 1 Kings 14:19, 29; 15:7, 23, 31; 16:5, 14, 20; 22:40. This is not the only time the Bible refers to outside works. Elsewhere, there is reference to "the Book of the Upright" (II Sam. 1:18) and "the Book of the Wars of God" (Num. 21:14).

a religious and educational message, interpreting events and evaluating them in accordance with the standards of the Torah.

TIMING PROBLEMS IN THE BOOK OF KINGS

One difficulty endemic to the book of Kings is numerical disparity; the years of the kings of Judah and Israel do not quite match up.

For example, in 1 Kings 15:1–2 we are told that in the eighteenth year of Jeroboam's rule over Israel, Abijam began his reign over Judah and ruled for three years. Next, we read in 15:9–10 that in Jeroboam's twentieth year, Asa reigned over Judah. But if Abijam was king for three years, Asa should have ascended the throne in Jeroboam's twenty-first year! This is a relatively minor example of years that seem to "go missing." There are three ways of resolving this and similar problems:

1. *Overlap of years* – Sometimes two kings reigned in a single year. This was probably the case with Abijam and Asa. If Abijam ruled for two years and four months, Kings refers to it as three years, as he died in the third year of his reign. At the same time, Asa ascended the throne in the third year of Jeroboam's rule, not the fourth. Thus, a single year is listed twice – for the deceased king and the ascendant one (or, phrasing it differently, a fraction of a year is considered a full year).

2. *Breaks in succession* – This possibility is the opposite of the previous solution; instead of one rule ending and the next beginning the same year, there is a break between rulers. For example, in 16:15, we read that in Asa's twenty-seventh year, Zimri reigned over Israel for seven days. In 16:23, we are told that in Asa's thirtieth year, Omri ruled. What happened to the missing three years? In this case, the text gives us a clear indication:

> Then the people divided into two, half following Tibni son of Ginath to crown him, and half following Omri. And the Omri faction was stronger…and Omri ruled. (16:21–22)

In this case, there was a break in succession, as the leadership struggle endured for three years.

3. *Two kings concurrently* – One example may be found regarding the reign of King Jotham. II Kings 15:30 speaks of the twentieth year of Jotham, but 15:32 informs us that he reigned for only sixteenth years! Was he king for sixteen years or for twenty? The answer lies in the following detail about his father, Uzziah:

> The Lord struck the king with a plague, and he was a leper until the day of his death; he lived in isolated quarters, while Jotham, the king's son, was in charge of the palace and governed the land. (15:5)

In one verse, the years of Jotham's reign are considered as if he ruled during his father's lifetime; in the other, his rule is enumerated from the moment he ascended the throne in his own right, after his father's death.

The first occurrence of this phenomenon is actually in the first chapter of Kings, when Solomon is crowned during David's lifetime. How are the years of Solomon and David recorded in the duration of the overlap between the two kings? Are the years of a single king counted, or do both father and son add the overlapping time to their respective reigns? Kings offers no clarification of this historical lacuna.

THE BOOKS OF KINGS AND CHRONICLES

Many historical events narrated by the book of Kings have parallels in the book of Chronicles. However, there are significant disparities in both style and substance. At times, Chronicles abridges stories, but it is frequently more expansive, detailing events unknown to us from Kings. Furthermore, Chronicles and Kings offer diverging assessments of certain figures. As we will refer to Chronicles intermittently in our discussions, it is worthwhile to include a few introductory statements about our prime parallel source.

The following are some characteristics of Chronicles:

1. Chronicles tells the story of Judah, the southern kingdom, referring to the northern kingdom only in passing and when

relevant to Judah. Moreover, the northern kingdom is viewed as fundamentally illegitimate; Chronicles seeks the unification of the kingdoms under Judean sovereignty.[14] And yet, Chronicles is strongly committed to the notion of the unity of Israel, as its opening chapters comprehensively detail the genealogies of all twelve tribes.

2. In Chronicles, the institution of the Temple is of paramount importance as a place of celebration and religious revival. The book extensively describes religious gatherings and national celebrations at the Temple, including a detailed record of prayers recited on those occasions.

3. Whereas the books of Samuel and Kings record the sins of David and Solomon, Chronicles overlooks their great misdemeanors completely, portraying the founders of the kingdom and the Temple as essentially flawless. It is as if the book wishes to convey that the roots of the kingdom and Temple are untainted by sin.

4. Repentance: Regarding the other nineteen kings, however, Chronicles frequently informs us of faults and failings. But in further contrast to Kings, Chronicles revels in royal repentance, celebrating any monarch who engages in religious repair or remorse and describing it in great detail.

How might we explain the discrepancies between the two books? The key to the differences between Chronicles and Kings relates to the period in which each was compiled. Kings is written in the wake of the Temple's destruction and the dispersion of the nation; it looks to explain tragedy and exile. Chronicles, traditionally attributed to Ezra, was penned during the formative era of the return to Zion, the early years of the Second Temple.[15] It seeks to inspire national reconstitution and religious rehabilitation.

---

14. II Chronicles 11:13, 15:8–9, 30:11, 34:6–9.

15. Academic scholars debate the precise period of authorship, but all estimates range from the fifth to third centuries BCE. Similarly, scholars now question the joint authorship of Ezra-Nehemiah and Chronicles, noting significant theological

After the return to Zion, despite the rebuilding of the Second Temple, Jerusalem languished in ruins, its walls dilapidated, still bearing the scars of the Babylonian attack that destroyed the city and its Temple.[16] Religiously, the nation was plagued with problems such as intermarriage and Shabbat desecration. Chronicles addresses a nation that did not believe it could restore itself to the stature and glory days of the First Temple. Although written as a retrospective of the First Temple period, the book aims to harness history as a means of addressing contemporary problems, boosting the nation's confidence, and strengthening its religious and political resolve.[17]

One problem was that the Jews who returned to Zion felt condemned by the past, weighed down by the sins of earlier generations: "Our fathers sinned and are no more; and we must bear their guilt" (Lam. 5:7). Chronicles challenges this view, offering ample precedent for repentance as a well-established national gesture. Past sins may be repaired, and a society can begin anew.[18]

If this was a period in which the Temple was faltering, Chronicles responds by emphasizing the centrality of the Temple as the prime national institution, thereby encouraging its revitalization.

Regarding Chronicles' eclipse of the northern kingdom, Radak suggests (in his introduction to Chronicles) that the history of Israel was deemed inconsequential due to the exile and disappearance of the ten

---

differences between them. For a concise introduction to the academic approach, see David Rothstein's introduction to I and II Chronicles in Adele Berlin and Marc Zvi Brettler, *The Jewish Study Bible* (New York: Oxford University Press, 2004), 1712–16.

16. See Nehemiah 1:3.

17. A useful article on this topic is Dr. Zippora Talshir, "The Perception of the Division of the Kingdom in Kings and Chronicles," *Al HaPerek* 7 (Israel: Ministry of Education, 1994), 34–52 [Hebrew].

18. See Sarah Yefet, *Beliefs and Opinions in the Book of Chronicles* (Jerusalem: Bialik Institute, 1995), 131–50 [Hebrew], who suggests that whereas Kings reflects a dynamic of collective reward and punishment, in which future generations classically suffer for the sins of earlier eras, Chronicles presents a model of divine justice in which reward or punishment is always exacted from the sinner himself. The theological implication is that God will not afflict a generation for sins that they did not perform. For the people of Ezra's generation, they could feel unburdened by the great sins of the past.

northern tribes. However, there could be a spiritual rationale. Jeroboam had rejected Jerusalem and its Temple; moreover, the north had established alternative sites of worship. As such, Chronicles sees its kingdom as fundamentally sinful, and is averse to recording its history unless it pertains to Judah. And yet, we stress that Chronicles boldly upholds all the tribes as an organic part of the nation of Israel. Others propose that, since Israelite settlement in Second Temple times is in Judea, around Jerusalem, with the north in the hands of the rival Samaritans, Chronicles chooses to ignore the northern state as a political entity.

So we see that Chronicles takes the same history as Kings but selects a different emphasis, a new agenda that responds to the timely national need.

Throughout this work, we shall periodically utilize Chronicles as a parallel to Kings. At times Chronicles will function as a complementary source. At other times we shall probe the contrasting information, evaluating whether the differences are indeed contradictory.

The Era of the Kings: A Graphic Summary

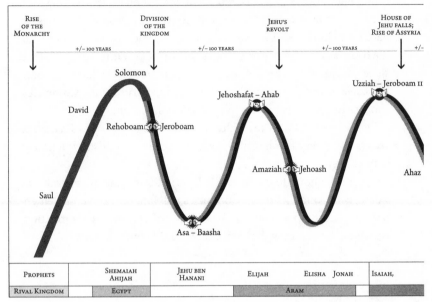

RISE OF THE MONARCHY	DIVISION OF THE KINGDOM	JEHU'S REVOLT	HOUSE OF JEHU FALLS; RISE OF ASSYRIA	

+/– 100 YEARS   +/– 100 YEARS   +/– 100 YEARS   +/–

Solomon

David

Rehoboam — Jeroboam

Saul

Jehoshafat – Ahab

Uzziah – Jeroboam II

Amaziah — Jehoash

Ahaz

Asa – Baasha

PROPHETS	SHEMAIAH AHIJAH	JEHU BEN HANANI	ELIJAH	ELISHA JONAH	ISAIAH,
RIVAL KINGDOM	EGYPT		ARAM		

Based on the Hebrew chart in the booklet, I Kings: Worksheets for the Student and Teacher (Alon Shevut: Herzog College, 2008), with special thanks to Herzog College for permission to use it.

The book of Kings spans over four hundred years of history and it is easy to get lost in the details. This visual representation offers a perspective on the wider historical context.

The chart records the basic historical units of the book, the highs and lows of the kingdom, the kings who engaged in civil war and those who collaborated with each other, the prophets for each period, and the rival powers with which Israel contended. Let us address a few central observations.

Israel experiences a high point – economic prosperity and a state of peace – when neighboring powers are at their low point. As rival states gain power, Israel finds it harder to flourish. Hence, David and Solomon's dominance of the region ends as Egypt flexes it muscles with King Shishak's invasion. Likewise, the lull between the fall of Aram and the rise of Assyria allows the heyday experienced by Uzziah in Judah and by Jeroboam in the north. Similarly, as the Assyrian empire wanes and before the Babylonian Empire has

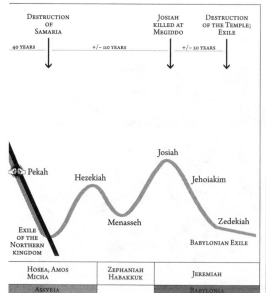

DESTRUCTION OF SAMARIA	JOSIAH KILLED AT MEGIDDO	DESTRUCTION OF THE TEMPLE; EXILE
40 YEARS	+/– 110 YEARS	+/– 20 YEARS

Josiah

Pekah

Hezekiah

Jehoiakim

Menasseh

Zedekiah

EXILE OF THE NORTHERN KINGDOM

BABYLONIAN EXILE

HOSEA, AMOS MICHA	ZEPHANIAH HABAKKUK	JEREMIAH
ASSYRIA		BABYLONIA

	Collaboration between kingdoms
	War between southern and northern kingdoms
▬▬	United kingdom
▬▬	Northern kingdom
▬▬	Southern kingdom (Judea)

reached its peak, Josiah manages to lead the kingdom to an era of relative prosperity. An exception to this is the period of Ahab and Jehoshaphat, in which the kingdom flourishes despite the power of Aram. Israel's internal strength and Ahab's alliance with Phoenicia allow Israel to defeat Aram and to dominate other kingdoms, such as Moab and Edom.

Interestingly, prophets often appear during the best of times: Ahijah the Shilonite at the end of Solomon's reign, Elijah during the period of Ahab, Isaiah and Amos during the heyday of Uzziah and Jeroboam II. It would seem that the prophets come to warn the people that the good times are the result of geopolitical factors, rather than God's satisfaction with the national culture. Frequently, prophets come to warn that hard times are approaching, or to caution against alliances with superpowers that will exact a steep cultural and moral price. Conversely, in hard times, prophets tend to offer solace and hope for the future, along with a call to return to God as a key to a better future.

Places mentioned in 1 Kings

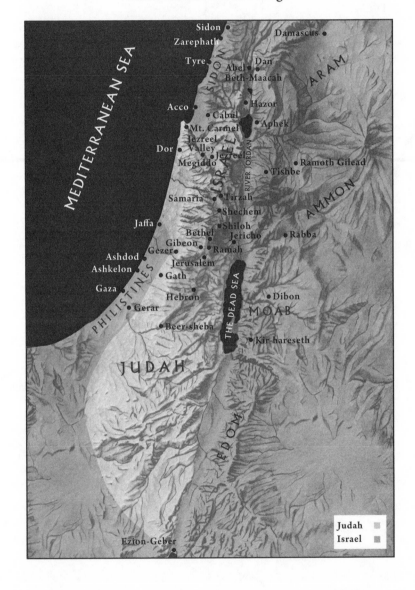

1 Kings 1

Race to the Throne

The book of Kings opens with a dramatic chapter of political intrigue and rivalry. King David is frail and elderly, but he has given no public instructions as to a designated heir.[1] Two sons of David contend for the throne: the dashing Adonijah, the hereditary heir, and his younger brother, Solomon. It is Adonijah who makes the first move, instigating his own celebratory coronation at Enrogel, just outside the walls of Jerusalem. He is supported by Joab, the army chief, and by his royal siblings. In response, Solomon's supporters – Nathan the prophet and Bathsheba, King David's wife and Solomon's mother – mobilize quickly to thwart Adonijah's coronation. In a carefully choreographed series of political machinations, they approach the ailing King David and insist that he honor an earlier promise to have Solomon crowned. The king accedes to their request, and Solomon is led to the Gihon spring in a royal procession and anointed as the monarch. Celebration erupts in the capital, surprising Adonijah's rival gathering and throwing his faction

---

1. This chapter is the *haftara* for *parashat Hayyei Sara* as both episodes depict the succession from an aging father to his son. In this regard, Abraham and Isaac connect with David and Solomon.

into disarray and panic. The chapter ends with Adonijah fearful for his life, and he seeks sanctuary at the sacrificial altar in Jerusalem. Solomon agrees to spare Adonijah as long as he pledges fealty to the new king.[2]

THE PROBLEM OF ABISHAG

The problem presented at the outset of the chapter is the inability of the aged and ailing King David to get warm. The resolution is found in the appointment of Abishag as a "*sokhenet*," translated as a "companion." Abishag's role is to warm the king by sharing his bed.

This opening story is quite perplexing. Is this the simplest way to meet David's medical needs? Moreover, why are the precise details regarding Abishag relevant to the story? Furthermore, why was a search made of the entire country in order to find this young lady? The dignity of a king certainly demands a beautiful woman to serve his needs,

---

2. There is a great deal of discussion regarding the placement of these two opening chapters of the book of Kings. In general, the biography of King David is narrated in the book of Samuel. Why do two chapters describing David's old age appear in the book of Kings? Phrased differently, are chapters 1–2 a story about David, or do they, in fact, mark the beginning of the Solomon story, starting with his coronation and rise to power?

Some academic scholars have suggested that chapters 1–2 of I Kings are in a sense a footnote to the book of Samuel. They mark the end of David's life and resolve the fate of several key figures who appear in II Samuel (Joab, Barzillai the Gileadite, and Shimei son of Gera; see ch. 2, "Generating Stability"). Moreover, chapter 1 continues a prominent theme of Samuel – children seizing power and brotherly rivalry in the royal family.

On the other hand, there are good reasons to read chapters 1–2 as an independent story. First, Samuel already has an appendix of sorts in the form of chapters 21–24, an organic literary unit that ends the book. Two concluding "appendices" would be surprising. Moreover, the key elements of chapter 1 are noticeably absent from Samuel. There, Solomon is not a leading candidate for the throne, and the oath to Bathsheba is never recorded. Accordingly, these chapters form not a conclusion to Samuel, but rather an introduction to Kings.

This influences our thinking about the question with which we began: Is this a story about David or Solomon? Once we assert that these opening chapters do not close Samuel, but introduce Kings by narrating the ascent of the new king to the throne, we must evaluate the opening episode from the perspective of Solomon's biography rather than David's. The key question, then, is how these events affect our understanding of Solomon, his persona, and his reign.

but might not a suitable candidate have been found in a more limited locale – the province of Judah, for instance?[3]

We shall offer two approaches to resolving these questions, which offer alternate dimensions of understanding the chapter.

APPROACH 1: A POLITICAL CHAPTER

The opening paragraph regarding Abishag may be perceived as setting a political tone to the chapter. In the opening verses, an anonymous group of courtiers are mentioned: "And his servants said, 'Let a virgin girl be sought for the king'" (1:2). Who are these unnamed "servants" or palace officials who instigate this national beauty contest? A key to identifying them is their reappearance in verse 9, when "all the men of Judah, the king's servants," join Adonijah in his coronation party. It appears that these palace officials, these "servants," are in fact aligned with Adonijah.

The proposal for a public, nationwide search for a woman to warm the sick King David's bed emerging from the headquarters of the Adonijah faction suggests that it is initiated as a publicity technique, a strategy in the campaign to crown Adonijah as king. The first stage of the campaign is to send a message to the entire country that the king is sick. This national beauty contest announces loud and clear that David cannot maintain his body temperature. The message is simple – the king is dying. Naturally, the nation will become quite concerned when the monarch's death appears imminent and a suitable heir has not yet been designated.[4]

Adonijah's supporters achieve their goal surreptitiously in order to obscure their motives and avoid accusations that they are usurping the throne. Nevertheless, it is clear that the Abishag story is directly related to Adonijah's self-election. With the heightened anxiety and urgency prevailing in Jerusalem, one imagines that all the talk is about

---

3. This story mirrors the search for a wife for Ahasuerus in the book of Esther. The similarity of the storyline is corroborated by some parallel language: The phrases "the king's servants" and "let them seek" (*yevakeshu*) appear both in 1 Kings 1 and in Esther 2:2. Ahasuerus, however, is a lecherous king who invites a new virgin into his bed each night for over a year. King David is the very antithesis, as we read, "...and the king did not know her" (1 Kings 1:4).

4. I heard this approach from my teacher, Rabbi Menachem Leibtag.

the pressing need to appoint a successor before the king dies. The stage is open for David's son to assume power.

Adonijah and His Coalition

> Now Adonijah son of Haggith went about boasting (*mitnasei*), "I will be king!" He provided himself with chariots and horses, and an escort of fifty runners. His father never scolded him, "Why did you do that?" He was the one born after Absalom and, like him, was very handsome. (1:5–6)

In treating this as a political story, we observe that the text here introduces Adonijah in the most pejorative terms. The phrase "*mitnasei*," translated here as "went about boasting," indicates a certain presumptuousness, as well as excessive pride. Even more significant is the way that the text compares Adonijah both explicitly and by allusion to his elder brother, the renegade Absalom.

Absalom ranks as one of the most infamous figures in the Bible. He murdered his brother Amnon in a calculated act of family vengeance;[5] worse still, he sought to depose his father, David, and kill him.[6] He is the rebellious son who, in a bid to demonstrate that he had assumed his father's place, pitched a tent on the palace roof and slept with David's concubines.[7]

There are several points of comparison between Adonijah and Absalom:

1. They are both described by their impressive good looks (1 Kings 1:5 and 11 Sam. 14:25).
2. Most significantly, they both instigate an attempt to crown themselves as king during their father's lifetime.
3. Each is the heir to the throne at the time of his self-coronation.[8]

---

5. 11 Samuel 13.
6. Ibid. 15–19.
7. Ibid. 16:22.
8. See the line of succession in 11 Samuel 3:2–4: "Sons were born to David in Hebron:

4. Adonijah uses David's ailments and the search for Abishag to discredit the king's health and to make him seem infirm. In a similar manner, Absalom paves the way to his self-coronation and raises public support by discrediting David's sense of justice (II Sam. 15:2–6).
5. Both Absalom and Adonijah make for themselves "chariots and horses and an escort of fifty runners" (I Kings 1:5 and II Sam. 15:1). Rashi views this practice as the result of foreign influence, alien to the Jewish ethic of the king.[9]
6. Absalom's sleeping with his father's ten concubines (II Sam. 16:20–22) parallels Adonijah's eventual request to marry Abishag (I Kings 2:13–22).

In equating Absalom and Adonijah, our chapter is directing us to a similarly unfavorable assessment of Adonijah.

Adonijah begins with a distinct advantage. His coalition is made up of David's oldest and most loyal associates: Joab, the army chief; the royal family; Abiathar, a veteran priest; and David's close advisers (*avdei hamelekh*). There is no intention of a rebellion, merely a deep concern for the stability of the kingdom. In a situation in which David appears to be dying, this well-connected group seeks to promote the hereditary heir, Adonijah, as a man who projects a strong leadership image, thereby ensuring national stability.

His firstborn was Amnon, to Ahinoam of Jezreel. His second, Chileab, to Abigail…; the third was Absalom son of Maacah…. The fourth, Adonijah son of Haggith…." See also ibid. 5:13–15. At the start of the book of Kings, Amnon and Absalom are both dead. We know little about Chileab, whose identity is something of an enigma; in I Chronicles 3:1–2, he is known by the name Daniel. We have no biographical information about Chileab/Daniel, and he never appears as a candidate for the monarchy, although the Talmud (*Berakhot* 4a) describes him as a Torah scholar.
9. I Samuel 8:12 suggests that the king's rights are to have soldiers running before his chariot; however, these two personalities provide the only instances in which we see so large a number of heralds. The negative dimension here would appear to be the large number of runners. In II Kings 1:9, 11, we see that fifty soldiers constitute an entire platoon. Even for Adonijah and Absalom, the crown prince, this would appear excessive. See also 18:41, in which it appears that only Elijah is running ahead of Ahab's chariot.

At a disadvantage are the group that is "uninvited" to Adonijah's coronation: "Nathan the prophet, Benaiah and the warriors, and his brother Solomon" (1:10). From the fact that these key figures are significantly omitted from the guest list, we may surmise that there has already been some contention as to the appropriate successor to David. This explains why Adonijah wishes to expedite his coronation – the stakes are high. There is further awareness that if Adonijah is crowned, Solomon's life is in peril (1:12).

Yet, if we line up the various coalitions, we can see that there is something missing in Adonijah's group (1:7–9):

	Adonijah	Solomon
Army	Joab	Benaiah
Priest	Abiathar	Zadok
Coalition	Royal family and servants of the king	Bathsheba, Shimei and Rei, and the warriors of David
Prophet	–	Nathan

The glaring omission of a prophet from Adonijah's team informs us that he is not concerned about receiving the messages of God – or, alternatively, that no prophet would associate with him!

Palace Intrigue

The chapter describes how, unexpectedly, the pendulum swings in favor of Solomon. Nathan and Bathsheba masterfully choreograph their approaches to King David in order to alert him, and possibly alarm him, to events happening just a few hundred yards from his bedside, at the spring of Enrogel (just outside the city of David). The manner in which Bathsheba enters the king's chamber, only to be interrupted by Nathan, who heralds the "news" of Adonijah's imminent coronation, works perfectly in bringing King David to a point of absolute lucidity.[10]

---

10. For analysis of the carefully crafted repetitions in this chapter, see Nehama Leibowitz, "Rebellion of Adonijah," in Leibowitz, *Studies in Bereshit (Genesis)*, 3rd ed.

Bathsheba recalls an oath that David had made some years earlier: "Your son, Solomon, shall reign after me and will sit on my throne in my stead" (1:17).[11] In fact, the reader might very well question the veracity of this claim, being that it has never been mentioned previously in the Bible. Did David ever utter such a promise, or is Bathsheba somehow taking advantage of David's feeble state of mind? Yet the king's reaffirmation of the oath to Bathsheba and his detailed instructions regarding the procedure for Solomon's coronation – nine command phrases in quick succession (1:32–36) – demonstrate a lucid, quick-thinking, detail-oriented King David who is in full control of his mental faculties.[12]

We noted above the presence of Nathan the prophet in Solomon's faction, but the absence of an **act of prophecy** is quite striking. Nathan does anoint Solomon, but in this atmosphere of such confusion and disarray, one might have anticipated a divine pronouncement or a prophetic verification as to the designated identity of the monarch. What should we make of Nathan's surprisingly non-prophetic role? Moreover, all the palace intrigue and machinations make one wonder what this story is telling us. Is Solomon crowned as king because the people around David know how to manipulate him?

The style of the chapter is of a distinctly secular, political story – but this may very well be the point. The fundamental decisions are made in David's palace. Once the king, however frail, has decided who his heir will be, and once Solomon has been anointed and has ascended the king's throne, he is the king, undisputedly and without question. This is the power of central government, of the palace – the robustness of hereditary transmission.

In this vein, we should take note that this story takes place at two parallel locations, two water springs: Enrogel, **outside** the city walls, and the Gihon spring – the central water source **inside** Jerusalem. There

---

(Jerusalem: World Zionist Organization, 1976), 250–57; and Robert Alter's fine reading of this story in his book *The Art of Biblical Narrative* (New York: Basic Books, 1981), 98–100.

11. Interestingly, the name Bathsheba can be understood as meaning "Daughter of Oath," rather suitable for this chapter. For more possibilities regarding this oath, see 1 Chronicles 22:9.

12. According to *Sanhedrin* 22a, David's sexual virility returned at this point as well.

are two zones here: the official zone – the city; and the unauthorized – Enrogel. Adonijah's illicit coronation takes place **outside** the city. Solomon's ceremony, in contrast, bears the stamp of officialdom. It is not surprising, then, that the very moment that Adonijah's faction – which wields greater political clout than Solomon's – realizes that Solomon has been seated upon the king's throne, its coronation party immediately dissolves. Instantaneously, it becomes clear to Adonijah that his life is in peril, and he rushes to the altar to protect his life.

In a breathtaking reversal, the chapter culminates not merely with Solomon mercifully extending clemency to Adonijah, but in a scene in which Adonijah bows to King Solomon, officially accepting his new status and his governance. Indeed, the phrase "King Solomon" is restated four times in the space of three verses (1:51–53). A decision has been made and it is final, and Adonijah is forced to concede. We have no sense that Solomon feels vulnerable or threatened by this rival contender for the throne. He allows Adonijah to live; Solomon is absolutely secure in his position.

How does a situation that a moment ago seemed so contestable, inconclusive, and undetermined become instantaneously resolved? Ironically, the message that emerges from this story is precisely the stability of the monarchy, the power and force of sovereign government. In earlier periods of Israelite history, both Saul and David were anointed in secret, and their rule was accepted only after they gradually gained public support. Solomon represents a new model, ascending the throne without question, in public. The moment the king has issued his official declaration – even if other powerful candidates exist – there is an absolute transfer of power.

We remain intrigued as to the choice of Solomon, whose persona is totally absent from this drama; instead, others act on his behalf. The lack of any detailing of Solomon's character implies that he pales in comparison to the flamboyant Adonijah. While Solomon appears to be the subject of this story, his persona is essentially unimportant. What is critical is David's declaration that Solomon "will sit on my throne and will rule in my stead" (1:35). Solomon's new status is unshakable as he is saluted (in the presence of his father), "May Solomon's rule be **greater** than David's rule" (1:37, 47).

APPROACH 2: THE SHADOW OF DAVID'S SIN

There is a second approach to this story that maps the chapter from a spiritual, rather than political, perspective.

In an enigmatic commentary on the opening line of the book, "King David was old...and though they covered him with bedclothes, he never felt warm" (1:1), the Talmud comments:

> Our rabbis taught: Anyone who ridicules clothes will eventually not benefit from them. This, because David tore the corner of Saul's cloak. (*Berakhot* 62b)

In other words, David's intolerable cold and the failure of blankets to warm him is a punishment for the disrespect that he demonstrated to clothing when he cut the corner of King Saul's cloak (1 Sam. 24:5).

This Talmudic lesson is harsh, although typical of the midrashic rabbinic style. One wonders why Ḥazal felt the need to dredge up David's sins of yesteryear in the opening lines of a book that focuses on the history beyond David. Ḥazal appear to be implying that there is a deeper meaning to the events of this chapter; they are intimately related to David's past.

The Sin of David and Bathsheba

Upon this backdrop, we may identify several points of contact between our chapter and David's most devastating sin – the episode of Bathsheba and Uriah (11 Sam. 11–12):

1. There are only two stories which feature the three characters of David, Bathsheba, and Nathan – our chapter and the episode of David's sin with Bathsheba and Uriah.
2. The phrase in our chapter indicating that Abishag will "lie in your bosom" ("*veshakhva behekeikha*") (1:3) echoes the Bathsheba episode, in the prophet's analogy of the little ewe lamb that "nestled in the bosom" ("*uveheiko tishkav*") of the poor man – a direct reference to Bathsheba (11 Sam. 12:3).
3. "Bathsheba went to the king, to his chamber; the king was very old, and Abishag the Shunammite was serving the king" (1:15).

This verse is particularly awkward. Why is it relevant that Abishag was "serving the king"? She was in his bed, warming him! One cannot read this verse without being startled by the image of Bathsheba, wife of the king, entering the bedroom to see King David with Abishag. Of course, the text reminds us that "the king was very old," and we recall that "the king did not know her," yet this scene raises the stark contrast between the young, virile David, who could not resist the temptation of Bathsheba, and his current feeble and impotent state. The coalescence of the images gives the impression of David broken and wasted, his strength having left him.

4. Bathsheba mentions David's oath to her that Solomon would be his successor. When was that oath made? As we noted above, it is not mentioned explicitly in the Bible. Radak makes the following interesting comment:

> And why did he [David] make an oath to her? After their child died, Bathsheba said: "The child died because of [our] sin. Even if we have a son who lives, he will be ridiculed by his brothers as an object of sin." And she refused to be intimate with David until he vowed that her firstborn son would succeed him as king.

According to Radak, the oath to Bathsheba was a direct outgrowth of the overwhelming burden of guilt engendered by the dreadful sin of David with Bathsheba. Again, however, this oath is mentioned only now.

The specter of David's sin resurfaces over and over in our chapter. We may conclude, therefore, that behind the overt political drama, there is a subtext that places David's sins as a background to this story. Why?

The Controversy of Solomon

Of all David's wives, Bathsheba is entangled in scandal, and her son, Solomon, would at first glance be a contentious and unlikely candidate for the succession, tainted as he is by his parents' sin. The text cannot ignore this problem. Can Solomon move beyond the past?

The conclusion is a resounding "Yes." This chapter teaches us that

Solomon is the suitable successor. This fact has already been affirmed by the book of Samuel, in verses that may have formed the textual basis for Radak's interpretation:

> David consoled his wife Bathsheba, he went and lay with her, she bore a son, and she named him Solomon; the Lord loved him. And He sent a message through the prophet Nathan, and he called his name Jedidiah (Beloved of God) at the instance of the Lord. (II Sam. 12:24–25)

These verses affirm that despite the illicit beginnings of the union between David and Bathsheba, Solomon is the "Beloved of God."

David's Withdrawal

But the shadow of the Bathsheba episode looms over David as well. A reading of II Samuel demonstrates that David has been plagued by death and ruin ever since the sin of Bathsheba. In that episode God condemned David to a terrible fate: "The sword will never leave your house...I will raise up a calamity against you from within your house; I will take your wives before your very eyes and give them to your neighbor..." (II Sam. 12:11–12). Starting with the death of Bathsheba's baby, the family is afflicted by rape, murder, treason, and revolt; four of David's children die under tragic circumstances.[13]

We suggested earlier that this chapter focuses on the power of the king, the stability of central government. But could the heir not have been named before David's old age set in? Did everything have to be decided in a haphazard scramble of backroom diplomacy?

I believe that we are witness here to a symptom of David's response to his sin. Ever since the episode of Bathsheba, David exhibits a distinct lack of involvement in public life. Unless his very survival is on the line, he seems almost resigned to the events that befall him.[14] One senses that he feels paralyzed, weighed down by his past sins.

---

13. See Prof. Avraham Grossman, "David's Old Age and his Will," http://www.daat.ac.il/daat/Tanach/rishonim/grosman1.htm [Hebrew].

14. King David seems to allow himself to be manipulated by Joab to reaccept his son

This withdrawal also affects his guidance of his children. David fails to rebuke Amnon for his rape of Tamar. He never confronts Absalom for his murder of Amnon. How can he rebuke his son for sexual crimes, when he is guilty of them? How can David scold his murdering son, when he bears the weight of Uriah's death? As the text specifies regarding Adonijah, "His father never scolded him: 'Why did you do that?'" (1:6).

Additionally, King David has left a political vacuum; he has failed to designate a successor.[15] His indecision and withdrawal from public life are a direct outgrowth of his sense of guilt.

These strands all come together in our chapter. The characters of the saga of David and Bathsheba are reassembled yet again, and the choice of language recalls that terrible sin from our subconscious. Our opening chapter revisits David, paralyzed physically and inactive in the sphere of national decision-making, the very opposite of his youthful, dynamic persona.

What is our chapter communicating by presenting David in this manner? First, it informs us that David has suffered terribly for his sins. The opening chapter of 1 Kings is the final episode of his awful punishment, as the fourth of his sons is to be killed. In the words of Abarbanel:

> David sinned greatly, admitted his sin valiantly, repented fully, and received his punishment, and through this, his sins were atoned.

(11 Sam. 14). When Absalom rebels, he doesn't fight, but instead flees, avoiding confrontation (15:13). In the same episode, David allows himself to be attacked and insulted, claiming it as a punishment from God (16:9–12), and he asks Joab and his generals to "deal gently with my boy, Absalom, for my sake" (18:5), thereby sabotaging his own cause. The wide support for two rebellions – of Absalom and Sheba son of Bichri (1 Sam. 20:1) – reflects a sense of dissatisfaction with David's national administration.

15. I have suggested that David's indecision regarding a successor is a sign of being weighed down by sin. It is possible, however, that there could have been simple personal and political reasons for his failure to designate an heir, as contemporary royal life attests. King Hussein of Jordan changed his mind in the final year of his reign, as he was dying, and designated a new heir – his son Abdullah instead of his brother, Hassan.

As David honors his oath to Bathsheba, he affirms that despite the problematic past, he has paid for his various sins. Most importantly, Solomon ascends the throne clear of past complications; there is no residual stain on his monarchy.

> David pleaded before God: "Master of the Universe, forgive me for that sin." God said: "You are forgiven." David responded: "Make me a sign [of forgiveness] in my lifetime." God said: "I will not publicize it in your lifetime, but I will publicize it in your son Solomon's lifetime."
>
> When Solomon built the Temple, he sought to install the Ark in the Holy of Holies, but the gates cleaved to each other. Solomon recited twenty-four prayers but was not answered.... When he [Solomon] said:..."O Lord, God, do not turn away Your anointed one, remember Your kindness to David," immediately he was answered [and the gates opened].... Then all of Israel knew that God had forgiven him for that sin. (*Shabbat* 30a)

The ascent of Solomon as David's successor and his building of the Temple is the clearest affirmation that David and Solomon are untainted by David's sin. David has paid his price, and the sin is absolved.

An additional lesson comes to mind in this connection. No king is immune to the consequences of his actions; even the greatest king will pay for his misdemeanors. As we shall see, this is a critical message for the book of Kings, a book in which kings perpetrate devastating crimes.

1 Kings 2

Generating Stability

This chapter narrates a sweeping drama of intrigue and violence. In the opening scene, we witness a dying King David imparting his final instructions and guidance to his son and heir, Solomon.[1] In the second section, Solomon acts to stabilize his rule, eliminating his enemies and defusing the forces that threaten his new sovereign status. The two sections of the chapter are separated by the transitional event of King David's death.[2]

---

1. This chapter is the *haftara* for *parashat Vayehi*. *Vayehi* describes Jacob's deathbed scene and his final words, his blessings and curses, to his children. Similarly, David voices his parting message to Solomon, his son and successor.
2. The chapter is carefully constructed:
   2:1–9 David's parting instructions to Solomon
   2:10–11 David's death
   2:12–46 Solomon's actions (based on David's directives)
   Each section is delineated through a technique of literary bracketing. The first section begins, "And David's days were approaching death," and ends, "And the days that David reigned..." (2:11). The second section begins, "And Solomon sat on David's throne...and his rule was firmly established" (2:12), and it ends, "And the kingdom was established in the hands of Solomon" (2:46).

David addresses several critical points in his last advice to his son. First, he instructs Solomon, "Be strong and act as a man" (2:2). Solomon depicts himself at this point of life as "a young lad with no experience in leadership" (3:7). David informs him that events will swiftly test Solomon's resolve and decisiveness, including the exercise of force and violence. Solomon must grow up – quickly! Strength and the maturity of adulthood are of the essence.

Second, David enunciates the centrality of Torah, advising and cautioning Solomon that dedicated adherence to God's law constitutes the key to his personal success, and ensures the perpetuation of the royal house of David.[3]

The bulk of David's behest, however, concerns a series of personalities who played critical roles in David's life: Joab, Barzillai, and Shimei. There is some "unfinished business" regarding each, and David charges Solomon with a number of responsibilities:

1. to ensure that Joab, David's army chief, does not die a peaceful death
2. to care for David's friend and supporter, Barzillai the Gileadite
3. to kill Shimei son of Gera

FRAMING THE CHAPTER: JUSTICE, VENDETTA, OR POLITICS?

There are two fundamental approaches that we may take when approaching this set of instructions. The first approach sees David as encouraging

---

3. This straightforward instruction of David's takes on a sinister, foreboding hue when we read of Solomon's religious deviance in chapter 11, as he "was not devoted to the Lord, God, as his father, David, had been" (11:4). There, God accuses him of abrogating the "covenant and the laws…" (11:11).

In the book of 11 Samuel, God assured King David that the house of David would continue forever. In that prophecy, God said that a king who failed in his dedication to Torah would be duly punished, but the royal line would remain intact (11 Sam. 7:13–14). David, however, communicates a more sober message (reiterated by Solomon himself in 8:25 and echoed by God in 9:5) – the sinning king will be "cut off from the throne," thereby jeopardizing the continuity of the entire Davidic line. This underscores the conditional nature of the monarchy (a message germane to the book of Kings) and of the house of David in particular.

Solomon to dispense reward and retribution as his opening royal action. This is a mandate to act in the name of justice:

> "And also" – The phrase "and also" states that beyond...that he [David] commanded him [Solomon] to walk in the paths of God, he wanted to say that this too is God's path: to destroy evil individuals. (Radak, 2:5)

Following this logic, the Talmud and traditional commentaries debate if Joab was, in fact, legally culpable in his assassination of Abner and Amasa according to halakhic standards and rules.[4]

However, this perspective is problematic. If David acts in the name of justice, then we would expect him to judge and sentence Joab and Shimei in a court of law! Moreover, David's appeal to Solomon's acumen seems to imply that he is prompting Solomon to trap Joab and Shimei, to engage in an underhanded and deceitful vendetta. Furthermore, David has sworn not to harm Shimei (see 2:7–8); can this oath simply be circumvented by passing the act of retribution to his son? Even if such an act is deemed legally sound, it certainly sounds ethically duplicitous.

In addition, why does David deposit these tasks upon his young son? Would a freshly crowned and inexperienced Solomon be in a better position than David to confront prominent national statesmen? As Abarbanel puts it:

> He would not have given his young, newly anointed son such a dangerous piece of advice as to kill top military figures at the very inception of his rule.

Abarbanel suggests a different approach, which perceives each of David's instructions as representing a piece of guidance, a forewarning based upon David's wealth of experience:

> David did not command Solomon to execute Joab and Shimei for earlier crimes, for which he himself did not have them executed....

---

4. *Sanhedrin* 49a.

Rather, his thinking and intention was to inform Solomon of the manner in which Joab and Shimei had acted against him in order to caution him not to appoint them to high office out of concern that they could manipulate him [Solomon] and act in a manner similar to the way that they had behaved to him [David]. The purpose of this bequest was counsel and education – that he should be wary of them and punish them vociferously should they betray him.

Accordingly, David's message pinpoints potential threats to Solomon's stability. David knows that once he has left the scene, political forces will be unleashed. Factions and interest groups that have remained concealed due to David's presence and authority will move quickly to out-maneuver or even unseat the young, fledgling king. This is why David opens his speech with the phrase "Be strong and act as a man." David's speech is an appeal to Solomon's wisdom and acumen (2:6, 9), rather than a legal pronouncement.

PUTTING AN END TO THE CONSPIRACY

A look at the structure of the chapter reinforces Abarbanel's understanding:

2:1–11 David's instructions	1. Torah	2. Joab	3. Barzillai	4. Shimei
2:12–27	Execution of Adonijah Exile of Abiathar			
2:28–47 Solomon's fulfillment		1. Joab		2. Shimei

The section of Adonijah's request to marry Abishag, his subsequent execution, as well as the exile of Abiathar the priest constitutes an interruption in the smooth flow of the chapter; it is wedged between David's parting instructions and Solomon's fulfillment of them. In chapter 1,

Adonijah was the prime contender for the throne. Adonijah's fresh approach to Bathsheba, while appearing as an innocent request, was a direct attack on Solomon's newfound status as king, and thus constituted an act of treason. But Adonijah had not acted alone; there is a conspiracy in the air. Solomon says so explicitly to Bathsheba: "…he is my older brother, and Abiathar the priest and Joab son of Zeruiah are on his side" (2:22). Joab understands it too: "The news reached Joab" (2:28). When Solomon executes the relentless renegade Adonijah, Joab understands that he is also on the firing line, and he begins to flee.

As Abarbanel noted, David's instructions were not about a vendetta against his enemies, but were rather an alert to the forces that would seek to dislodge Solomon. David knew these people intimately and understood how they operated. He was instructing Solomon, on the basis of past experience, to be vigilant and to identify the warning signs at the moment that they surfaced – which he did most efficiently in thwarting a new conspiracy, by executing Adonijah and Joab, and exiling Abiathar. The central placement of Adonijah's attempt to unseat Solomon verifies Abarbanel's approach.

ADONIJAH AND THE CONCUBINE

Let us look more closely at Adonijah's appeal to marry Abishag, a poisoned act that costs Adonijah his life (2:22–23). Why is this seemingly reasonable request considered to be an act of treason?

There are several instances in the Bible in which a son engages in sexual relations with his father's concubine, and in each case, the son seeks to usurp his father's position. In these similar stories, the motive for this act is political rather than amorous. The assumption is that the son, in engaging in the ultimate intimacy with his father's concubine, is taking his place in the conjugal realm, and, by implication, assuming his father's position as king in the political sphere. The son is assuming the throne.

The most illustrative precedent is the story of Absalom, who temporarily deposed his father, King David. David was forced to abandon Jerusalem for fear of his life.[5] Absalom, keen to declare his unequivocal

---

5. As we noted in chapter 1, the story of Absalom is noticeably present in the backdrop

status as king, asks his advisers how he might publicize his new role as monarch. They reply:

> Lie with your father's concubines, whom he left to mind the palace; and when all Israel hears that you have dared the wrath of your father, all who support you will be encouraged. (II Sam. 16:21)

In a similar story, Abner took Saul's concubine after his master's death and was accused of attempting to usurp the throne (ibid. 3:7).[6] A further example of this dynamic is the disturbing episode, narrated briefly in Genesis, involving Jacob's son Reuben: "When Israel dwelt in that land, Reuben went and slept with Bilhah, his father's concubine; Israel heard" (Gen. 33:32). Here too, we have a son who seeks to establish his place in the family through sexual relations with his father's concubine.[7] Needless to say, this act is severely criticized in Jacob's final words (49:2–6).

This background explains Adonijah's request. Adonijah previously attempted to seize the throne directly. Now, a furtive and devious

---

to this chapter. Not only is his name strangely referenced in 2:28 (and more logically in 2:7), but both Shimei and Barzillai are major characters from the story of his rebellion. Ralbag further claims that Joab is to be killed not only because of his guilt in the deaths of Abner and Amasa, but also for the killing of Absalom.

6. The return of David's wife Michal, Saul's daughter (II Sam. 3:13–16), appears to fit into this category as well.

7. A straightforward textual reading of the story might explain the events in the following manner: Rachel has recently died. While Rachel was alive, she was the favorite wife, and her children were similarly preferred. But with Rachel's death, the sons of Leah seek to stake their leadership claim in the family. Through his illegitimate intimacy with Bilhah, Reuben – firstborn of Leah – is emphatically stating that he intends to succeed his father as the family leader. This aggressive act conveys the message that the children of Leah, rather than Rachel's sons, will take the place of their father, Jacob. According to one rabbinic reading, Reuben did nothing more than adjust Jacob's sleeping arrangements (see Rashi on Genesis 33:32). To understand more about the relationship between the midrash on the Reuben story and the *peshat*, see my essay, "Reuven: Cover-up or *Peshat*," The Virtual Beit Midrash, http://vbm-torah.org/archive/intparsha67/08-67vayishlach.htm.

Adonijah asks Bathsheba to approach the king with a request to marry King David's concubine Abishag.[8] Solomon responds, outraged:

> "Why request Abishag the Shunammite for Adonijah? Request the kingship for him!" ...Thereupon, King Solomon swore by the Lord: "So may God do to me and even more, if broaching this matter does not cost Adonijah his life... Adonijah shall be put to death this very day!" (1 Kings 2:21–24)

Solomon reads the situation correctly, unhesitatingly identifying this as a move to unseat him – an unqualified act of treason.

ABIATHAR

Solomon treats each member of the treasonous coalition differently. Adonijah – the pretender to the throne – has been executed, and Joab will also be put to death. Abiathar the priest, however, is not killed. Why not? Abarbanel explains:

---

8. Adonijah exposes his state of thinking in his appeal to Bathsheba (1 Kings 2:15), incriminating himself quite clearly: "You know that the throne was mine, and all Israel had turned [its] face to me as king; but the kingship was rechanneled to my brother." It is interesting that Adonijah approaches Bathsheba in particular. *Da'at Mikra* assumes that she holds an official position; after all, Solomon has installed a throne for her next to his own (2:19). Some have suggested that this is the first instance of a *gevira* in Israelite royalty (see 1 Kings 15: Civil War, n. 9), though Bathsheba is never explicitly referred to by that title.

Nevertheless, it is curious that Adonijah approached Bathsheba. Did he not realize that he was signing his own death warrant? Two possibilities may be suggested. First, he may have failed to appraise Solomon's political acumen, assuming him to be a diffident and gutless novice. With the support of the wily Joab and Abiathar, he calculated that he still retained a realistic chance of assuming power. Alternatively, he was so obsessed by his dream of national rule that he was blinded to the possibilities of his own failure. He had to have the throne even at the price of his own death!

Likewise, Bathsheba, in her mere repetition of Adonijah's request, is either exceptionally naïve – a difficult thing to assume given her political manipulations and skill in chapter 1 – or intentionally acting innocent and unworldly, while in truth fully aware that her "small" request will frame Adonijah, and that Solomon will view it as an act of treason.

For an alternative reading of this episode, see Adele Berlin, *Poetics and Interpretation of Biblical Narrative* (Sheffield: Almond Press, 1983), 28–30.

Due to the fact that Abiathar was a high priest, he did not want to execute him, lest his house be treated like that of Saul, who killed the priests of Nob.

Perhaps Solomon was simply reluctant to kill a priest, but upon further investigation, we can identify a deeper connection between Abiathar, David, and the town of Nob.

Solomon himself explains his reluctance to kill Abiathar:

> To the priest Abiathar, the king said: "Go to your field at Anathoth; you deserve to die, but I shall not put you to death at this time, **because you carried the Ark of the Lord, God, before David, my father, and you shared all the hardships that my father endured.**" (1 Kings 2:26)

In what way did Abiathar carry the "Ark of the Lord, God" before David? Which hardships did they endure together? The story of Nob, the city of priests, as recorded in 1 Samuel 22, provides the background information. David, a fugitive from the king, had taken protection in the city of Nob. When Saul discovered that Nob had harbored David, he murdered all its inhabitants – men, women, and children. Only one person escaped – Abiathar:

> One son of Ahimelech... escaped; his name was Abiathar, and he fled to David. When Abiathar told David that Saul had killed the priests of God, David said to Abiathar: **"...I am the cause of the deaths of your father's house. Stay with me; do not be afraid, for whoever seeks your life seeks my life also; you will be in my care."** ... And when Abiathar... fled to David at Keilah, he brought an ephod with him. (1 Sam. 22:20–23, 23:6)

Why does Solomon not execute Abiathar? First, Abiathar had not been earmarked explicitly by David as a threat. Furthermore, Solomon also knows that David issued an explicit promise to take care of Abiathar. David felt a deep sense of guilt that his presence in the town of Nob had induced Saul to decimate Abiathar's family, and hence David sheltered this sole survivor, offering him protection. A third point is relevant as well. During the many long years that David and Abiathar had shared as fugitives from Saul, in caves and hideaways, Abiathar served a critical function to David and his group; he provided a direct link to God by means of the ephod that he carried. This ephod is referred to as the "Ark of the Lord, God" in our chapter.[9] It is clear that Abiathar had a lifelong history of loyalty to David, and the composite effect of these factors makes Solomon act differently toward Abiathar.

Solomon's treatment of Abiathar exhibits his characteristic wisdom. First, he marks Abiathar as a "dead man" (2:26); Abiathar must understand that he has been close to execution, and he is being formally cautioned. Next, Solomon removes Abiathar from the capital city, disengaging him from the networks of power and politics. Third, he commands him to devote his time to his farm and thus to cease functioning as a priest. By banishing Abiathar to Anathoth, Solomon successfully neutralizes any threat that Abiathar might pose.

One postscript is in order, however. In chapter 4, we read a list of Solomon's "cabinet," his government ministers, among whom are "Zadok and Abiathar – priests" (4:4). It appears that Abiathar is recalled to high office. Apparently, after the crisis of Adonijah, once the dust has settled, Solomon sees Abiathar as a worthy figure to occupy a leadership position in the Temple.

JOAB SON OF ZERUIAH

For forty years, throughout David's rule, Joab served as David's formidable military chief – "And Joab son of Zeruiah led the army" (11 Sam.

---

9. Rashi suggests that Abiathar's role of carrying the Ark relates to his flight from Jerusalem during the Absalom mutiny (see 11 Sam. 15:29 and 17:15). However, in that story, Abiathar is told to return the Ark to Jerusalem, not to "carry the Ark of the Lord, God, before" David. While he does function as an informer for David against Absalom, the profile of Abiathar in our verses does not fit the details of the Absalom story particularly well. I have adopted the approach of *Da'at Mikra* (see previous note) as regards Abiathar.

In the Tabernacle as described in the book of Exodus, the ephod and Ark are two totally different components; one is at the epicenter of the Tabernacle, and the other is worn by the high priest. In the book of Samuel, however, there appears to be some overlap between the two. See, for example, 1 Samuel 14:3, 18.

8:16) – leading the army in expanding the borders of David's kingdom to the size of an empire. Joab, David's nephew,[10] was a fearless warrior,[11] but beyond his immediate military role, Joab functioned as a senior government figure and a personal friend and adviser to David, sometimes addressing the king quite candidly and forcefully.[12]

However, it is equally evident that the relationship with Joab was not without a negative element. In this vein, no text is more blatant than David's final directive:

> You also know all that Joab son of Zeruiah did to me – what he did to the two officers of the hosts of Israel, to Abner son of Ner and to Amasa son of Jether, that he killed them, and shed the blood of war in peace, and put the blood of war upon his belt that was around his loins and in his shoes that were on his feet. Act according to your wisdom, and do not let him die a peaceful death of old age. (1 Kings 2:5–6)

In order to understand David's harsh assessment, we shall turn our attention to the two episodes specified by David – Joab's assassination of two rival military commanders, in which he "shed the blood of war in peace."[13]

---

10. Joab was David's sister's son: "Jesse begot Eliab, the eldest, and ... the seventh was David. And their sisters, Zeruiah and Abigail, and the sons of Zeruiah were Abishai, Joab, and Asahel – the three of them. And Abigail gave birth to Amasa ..." (1 Chron. 2:13–17).

11. It was Joab who captured Jerusalem; see 1 Chronicles 11:6.

12. See in particular the aftermath of the Absalom rebellion, in 11 Samuel 19:6–8 and 24:3. In both instances, Joab confronts the king and disagrees with him. There are also times when Joab's concern for the welfare of the king causes him to act deceitfully, manipulating David; for example, see 11 Samuel 14. Joab is also the king's confidant (and accomplice) in the killing of Uriah; see 11 Sam. 11:16–25. Joab was clearly a person whom David felt he could trust. Joab exhibits strong loyalty to David, for example, in 11 Sam. 12:27–28.

13. The commentaries add other sins and violent acts to Joab's crimes on the basis of the phrase "that Joab ... did to me" (1 Kings 2:5), apparently referring to an event with personal ramifications for David. For example: "'That Joab did to me': This refers to Absalom, when he [Joab] defied his [David's] expressed command and

The Murder of Abner

For seven years following the tragic death of King Saul, a state of civil war persisted; King David had been crowned by the tribe of Judah, but the other tribes retained their allegiance to Saul, led by Saul's son, Ishbosheth (II Sam. 2:10–11). Abner son of Ner had been King Saul's chief of staff, and during this period of civil war, Abner continued to function as the head of the army and was effectively the leader of Ishbosheth's administration (II Sam. 3:1).

In the thick of one particularly bloody clash in the course of the war between the house of David and the house of Saul, Abner found himself hotly pursued by David's forces, and specifically by the young warrior Asahel son of Zeruiah, Joab's brother (II Sam. 2:18–23). Abner killed Asahel in self-defense.[14] This detail is critical to understanding the events that follow.

Some years later, Abner traveled to Hebron, seeking to strike a pact and thereby unite the nation under King David's rule. Abner signed a peace agreement with David. But then:

> Joab came to the king and said: "What have you done? Behold, Abner came to you – why did you then send him, so he is gone away? You know Abner son of Ner, that he came to seduce you, and to know your going out and your coming in, and to know all that you are doing!" And Joab went out from David and sent messengers after Abner, and they brought him back from the well of Sirah, but David did not know of it. So Abner returned to Hebron, and Joab took him aside inside the gate to speak to him in private,[15] and he struck him there in the belly, and he died, for the blood of Asahel his brother. (II Sam. 3:23–27)

---

killed him" (Ralbag ad loc.). Similarly, Rashi mentions that Joab disclosed personal correspondence between himself and David to his subordinates in the episode of the death of Uriah.

14. Abner was clearly distressed at the prospect of killing Asahel: "How will I be able to look your brother Joab in the face?" (II Sam. 2:22). He tried to convince Asahel to abandon his pursuit, but when Asahel persisted, he killed him.

15. David instructs Solomon to "put the blood of war upon his belt that was around

In murdering Abner, Joab threatened to scuttle the newly signed peace deal between David and Abner, jeopardizing national unity and possibly thrusting the factions into a renewed state of conflict.

---

his loins and in his shoes that were on his feet" (1 Kings 2:5). This unusual phrase referring to Joab's shoes bewildered the commentators. The "belt around the loins" always refers to an instrument of war; "girding of loins" refers to tightening this belt at the waist. This belt (a) held weapons on the body; (b) lifted up the robes of the warrior, affording him greater movement, so that he could run fast; and (c) firmed up the body (just as weightlifters use belts nowadays) and assisted in fighting. But what is the relevance of shoes in this context?

It is possible that shoes also relate to war. For example, Isaiah is instructed to dress like a prisoner of war and present himself "naked and barefoot" (Is. 20:2). A barefoot person cannot escape; shoes or boots are part of army apparel. (In this regard, see also Isaiah 5:27, which also links belt and shoes in the context of the warrior.)

Ḥazal developed a fascinating and fantastic reading based on this unusual reference to footwear:

> He [Joab] asked him [Abner] guilefully: "A widow who frees her brother-in-law of the obligation of *yibbum* (levirate marriage) – if she has no hands, how does she perform *halitza* [a ritual in which the widow removes the brother-in-law's shoe]?" He [Abner] began telling him and showing him: "She takes his shoe thus, with her teeth…." And he [Joab] drew his sword and killed him. (Rashi, *Sanhedrin* 49a)

In this midrash, Ḥazal take the reference to "shoes," connecting it to another place in which shoes are mentioned – the command of *halitza*. In the image painted by this midrash, as he draws Abner into the gateway – the place of the judges (see Deut. 16:18), and hence the place of Torah analysis – Joab engages him in a detailed halakhic discussion as a ruse to divert his attention. When Abner's mind is otherwise occupied, Joab murders him.

Interestingly, the midrash portrays this group of army generals as steeped in Torah, discussing halakhic minutiae even at a chance meeting in a deserted alley. This reinforces the rabbinic portrayal of David and his men as highly spiritual characters (see, for example, the depictions of David in *Berakhot* 3a–4b).

The specific reference to *halitza* is also interesting. After all, *halitza* is performed to release a woman when her husband dies childless and she is supposed to marry his brother so that she may perpetuate her husband's name. Here, too, Joab wishes to finish the incomplete work of his brother Asahel. Moreover, the transfer of Abner from Saul to David may be seen as a *yibbum* of sorts, as the general of the dead King Saul – the figurative dead brother – now binds himself in a "covenant" with a new master. It is this "*yibbum*" that Joab finds suspect.

Why did Joab kill Abner? There are three logical possibilities:

1. *Vengeance* – He sought to avenge the blood of his brother Asahel.
2. *Personal interest* – It was likely that with Abner in alliance with David, Abner would be promoted to the top military post. This would remove Joab from his position as chief of staff.
3. *National security* – Joab may not have trusted Abner. In the verses cited above, he expressed his suspicions regarding Abner as a substantial national threat. Joab felt that David, in his pursuit of national control, had let his guard down and made a deal with a deceitful man who would eventually betray him.

When examining the textual evidence, Joab's speech to David expressed deep mistrust of Abner; he suspected Abner's peace deal was a deception, a ruse. On the other hand, the text of the book of Kings, in evaluating Joab's motives, informs us that Joab murdered Abner "for the blood of Asahel his brother" – as revenge. Did Joab act in personal vengeance and malice or for the higher values of the kingdom?

Although Joab's motives were certainly complex, David's response to his act was unequivocal. David marched at the head of Abner's funeral procession, declaring his innocence and his administration's repudiation of this act of violence. David eulogized Abner and took upon himself the rites of mourners. He cursed Joab openly with a litany of terrible misfortunes:

> David heard afterward, and he said: "I and my kingdom are guilt-less before God forever for the blood of Abner son of Ner. It shall rest upon the head of Joab and all of his father's household: May Joab's house never be without someone suffering from a discharge or an eruption, or a leper, or a male who handles the spindle, or one slain by the sword, or one lacking bread." (II Sam. 3:28–29)

This profession of innocence on David's part is echoed in the book of Kings in a clear and beautifully crafted statement by Solomon, when he commands that Joab be put to death (I Kings 2:31–33):

	A1	Remove the innocent blood from me and my father's house
	B1	And let the blood guilt be returned on his [Joab's] own head
	C1	For he attacked two righteous and good men and killed them by the sword
	D	**And my father did not know**
	C2	Abner son of Ner, the army commander of Israel, and Amasa son of Jether, army commander of Judah
	B2	Let their blood be returned on Joab's head and on the head of his descendants forever
	A2	And for David and his descendants, for his house and his throne, may there be peace from God forever.

This perfect chiasm has at its axis, at its apex, the clear statement that "my father did not know." This was Joab's act, and his alone.

Amasa

In a similar scenario at a later point in David's life, after Absalom's revolt, David revisited his strategy of placating the malcontents by embracing and promoting a rival military chief. In this story, David appointed Amasa, Absalom's senior commander, to be chief of staff of his army. Once again, Joab became suspicious and took unauthorized action:

> Joab said to Amasa: "Are you well, my brother?" And Joab grasped Amasa's beard with his right hand to kiss him. And Amasa took no heed of the sword in Joab's hand, and he smote him…. (II Sam. 20:9–10)

This story is similar to that of Abner. First, both represent betrayal of and dishonor toward the king, as Joab subverts the king's plans and undermines David's peaceful political strategy. Furthermore, both attest to Joab's dangerous political meddling. David seeks to heal national wounds and bridge divisions through appeasement, by appointing rival officers to the leadership of his military; Joab murders them, jeopardizing and undermining the prospect of national peace and unity.

Unlike the case of Abner, Amasa's murder could not have been motivated by family vengeance. Joab harbored a pathologically suspicious mind, viewing any rival as a potential threat to David and his leadership. Joab rejected the risks that David took for peace; he felt secure only when he had eliminated the enemy absolutely. Joab ignored royal commands and followed his own agenda.[16]

This man constituted a formidable political liability for Solomon. With the unscrupulous Joab supportive of Adonijah, any act would be possible. As soon as Adonijah's rebellion moved into action, Solomon knew that he had to execute Joab.

War and Peace

In his warning to Solomon, David states that Joab "shed the blood of war in peace" (I Kings 2:5). The words "blood" and "peace" recur in the next verses. An intertextual examination of these words reveals how relevant they are in framing King Solomon's reign.

Chronicles describes David's perception of Solomon's era, as opposed to his own reign:

> David told his son Solomon: "I had my heart set on building a temple for the name of the Lord, God. But this word of God came to me: 'You have shed much **blood** and have fought great **wars**; you are not to build a house for My name, because you have shed much **blood** before Me. You will have a son who will

---

16. David repeatedly remarks about the violent tendencies of the "sons of Zeruiah" (see II Sam. 3:39), but it is Abishai's violent streak that David must restrain more than others; see I Samuel 26:8–9 and II Samuel 16:9.

It is notable that these are not the only two occasions in which Joab acted independently, intervening and redirecting situations critical to the future of the nation and aggressively pushing his own personal agenda forward. After the king distanced his son Absalom, Joab resorted to subterfuge to have him returned, clearly manipulating national politics and his position of power. In the war against Absalom, the king explicitly instructed the troops not to kill Absalom. When Absalom was seized, no foot soldier would dream of attacking him against David's direct orders. But Joab had his closest soldiers execute Absalom. Later, Joab backed Adonijah's bid for the monarchy, apparently without consulting David. Thus, there is a convincing case that Joab repeatedly acted against the expressed wishes of the king.

be a **peaceful** man; I will give him **peace** from all the enemies around him; his name will be **Solomon (peace is his)**, and in his time I will give Israel **peace** and quiet. He shall build a house for My name … I will establish the throne of his kingdom over Israel forever.'" (1 Chron. 22:7–10)[17]

Solomon's name, his identity, his generation is one of peace. His agenda is not military or violent, but rather a peaceful environment in which a Temple will be built so that the nation may turn its attention to God.

Joab, on the other hand, is a man of blood and war. He belongs to a different age. Joab does not know how to end the war; he cannot recognize peace. He places the "blood of war in peace." In other words, he cannot allow peace to be born; violence is his method of solving problems.[18] Accordingly, Joab as a central governmental figure is incompatible with Solomon, especially in this inaugural period as "a young lad with no experience in leadership" (1 Kings 3:7).[19] Joab and Solomon are opposites, and Solomon's era, designated as a time in which Israel will live in peace and quiet, finds its antithesis in Joab.[20] Joab has no place in the world of Solomon.

---

17. This chapter in 1 Chronicles has a strong connection to our chapter in Kings. So does 11 Samuel 7. In these chapters, God outlines why David is unsuitable for the task of building the Temple, a project that will constitute the primary accomplishment of his son Solomon.
18. The repetitive usage of the word *"shalom"* in the passage of Abner's murder in 11 Samuel 3, and its deliberate omission by Joab, is instructive in this regard.
19. This is the New Jewish Publication Society (NJPS, 1985) translation of 1 Kings 3:7, in which Solomon describes himself as *"naar katan."* This is an interesting self-depiction, and it finds parallels elsewhere in the David-Solomon stories. Solomon is repeatedly referred to in his inaugural stage as "young" (*naar*) and "tender" (*rakh*); see 1 Chronicles 22:5 and 29:1. Interestingly, David describes himself with the latter term in regard to the violence of Joab: "And I am this day tender (*rakh*), although anointed king, and these men the sons of Zeruiah are too savage for me; the Lord shall reward the doer of evil according to his wickedness" (11 Sam. 3:39). According to the commentaries, Solomon is only twelve years old when he ascends the throne; see the comments of Rashi and Radak on 1 Kings 3:7, in which they analyze the timeline.
20. Interestingly, the Talmud sees a similar dichotomy – and partnership – between Joab and David: "If not for David's Torah study, Joab would not have succeeded in war;

Flight to the Altar

When he realizes that his life is in danger, Joab flees to the altar, as Adonijah does in chapter 1 after his failed attempt to appoint himself king.[21] What is the origin of this act, and how does it work?

In its discussion of murder, the Torah instructs: "And if a person comes maliciously against his fellow to kill him with guile, you shall **take him from My altar to die**" (Ex. 21:14).[22] It seems that this is a reference to an ancient tradition predating even *parashat Mishpatim*, which perceived the sacrificial altar, a classic instrument of atonement, as able to offer protection to fugitives from the law.[23] The Torah, however, does not accept this mode of escape. The law in *parashat Mishpatim* explicitly rejects this arrangement of asylum, stating that even when criminals seek protection at the altar, they will be taken from there to their deaths.[24]

If Jewish tradition rejects this practice, why do Joab and Adonijah run to the altar? Moreover, if this institution of asylum was widely known, why have we never encountered it elsewhere in the Bible?

Importantly, Rambam applies the law of "take him from My altar to die" in a particular context:

---

and if not for Joab's effort in battle, David would not have been able to learn Torah. As it is written, 'David administered justice and charity for all his people, and Joab was over the host' (II Sam. 8:15)" (*Sanhedrin* 49a).

21. It seems that both Adonijah and Joab ran to the altar in the tent that was pitched for the Ark of the Covenant in the city of David (Jerusalem); the *Metzudat David* commentary says so explicitly.

22. Ḥazal learn a variety of things from this verse; see *Mekhilta* and Rashi ad loc. Among these teachings: "'From the altar' – the Temple service is suspended to extract a murderer from the Temple." Another opinion sees this verse as teaching that the Sanhedrin should convene near the Temple altar.

23. Indeed, later in history, this right of asylum became a law of the Christian Church, granting protection to criminals and runaway slaves who took refuge in the church. A modern illustration of the power of a church to harbor criminals was the siege at the Church of the Nativity in 2002; Palestinian terrorists took shelter in the church, and the IDF was unwilling to attack it.

24. For a deeper understanding of this verse in *Mishpatim*, see Rabbi Yaakov Medan, "Murdering with Guile," The Virtual Beit Midrash, http://vbm-torah.org/archive/parsha65/18-65mishpatim.htm.

> An individual who is afraid to be killed **by order of the king** or by emergency order of the court, and escapes to the altar and leans on it, even if he is not a priest, he is saved. We do not ever take him from the altar to die, unless he is liable for the death penalty by the court with complete testimony and forewarning, like others who are executed by the court at all times. (Laws of the Murderer and Protection of Life 5:14)

In other words, the right of asylum is not extended to criminals liable in a court of justice; it applies exclusively to people who are entangled with the ruling powers. A murderer will be tried in court, and the altar offers no protection, but fugitives from the king on account of treason have the advantage of the protection of the Temple. What is the logic behind this distinction? Perhaps the Temple, the altar, is in some way extraterritorial; it is under divine hegemony and not under the jurisdiction of the king. Torah law may apply at the altar (the Sanhedrin, after all, sits adjacent to the altar), but the authority of the king has no place in the palace of the King of Kings.

By fleeing to the altar, Joab seeks to declare that his offense is a crime against the king alone; he is not guilty of murder in the standard sense. Solomon, however, insists that he be treated like a willful murderer; he is guilty as a criminal and must pay for his crimes.

SHIMEI SON OF GERA

The third personality on David's list is Shimei son of Gera, a relative of Saul who took advantage of David's lowest moments, when he was on the run from Absalom, to curse the king publicly, hurling stones at him and humiliating him (11 Sam. 16:5–13). Later, when David regained the throne, the same Shimei led a delegation of one thousand men from the tribe of Benjamin to greet David and support him. Shimei apologized publicly, and David, uninterested in exacerbating tensions with Benjamin, promised not to harm him (19:16–23).

What danger does Shimei pose to Solomon? As a leader of the northern tribes, Shimei commands significant political leverage. David is concerned that Shimei will stir up old grievances, the old tribal animosity between the house of Saul and the house of David, between Benjamin and Judah.[25]

Solomon keeps Shimei under "house arrest," under surveillance. But Shimei makes a wrong move; when "two of Shimei's servants flee to Achish...king of Gath" (1 Kings 2:39), he pursues them, and Solomon has him executed for violating his probation. At first glance, it seems that Solomon is overreacting; after all, if this is an innocent act of retrieving runaway slaves, then Solomon is exacting an extreme price for a simple and innocuous act. Upon closer examination, however, the mention of "Achish son of Maachah, king of Gath" by his official royal title leads us to believe – along with Solomon – that this is a venture of political meddling on Shimei's part. Shimei has made an appointment with a rival king, not an innocent journey to retrieve lost slaves. Shimei, vacillating and unreliable, who has huge influence in the tribe of Benjamin and who curses people when they are down and apologizes when his adversary is ascendant, is not to be trusted. Solomon does not wait to find out what lies behind this visit. Instead, he sends a clear message to Benjamin and other political factions as to who is in command.

IN CONCLUSION

Our chapter ends on a high note: "And the kingdom was established in the hands of Solomon" (2:46). These opening two chapters have narrated the tale of Solomon's rise to power and the elimination of his enemies. We are curious about this fresh young king. What drives him? What does this portend for this new era? Chapter 3 will give us a good indication of Solomon's central concerns and passions.

---

25. Solomon is planning to move the central altar from Gibeon, in the territory of the tribe of Benjamin, to Jerusalem, in the portion of Judah; see the next chapter. The political fallout of such a move could be devastating if there are parties interested in stirring up the "insult" to the tribe of Benjamin.

1 Kings 3

The Gift of Wisdom

As we open chapter 3, we have left Solomon's nascent leadership struggles behind, and we begin to view him as an independent figure. What type of personality shall we encounter in this young and promising king? How does the book of Kings depict Solomon?

INTRODUCTION TO THE SOLOMON CHAPTERS (3–11)

The opening perspective is highly positive: "Solomon **loved God, following the practices of his father, David**" (3:3). Solomon is a lover of God, committed to His law in the same manner as his father. The next nine chapters will detail the formidable achievements of this king and the magnificent empire that he commands. Chapter 3 is dedicated to Solomon's intimate relationship with God and the special gift of wisdom bestowed upon him. The following chapters reinforce this glowing assessment, listing Solomon's accomplishments and depicting the unprecedented grandeur of his rule.

Yet even a cursory acquaintance with Solomon's biography must take into account his tragic end. In a painful inversion, or even undoing, of Solomon's magnificent achievements, we read the reversal of the phrase that so positively described his beginnings:

And King Solomon loved many foreign women…. And in Solomon's old age, his wives caused his heart to stray after other gods, and **he was not wholeheartedly devoted to the Lord, his God, as his father, David, had been**…. (11:1, 4)

The love for God that characterized Solomon's youth is replaced by his love for foreign women, who lead him to idolatry.[1]

The Solomon chapters are structured to depict Solomon's rise and his eventual decline. Chapters 3–5 describe his successful administration and its accomplishments. This section has its corollary in chapters 9–10, which lead to chapter 11, dedicated to Solomon's sins and to the forces that threaten to destroy the peace and wealth of his kingdom. At the center of this structure is Solomon's crowning achievement – namely, the Temple:

Rise of an Empire	Ch. 3	God appears to Solomon; gift of wisdom
	Ch. 4	Organization of the nation into twelve districts
	Ch. 5	Power, wealth, international relations, Hiram
The Temple (and the King's Palace)	Ch. 6	Construction of the Temple
	Ch. 7	Royal buildings, crafting of Temple vessels
	Ch. 8	Temple dedication ceremony
Decline of an Empire	Ch. 9	God appears to Solomon
	Chs. 9–10	Power, wealth, international relations, Hiram
	Ch. 11	Solomon's sins

If we are aware at the outset of an eventual decline in Solomon's kingdom and his commitment to God, then how should we read these chapters and correctly appraise his persona? Our approach will be to follow the

---

1. A key question here is whether Solomon abruptly turned away from God in his old age as a sharp reversal of his former self, or whether this was a steady process, with the roots and seeds of the problems of Solomon's later years already present at an earlier stage. In addressing this question, we should note that numerous textual hints and innuendos throughout the early chapters harbor a hidden critique of

thrust of the text. The early chapters portray Solomon in a spirit of admiration and approval; the latter chapters expose problematic elements of his rule; the final chapter makes his sins explicit. Our approach will be to flow with the contours and mood of the text, reveling in the rise of Solomon and feeling disappointment and frustration at his decline.

JOURNEY TO GIBEON – MOVING THE TEMPLE

The beginning of chapter 3 describes Solomon's inaugural undertaking:

> Solomon went to Gibeon to sacrifice there, for it was the central altar; Solomon offered one thousand burnt offerings on that altar. In Gibeon the Lord appeared to Solomon.... (3:4–5)

Why does Solomon travel to Gibeon to offer one thousand sacrifices? He could have sacrificed at the altar in Jerusalem![2] And why does God appear to Solomon in a nighttime vision at this specific juncture? The key to understanding Solomon's public spectacle at Gibeon is that it is the announcement, or "launch," of the initiative to transfer the sacrificial service from Gibeon and build the Temple in Jerusalem.

To substantiate this theory, some background is necessary. The preceding verses explain the state of sacrificial worship prior to Solomon's era:

> The people, however, continued to offer sacrifices on *bamot* (local altars), for up to that time, no house had been built for the name of God. Solomon loved God, following the practices of his father,

---

Solomon, even in his earlier life. One classic example is the phrase that opens our chapter (3:1), referring to Solomon's marriage to the daughter of Pharaoh. Rashi's negative reading of 3:1 is contested by Radak and Malbim, who view their union as religiously insignificant at this stage of Solomon's life. However, as we read on, this marriage punctuates the story at regular intervals (7:8, 9:16, 11:1, 11:26–27). We will address this relationship directly in our discussion of chapters 9–11. For more regarding these subversive textual undercurrents, especially in chapter 3, see Yoav Barzilai, "The Prologue to Solomon's Kingship," *Megadim* 11 (1990): 73–98 [Hebrew].

2. An altar had already been built in Jerusalem by David, as described in II Samuel 6:17.

David; however, he sacrificed and offered at the *bamot*.[3] And
Solomon went to Gibeon... (3:2–4)

The Torah legislates a single, central place – a Tabernacle or Temple – which functions as the sole location of the sacrificial service (Deut. 12:1–17). However, in the absence of a central place of worship, local sacrificial altars – *bamot* – are permitted:

> Until the Tabernacle was erected, *bamot* were permitted....
> After the Tabernacle was erected, *bamot* became forbidden....
> They came to Gilgal and the *bamot* were permitted....
> [When] they came to Shiloh, the *bamot* were forbidden....
> [When] they came to Nob and to Gibeon, the *bamot* were [again]
>   permitted....
> [When] they came to Jerusalem, the *bamot* were [again] forbidden, and were never again permitted.... (*Zevaḥim* 14:4–8)

---

3. The language in this verse is part of the standard, "form" language of the book of Kings. As noted, Kings uses fixed textual formulae to introduce each king. One purpose of this formulaic language is to assess each king spiritually – whether he does "that which is right in the eyes of the Lord" or "that which is evil." This assessment is largely a function of his record in the area of idolatry and cultic worship, as opposed to loyal service of God. Even for several "good" kings, part of the standard template, the recursive formulaic language, relates to the *bamot*. See, for example, regarding Asa (I Kings 15:14), Jehoshaphat (22:44), Amaziah (II Kings 14:4), and Uzziah (15:4): "But the *bamot* were not removed; the people continued to sacrifice at the *bamot*." This statement occurs in particular regarding the kings of Judah.

During the time of Solomon, before the Temple was established as the exclusive sacrificial site, *bamot* were permitted; therefore, this statement seems awkwardly out of place. One resolution may be that it is a standard formulation and hence included here as well, but the truth is that this rigidity of style is not applied so comprehensively as to explain it in this context. Perhaps, then, this deliberate reference to *bamot* at the start of chapter 3 is an attempt to set the scene for Solomon's action at Gibeon, which, as we shall see, is directed at building the Temple and eliminating the *bamot*. This formulaic language, which standardly resonates with negative associations, is used to underscore the pressing need for a Temple.

Alternatively, this reference to *bamot* is an allusion to the sins of Solomon; see his building of a *bama* to the gods of Moab and Ammon in 11:7.

In Joshua's time, the Tabernacle stood at Shiloh. However, since its destruction in the days of Eli,[4] the central national sanctuary had been in a state of rupture, with its two central ritual objects – the Ark of the Covenant and the altar – in separate locations.[5] The Ark was housed in Jerusalem, while the altar stood in the city of Gibeon.[6] The "great altar" at which Solomon offers sacrifices in Gibeon is the site of the national sacrifices. This situation is clearly undesirable; Gibeon is a poor substitute for a full-fledged Temple.

Solomon's state visit to Gibeon is described as an event of national importance, not a private undertaking. It is accompanied by fanfare and celebration:

> Solomon summoned all Israel – officers of thousands and hundreds, and the judges and chiefs of all Israel.... Then Solomon and the assemblage that was with him went to the altar at Gibeon, for the Tent of Meeting...was there. But the Ark of God David had brought...to the place that David had prepared for it...in Jerusalem. (II Chron. 1:2–4)

---

4. See I Samuel 4, Jeremiah 7:12, and Psalms 78:60.
5. The Ark is the seat of God's presence, and the first ritual vessel mentioned in the Tabernacle construction. The altar is the location of sacrifices. Both are situated on the Temple's central axis. Whereas Maimonides rates the altar as the most critical ritual vessel (the Second Temple had no Ark at all, he notes), Nahmanides sees the Ark as the highest in stature. In my article, "*Ohel Mo'ed* – Meeting God," The Virtual Beit Midrash, http://vbm-torah.org/archive/intparsha72/19-72teruma.htm, I have argued that the Ark is where God approaches man, whereas the altar is the site at which man approaches God.
6. See I Chronicles 16:37–40, which is more explicit. Archaeologists have identified Gibeon as the city of El-jib, just north of Nebi Samuel, a few miles from Jerusalem of today. Impressive archaeological finds of many wine jar handles bearing the word Gibeon (GVN), along with the Arabic preservation of the name, make the identification of the site relatively certain. Archaeologists have also found impressive water systems and one huge cistern from the Iron Age – the twelfth century BCE, the time of Joshua. Some have speculated that this cistern could be the "pool" mentioned in II Samuel 2:13.

These verses, which inform us of the excitement surrounding Solomon's mission, also highlight the internal division of the "Tent of Meeting," in that the altar is separated from the Ark. Immediately following his sacrifices at Gibeon, Solomon expresses his intent to unify the house of God:

> And Solomon awoke, and, behold, it was a dream; and he **came to Jerusalem** and stood before the Ark of the Covenant of God, and offered burnt offerings, and offered peace offerings, and made a feast for all his servants. (1 Kings 3:15)

Solomon sacrifices first in Gibeon, then in Jerusalem. The sacrifices in Gibeon are a sign of respect to the "old" altar. By immediately traveling to Jerusalem to offer sacrifices there, he demonstrates his intent to build the Temple.

Malbim indeed suggests:

> He took the copper altar and the entire Tent of Meeting with him [from Gibeon] to Jerusalem…, and from this point on, they sacrificed in Jerusalem.

According to this reading, when God appears to Solomon in a nighttime vision at Gibeon, He is rewarding him for initiating and undertaking the historic decision to construct the Temple.[7] If this assessment is correct, then it is Solomon's devotion to God and His worship that grants him the gift of wisdom. Solomon's exceptional wisdom is predicated upon his religious commitment.

---

7. Rashi (1 Kings 3:2), quoting *Seder Olam*, suggests that this event takes place four years into Solomon's reign. Rashi criticizes him for delaying the Temple's construction that long. It is likely that Hazal derived this chronology from the fact that the story of Shimei in chapter 2 takes place in the third year of Solomon's reign, and this is the very next story. However, if we follow the flow of the chapter both here and in Chronicles, it is possible that this journey to Gibeon is the first act of Solomon's monarchy. In Chronicles, the building of the Temple is an explicit aim of the visit to Gibeon.

SOLOMON REQUESTS WISDOM

A different reading is suggested by Ralbag, who explains that Solomon traveled to Gibeon and offered one thousand sacrifices with the objective of inducing a prophetic experience:

> For offerings have a powerful effect in generating prophecy, as we have explained with the story of Balaam.

Solomon's first deed, then, is to instigate a connection with God, seeking an audience with the divine. This pattern – sacrifices followed by revelation – is a classic paradigm elsewhere in the Bible; Noah received revelation after offering sacrifices in the wake of the flood,[8] and God spoke to Jacob after he offered sacrifices on his way to Egypt.[9]

Why does Solomon need an audience with God? What is the request that he wishes to make?

> I am a young lad with no experience in leadership[10].... Grant your servant an understanding mind to judge Your people, to distinguish between good and bad.... (3:7–9)

Imbued with a sense of public service, personal mission, and humility, Solomon requests the wisdom to "judge Your people, ...for who can judge this vast people of Yours?" (3:9). This unusual request is uncharacteristic of royalty. The Torah has already warned us that the king has a tendency and temptation to indulge in the trappings of luxury and power.[11] The youthful Solomon is wary of these pitfalls; he requests neither

---

8. "Noah built an altar to God...and offered burnt sacrifices on the altar. And God smelled the sweet smell, and God said...and God blessed Noah and his sons..." (Gen. 8:20–9:1).
9. "He came to Beersheba and offered sacrifices to the God of his father, Isaac. And God spoke to Israel in a nighttime vision..." (ibid. 46:1–2).
10. This is the NJPS translation. See the previous chapter, "Generating Stability," n. 19, where we examined this phrase. According to Rashi and Radak on I Kings 3:7, Solomon was only twelve years old when he took the reins of leadership.
11. See Deuteronomy 17:14–20, which outlines the laws of the king. The key phrase,

wealth nor military prowess a long life, but only wisdom – wisdom to be applied in the service of his nation. Solomon seeks to dispense justice, not aggregate power. God welcomes his request:[12]

> And God said to him: Because you have asked for this –
> you did not ask for long life,
> you did not ask for riches,
> you did not ask for the life of your enemies,
> but you asked for discernment in administering justice –
> I now do as you have spoken.
> I grant you a wise and discerning heart;
> there has never been anyone like you before,
> nor will anyone like you arise again. (3:11–12)

THE TRIAL

Solomon's dream is followed by the famous trial in which two women contest the identity of a newborn baby, each claiming it to be her own. Solomon resorts to a shocking solution, employing a dangerous and unorthodox extralegal decision – "Cut the live child in two..." (3:25) – thereby solving what would appear to be an irresolvable case. This story is an exemplar of Solomon's God-given gift of wisdom. It makes a deep impression upon the nation:

> When all Israel heard the decision that the king had rendered, they stood in awe of the king, for they saw that he possessed

---

repeated three times, is "he may not amass for himself." The verses specifically limit the king from accumulating military power, wives, and money: "He may not amass horses for himself.... And he may not amass wives for himself, lest his heart go astray; nor may he amass silver and gold to excess for himself."

12. Note God's warning that Solomon adhere to the "laws and commandments" (1 Kings 3:14), reminiscent of David's instructions in 2:3–4. This reiterated notion – that blessings and success are predicated upon commitment to Torah observance – is a reflection of Jewish values. These verses, innocuous in context, become rather ominous in hindsight, as we realize how susceptible Solomon is to negative influences; see note 2, above.

divine wisdom to execute justice. And King Solomon was king over all Israel. (3:28–4:1)[13]

We will make two brief comments about this highly unusual court hearing.[14] First, it is notable that this story is about two women from the lowest stratum of society. Two prostitutes present a case, and they receive an audience with the king! This should not be taken for granted; it is apparent that there is a policy of open access to the king in adjudicating civilian disputes. This may be illustrated in other episodes in the Bible:[15]

> Once when the king was walking on the city wall, a woman cried out to him: "Help me, Your Majesty!" (II Kings 6:26)

> The woman of Tekoa came to the king, flung herself face down on the ground, … and cried out, "Help, O King!" The king asked, "What troubles you?" (II Sam. 14:4–5)

---

13. We have characterized I Kings 3 as the first episode of Solomon's independent reign, after solidifying his position as king. But the juxtaposition of these two verses – the connection between Israel's reaction to Solomon's judgment and the phrase that follows, "And King Solomon was king over all Israel" – indicates that even chapter 3 is in essence part of the foundational stage of Solomon's monarchy. Chapters 1–2 ensure Solomon's political survival within the higher political echelons; chapter 3 secures him the popular support and confidence of his subjects, of the entire nation of Israel. See Rashi, Radak, and especially Malbim, who all share this approach.

14. The story is complex and has been discussed at length elsewhere. Our presentation has been influenced by the literary analysis of this story by Moshe Garsiel, "Revealing and Concealing as a Narrative Strategy in Solomon's Judgment: I Kings 3:16–18," CBQ 64 (2002): 229–47; and Meir Sternberg, *The Poetics of Biblical Narrative* (Bloomington: Indiana University Press, 1985), 167–70.

15. See the original request for a king – "Appoint for us a king to judge us" (I Sam. 8:5) – although the intent may be in the broad realm of leadership more than specifically judicial functions. We see King David sitting in court as a judge (II Sam. 15:1–6), and one of our first impressions of Moses' relationship with the people is the image of their standing before him from morning to night, waiting for judgment (Ex. 18:16). Through these stories, we see that dispensation of justice is central to the leadership role. Another example of the king's being available to adjudicate legal matters appears in I Kings 21:39.

Evidently, regular citizens are granted access to the highest authority in the land, even outside the palace walls! Solomon's palace contains a courtroom, in which the king welcomes the entire gamut of citizens who seek his counsel.[16] Our story of the two prostitutes deliberately presents two women from the murkiest sector of society, exhibiting the fact that Solomon seeks to make justice accessible to the entire nation, not simply to the upper classes.

A second point of significance is that this dispute is held without a shred of corroborating evidence: "And there was none with us in the house" (1 Kings 3:18). Moreover, the manner in which the narrative is presented makes it impossible to identify which of the women is telling the truth; the verses refer obliquely to "the first woman" (3:17) and "the other woman" (3:22), with no obvious way of knowing which of the litigants is "the woman whose son was alive" (3:26). While scholars have attempted to decode the deliberately opaque and confusing language,[17] the text is delicately crafted to reflect the case itself – indecipherable and impossible to resolve. At first, the reader senses, along with Solomon, that the case is at an impasse; there is no conclusive evidence that might expose the identity of the true mother. Upon hearing Solomon's

---

16. 1 Kings 7:7.
17. The traditional commentators are intrigued by two questions: (1) Which of the women is telling the truth, the "first" or the "other woman"? (2) Has Solomon figured out the case before he resorts to the sword?

    In answering the first question, most commentators assume that the "first woman" is the truthful one, due to her polite language, "Please, my lord" (ibid. 3:17 and echoed in 3:26), as opposed to the coarse and terse rejections of the "other woman." Malbim contests this reading, however, preferring to see the "other woman" as truthful on the basis of the order of her words, "No, my son is the live one; your son is the dead one" (3:22), in which she speaks of the live child first, thereby indicating him to be her true concern. In contrast, the "first" woman states, "No! Your son is the dead one; my son is the live one" (ibid.); her attention is upon the dead child.

    Regarding the second question, Malbim suggests that Solomon had cracked the case prior to his decree to cut the baby in half. Similarly, Radbaz, Rabbi Yosef Kara, and Abarbanel claim that Solomon's astute and insightful observation of mother and child led him to deduce whose child was whose.

    Ralbag, however, proposes that Solomon was baffled due to a paucity of evidence. He sees the sword solution as a ploy to induce one of the women to confess. I believe that the manner in which the story is told gives credence to this option.

shocking decision, "Fetch me a sword" (3:24), the reader becomes confused and alarmed. But as the order is pronounced, "Cut the live child in two," the reader identifies with the terror felt by the mother of the baby:

> But the woman whose son was the live one pleaded with the king, for she was overcome with compassion for her son; "Please, my lord!" she cried. **"Give her the live child, and by no means kill him!"** The other insisted: "He shall be neither mine nor yours; divide him!" The king answered and said: **"Give her the live child, and by no means kill him!** She is his mother." (3:26–27)

The fact that Solomon pronounces the identity of the true mother using her own words, a verbatim repetition of her outcry, leaves us with no doubt that his design all along has been to tease this emotional outburst from the women. He has in essence elicited a confession; we realize that Solomon has arrived at the truth, the correct solution.

However, in a marvelous literary stroke, the account of the trial concludes without any verifiable means of deciphering which of the women is the true mother! The reader is deliberately left in the dark as Solomon solves the case, assured that he has discovered the truth and executed justice, even though the resolution is concealed and elusive! This literary device echoes the sense of wonder experienced by the nation as it marveled at the wisdom of the king.

THE IDEAL KING

The assessment of Solomon expressed in this story may best be put into context by means of a few famous lines from the prophet Isaiah, who paints a portrait of the ideal king:

> But a shoot shall grow out of the stump of Jesse,
> A twig shall sprout from his stock.
> The spirit of the Lord shall alight upon him,
> A spirit of wisdom and insight,
> A spirit of counsel and valor,
> A spirit of devotion and reverence for the Lord.
> He shall sense the truth by his reverence for the Lord;

> He shall not judge by what his eyes behold,
> Or decide by what his ears perceive.
> He shall judge the poor with equity (*tzedaka*),
> And decide with justice for the lowly of the land....
> Justice shall be the girdle of his loins.... (Is. 11:1–5)

This prophecy envisions an idyllic era in which "The wolf shall lie down with the lamb..." (11:6). This is messianic imagery. In an earlier chapter of Isaiah, the king is described in a similar fashion:

> For a child has been born to us, a son has been given us, and the authority has settled on his shoulders...a peaceable ruler... peace without limit, upon **David's throne** and kingdom. That it may be firmly established in justice and equity now and evermore. (9:5–6)

Solomon is not the only king who has been associated with the championing of justice,[18] but this is his foremost accolade. When we read Isaiah's messianic depiction, so reflective of the imagery and language used in the context of Solomon – the era of peace and justice, the sprout of Jesse – we sense that Solomon is the exemplar of the ideal concept of the monarchy. This is a formidable starting point.

---

18. One in particular comes to mind – Jehoshaphat (whose very name is evocative); see II Chronicles 19 and our final chapter, "I Kings 22: Jehoshaphat, King of Judah."

1 Kings 4

A Fresh National Agenda

The success of an empire is dependent upon effective government. In chapter 4, we find two separate lists of Solomon's administrative infrastructure, the first detailing the high officials who make up his government and the second an enumeration of twelve regional provinces, or administrative districts, into which the land of Israel is divided.

At first glance, these are nothing but a tedious series of names and places. However, when we encounter detailed technical information of this sort, our approach will be to mine it for the drama that lies between the lines.

SOLOMON'S CABINET

What can the roster of Solomon's government officials reveal about the agenda that he sets for the country and his national priorities? We will analyze Solomon's government by comparing it to a similar list of David's inner circle some years earlier:

	Solomon – 1 Kings 4:2–6	David – II Sam. 20:23–26
1	Priest	Army – chief of staff
2	Scribes	Cherethites and Pelethites
3	Secretary	Tax minister
4	Army – chief of staff	Secretary
5	Priests	Scribe
6	Minister of the provinces	Priests
7	"Friend" of the king	Priest for David
8	Minister over the "house"	
9	Tax minister	

We observe that for David, the leading official was the head of the military;[1] his second position was reserved for the king's personal guard, the Cherethites and Pelethites.[2] In contrast, Solomon's government lists the military (chief of staff) far lower, and the king's guard is entirely absent.

How can we explain these differences? David rose to fame as a military officer. During his era, the country had to wage war in order to secure its borders. By embarking upon a campaign of foreign conquest, David expanded his small kingdom into an empire. On the domestic front, he experienced mutiny and civil war. It is thus quite natural to see the military taking the prime position in David's agenda, with the king's guard occupying second place.

In contrast, national security is not the most pressing item on Solomon's agenda. The nation is at peace (5:1–5), Solomon's safety is uncontested, and we never see him go out to war. Instead, Solomon's top government position goes to the priest, with a further set of priests added later in the list. This emphasis on priesthood reflects Solomon's

---

1. This is also the case in another list of David's ministers, in II Samuel 8:16–20.
2. *Targum Yonatan* translates the Hebrew terms here, "*hakreti... hapleti*," as "bows and slingshots," whereas Josephus describes the Cherethites and Pelethites as David's bodyguards. *Da'at Mikra* adopts the view that they constitute the king's personal security regiment. See Yehuda Kiel, *Da'at Mikra, II Samuel* (Jerusalem: Mossad Harav Kook, 1981), commentary on 8:18 [Hebrew].

monumental project – the Temple – and the central role that religion plays in his world.

The second emphasis of Solomon's government is the central role of national administration. As opposed to David's war cabinet, the image projected by Solomon's list is that of a stately, civilian agenda. There is an increased administrative workload, and we accordingly see the domestic government team upgraded and expanded in the list. David had a single scribe, a secretary, and a tax collector; Solomon has two scribes, the minister over the provinces, the king's "friend,"[3] and the minister over the house. With its increased regional jurisdiction, Solomon's kingdom requires a larger and more sophisticated system of bureaucracy and governance.

The precise function of each of these roles is difficult to grasp. The scribe is described by Rashi as the king's chronicler and by the *Da'at Mikra* commentary as a sort of home secretary. These roles are well documented; archaeology has discovered parallel government positions in ancient Egypt and Mesopotamia. Later in the book of Kings, this threesome – the minister over the house, the scribe, and the secretary – conducts war negotiations with the Assyrians.[4] The book of Jeremiah records an "office of the scribe" situated in the Temple compound, in which "all the ministers sit."[5] We can thus say with some certainty that

---

3. The *re'eh hamelekh* (4:5) is a mysterious title about which there is little concrete information. Is this an informal position or an official one? *Targum Yonatan* translates it as *shushbin*, which usually refers to a bridegroom's best man. Radak speaks of some sort of companion who becomes a personal assistant to the king. The title of *re'eh* is applied to Jonadab (II Sam. 13:3, 32), who seems to be a royal courtier and who is described as "a very wise man." Chushai the Archite, "*re'eh David*," is another loyal consultant or adviser; see II Sam. 15:37, 16:16, and 17:5. Does the phrase thus indicate an official adviser to the monarchy? Some have pointed to the term *mere'ehu* in Genesis 26:26 in reference to Abimelech's entourage (similarly in II Samuel 3:8 and I Kings 16:11). Is there a connection?
4. II Kings 18:18, 19:2. For more on the scribe, see II Kings 12:11, 23:3, 25:19. I Chronicles 27:32 speaks of "Jonathan, uncle of David, a counselor, wise man, and scribe"; in II Chronicles 26:11, the "scribe" is responsible for the army. The "minister over the house" is found in I Kings 16:9 and as Ahab's closest adviser in 18:3; see also II Kings 10:5, 15:5.
5. Jeremiah 36:12.

these administrative offices remained in place throughout the First Temple period.

To summarize, Solomon's government, in the absence of military conflict, is free to turn itself toward a domestic agenda, to the Temple and affairs of state. This orientation constitutes a shift from earlier periods.

THE TWELVE ADMINISTRATIVE REGIONS (4:7–19)

At this point, the chapter moves on to the demarcation of the twelve administrative regions through which Solomon finances the country.

The number twelve is striking in that it recalls the classic tribal division that we have been accustomed to throughout Jewish history, since the Exodus and through the settlement period and the Judges. When we examine the list of districts, however, we discern that the geographical regions do not match specific tribes. In fact, only five regions (Mount Ephraim, Naphtali, Asher, Issachar, and Benjamin) correspond to tribal identities. It appears that Solomon has remodeled tribal borders and generated new regional boundaries.

What is the motive behind this division into administrative counties? What purpose does it serve? The text identifies these areas as regional tax zones:

> These officers financed King Solomon and all those who sat at King Solomon's table, each one for a month; they let nothing be lacking. Barley also and straw for the horses and swift steeds… every man according to his charge. (5:7–8)

But what is Solomon's objective in altering the ancient tribal divisions? And what are the implications of this reshuffling of tribal boundaries?

1. *Expanded territory* – One theory views the new division as a response to the capture and settlement of new areas, previously unpopulated by Israel in the times of Joshua and the Judges. Population shift requires the drawing of new civic lines. Some of these new areas, such as the region of Dor, with its lucrative port, were small, but generated significant revenue; this region was capable of competing financially with provinces much larger in

area and population. Solomon, understanding the new economic realities of Israel, restructures his country accordingly.

2. *A new national agenda* – Some suggest that we are witnessing an attempt to modernize the kingdom and discard the ancient tribal division.[6] The tribal period of the Judges has come to a close. Now, with one king and a united nation, the tribal identities seem archaic and superfluous. Solomon retains five tribal units, but creates seven new regions that muddle and modernize the traditional boundaries.

But rezoning the country has its hazards. Notwithstanding Solomon's intent, historic identities endure; ethnic statuses remain intact. Solomon's changes are most severe for the tribes of Ephraim and Manasseh, as they suffer from a more invasive subdivision, and hence a disproportionate tax burden. This uneven policy is possibly deliberate, intended to weaken the tribes of Joseph, who represent a potential source of opposition to the king, but this strategy has a devastating ripple effect in later years. The act that eventually tears Solomon's kingdom apart after his death is a demand for a reduction of the crushing tax burden, and the epicenter of the revolt is the tribes of Joseph.[7]

A further significant and troubling detail is that the tribe of Judah is not specified in this list of tax colonies. Some suggest that this omission is evidence that Solomon's own tribe is fully absolved of its tax burden. *Da'at Mikra* denies this favoritism on Solomon's part, asserting that such blatant favoritism would surely have featured prominently as an argument in Jeroboam's rebellion. *Da'at Mikra* therefore adopts an unconventional reading that merges verses 4:19 and 4:20, to read, "And one prefect who was in the land of Judah." In this reading, Judah constitutes a thirteenth province, with its own administrator and tax collector.

---

6. O. Bustenai and M. Garsiel, eds., *Encyclopedia of the World of the Bible, 1 Kings* (Tel Aviv: Davidson-Atai, 1994), 48 [Hebrew].

7. 1 Kings 11:27–28, 12:4; and A. Grossman, "1 Kings, Chapter 4: Solomon's District Governors," http://www.daat.ac.il/daat/tanach/rishonim/grosman2.htm [Heb].

1 Kings 5

Building an Empire

> Solomon's rule extended over all the kingdoms from the Euphrates to the land of the Philistines and the boundary of Egypt; they brought Solomon tribute and were subject to him all his life.... For he controlled the whole west of the Euphrates – all the kings west of the Euphrates from Tiphsah to Gaza; and he had peace on all his borders roundabout. (1 Kings 5:1, 4)

Solomon controls a vast tract of the Middle East, ruling an expansive empire that stretches from the border of Egypt to Mesopotamia. His power was uncontested, and all nations "brought Solomon tribute and were subject to him all his life."

We already know that Solomon has allied himself with Egypt – "Solomon married [the daughter of] Pharaoh, king of Egypt" (3:1).[1] Scholars suggest that this marriage, as well as the gift of the city of Gezer (9:16–17), reflects the fact that Solomon is the dominant regional power

---

1. Malbim views this marriage as an expression of a political alliance between Egypt and Solomon.

player.[2] Furthermore, Solomon's role as the market maker for Egyptian horses (10:28) demonstrates his financial influence. All of this brings unprecedented wealth and higher living standards to Israel:

> Judah and Israel were as numerous as the sands of the sea; they ate and drank and were content.... (4:20)[3]

THE ARMY AND BUILDING PROJECTS

Whereas David's army was made up primarily of reserves (II Sam. 24:9), Solomon has a sizable standing army of twelve thousand horsemen and forty thousand horses (1 Kings 5:6),[4] providing him with a defense force and a ready deterrent capability. The retention of such large forces is a colossal undertaking in that it necessitates the building of army bases and the employment of an enormous staff to service the military, beyond the fighters themselves – an infrastructure to provide food for the soldiers, cooks and maintenance workers, horse grooms, as well as the procurement of military hardware. The administration of this system expands the role of central government and its consumption extensively (5:7–8).

Three military centers are built for the chariotry (9:15 and 10:26): Hazor – the northern command; Megiddo, in the center of the country, controlling the Jezreel Valley, the trade routes, and the coastal plain; and Gezer – the southern command, controlling the southern approach to the country.[5] Solomon builds Bethhoron on the mountain pass that leads

---

2. See O. Bustenai and M. Garsiel, *Encyclopedia of the World of the Bible, 1 Kings* (Tel Aviv: Davidson-Atai, 1994), 36 [Hebrew].

3. See also 1 Kings 5:5.

4. Many note the flagrant violation of the directive addressed to Israelite kings that "he may not amass horses" (Deut. 17:17). Furthermore, the continuation of the verse there – the prohibition of trade with Egypt in order to procure horses – is also relevant, given Solomon's obvious contravention of that law in 1 Kings 10:28. These issues are not incidental; they are the heart of the excesses and ensuing downfall of Solomon, which we will examine at some length. See Hanan Gafni, "The Reign of Solomon – The Failure and Its Reasons," *Megadim* 31 (2000): 87–94 [Hebrew].

5. In the late 1950s and 1960s, Yigael Yadin uncovered impressive six-chambered gates in Tel Hazor, as well as in Megiddo and Gezer, and declared that they dated to Solomon's period. Since then, Amnon Ben-Tor has verified these findings, discov-

to Jerusalem to defend the capital (9:17), as well as other cities, giving him greater control over trade routes (9:18). He also constructs store cities to ensure the resilience of the imperial center (10:19). A strong country must have the wherewithal to withstand prolonged drought or siege; Solomon's warehouses and silos serve this objective.

In a project that could have been achieved only by the very strongest and wealthiest of kings, Solomon builds a port at Ezion-Geber, Eilat today (9:26–28, 10:11). The expense involved, the technical expertise and industry needed to build huge seafaring vessels, as well as the defense of the supply line stretching long distances through the desert to Eilat, exceed the economic and logistical capability of the average king.

Solomon's huge military commitment and extensive building demonstrate the extraordinary might of his kingdom.

CENTER OF WORLD KNOWLEDGE

> The Lord endowed Solomon with wisdom and discernment in great measure, with understanding as vast as the sands on the seashore. Solomon's wisdom was greater than the wisdom of all the children of the east country, and than all the wisdom of the Egyptians. He was the wisest of all men, … and his fame spread among all the surrounding nations. He composed three thousand proverbs, and his songs numbered a thousand and five. He discoursed about trees, from the cedar in Lebanon to the hyssop that grows out of the wall; and he discoursed about beasts, birds, creeping things, and fish. Men of all peoples came to hear Solomon's wisdom, [sent by] all the kings of the earth, who had heard of his wisdom. (5:10–14)

---

ering a fortified outer wall of the city that dates to the ninth or tenth century BCE. See Ben-Tor, "Excavating Hazor: Solomon's City Rises from the Ashes," *Biblical Archaeology Review* 25:2 (1999): 26–37, 60. More recently, Eilat Mazar has discovered a similar gate and remains of a wall in Jerusalem's Ophel excavation park, which she dates to the time of Solomon. See Eilat Mazar, *Discovering the Solomonic Wall in Jerusalem: A Remarkable Archaeological Adventure* (Jerusalem: Shoham Academic Research and Publication, 2011).

Solomon is an impressive thinker. The thousand and five songs and three thousand parables referred to may accord with at least some of the content of Song of Songs and Proverbs,[6] which are attributed to him;[7] Ḥazal add Ecclesiastes to his repertoire.[8] But his wisdom goes beyond that; the book of Kings notes his knowledge of trees and animals and his superiority over all other known scholars. Rashi interprets this as referring to his knowledge of natural sciences:

> "He discoursed about trees" – the health of each plant and the constitution of the timber; which is suited to what type of construction, what soil it needs. And likewise "about beasts" – their medicinal needs, reproductive techniques, and nutrition.

We gain the impression that Solomon is a master of philosophy and literature, botany and zoology, and that no sphere of human wisdom eludes him.[9]

How does Solomon amass this huge knowledge base? Can all this knowledge possibly be concentrated in one individual? And how is it possible for all those who come to seek wisdom from the king to study with a single man, who has many other responsibilities, let alone be mentored by him?

---

6. See Yehuda Kiel, *Da'at Mikra, 1 Kings* [Hebrew]. He details four possible definitions of the term *meshalim* (which we've translated as parables): (1) proverbs and idioms – wisdom in concise phrases; (2) prophetic visions, such as Balaam's *mashal* (see Num. 23:7, 18; 24:3, 15); (3) philosophical musings (as in Job 27 and 29); (4) victory songs (see Num. 21:27). What these all have in common is the songlike, poetic, figurative form of symbolic, evocative language. In addition, the *mashal* frequently conveys a message, a practical lesson.
7. See the opening verses of Proverbs and Song of Songs.
8. *Seder Olam* 15, *Eccl. Rabba* 1:1, and *Song Rabba* 1:6. Ecclesiastes opens by designating its author: "The words of Ecclesiastes son of David, king in Jerusalem" (1:1), and since Solomon fits that description, rabbinic sources standardly attribute the book to him. Reading Ecclesiastes 2:4–10, one is impressed with the biographical overlap between Solomon and Ecclesiastes. Moreover, 12:9 emphasizes Ecclesiastes' parables.
9. *Song Rabba* 1:8 suggests that Solomon's genius lay in the connections that he made between disparate disciplines. It was his multidisciplinary approach that made him unique.

We may answer this question with another question. When we say that Solomon's wisdom exceeded that of every civilization and scholar, are we speaking of Solomon the individual or his kingdom as a whole? When the text says that "Solomon built," we assume that the king planned, supervised, and financed the construction, not that he actually chiseled the stonework and cut the wood. Similarly, when we discuss Solomon's wisdom regarding trees, beasts, and fowl, we are speaking of the intellectual environment he has created in Jerusalem. Not all this broad knowledge need be attributed to Solomon personally.

IMPORTING EXPERTISE

Solomon's genius lies in his plan to harness all worldly knowledge and make Jerusalem the hub of all wisdom, be it scientific, artistic, techno-logical, or intellectual. Sometimes he achieves this goal by importing foreign expertise.

When approaching Hiram, the king of Tyre, in order to procure timber, Solomon specifies that "there is none among us who know how to cut timber like the inhabitants of Sidon" (5:20). Yet Solomon insists, "My servants will work with yours" (ibid.). His intention is that his men should learn this art, the work and skill of the lumberjack, from the Phoe-nicians. He imports not only cedar wood, but also the technical know-how, thus expanding the knowledge base and skill set of the nation. He pursues a similar strategy when building a fleet of ships:

> Hiram sent servants with the fleet, experienced mariners...to serve **with** Solomon's men. (9:26)

Likewise, Solomon imports artisans and experts in their various fields, appreciating their professional skill and technological advantage. One example is Hiram of Tyre,[10] an expert in the crafting of metals:

> King Solomon sent for Hiram and brought him over from Tyre. He was the son of a widow of the tribe of Naphtali and his father had been a Tyrian coppersmith; he was endowed with

---

10. This Hiram coincidentally shares the king's name.

skill, ability, and talent for executing all work with bronze;[11] he came to King Solomon and performed all his work. (7:13–14)

Beyond Solomon's personal genius and prowess, he pools the most advanced knowledge and scholarship in his kingdom. He establishes Jerusalem as the center of global expertise. He turns it into the Yale and Harvard, the Oxford and Cambridge of the ancient world. It thus becomes a magnet for intellectuals and students who seek to further their education at this crucible of knowledge.[12]

INTERNATIONAL RELATIONS

King Hiram of Tyre sent his officials to Solomon when he heard that he had been anointed in place of his father, for Hiram had always been a friend of David. (5:15)

Extensive international relations play a significant role in Solomon's empire. His relationship with King Hiram is a close one, and they collaborate in many areas, among them timber and shipping. We have already mentioned Solomon's alliance with Egypt, and we will hear further about his wives from the surrounding nations – a reflection of the political ties that he has forged throughout the region – as well as his interaction with the queen of Sheba, who visits the king in order to consult with him.

SURPLUS AND PROSPERITY

When Hiram, the king of Tyre, contracts with Solomon to supply him with raw materials for his building projects, Solomon pays Hiram out of his nation's agricultural surplus:

---

11. This language directly parallels the depiction of Bezalel in Exodus 31:3. The obvious intent is to portray Solomon's Temple as reflective of and equivalent to Moses' Tabernacle.
12. Although we are based here on 5:14, note the parallel with the messianic vision of Isaiah 2:2–3.

...twenty thousand measures of wheat, provision for his household, and twenty measures of finely pressed oil – thus Solomon
gave Hiram annually. (5:25)

This business transaction gives us a clear indication of an agricultural
boom that fuels the entire economy. In a tangible reflection of the
divine blessings listed in the Torah,[13] the country produces vast excesses
of grain and oil. The nation of Israel is described as sitting "every man
under his vine and fig tree" (5:5), a metaphor for calm, serenity, and a
high standard of living.

Moreover, the opulence of the kingdom bespeaks economic
power and plenty:

All of King Solomon's drinking cups were gold, and all the tableware of the Lebanon Forest house was pure gold; there was no
silver; it counted for nothing in Solomon's days.... The king made
silver as plentiful as stones in Jerusalem, and cedars as plentiful
as the sycamores in the coastal plain. (10:21, 27).

Everything Solomon does is on a grand scale. The Temple is made with
the finest stonework (5:31), overlaid with imported wood paneling
(6:15), engraved with intricate carvings (6:29), and plated with gold
(6:21). The Temple takes seven years to build, with verses describing
the "70,000 porters and 80,000 quarries in the hills...3,300 supervi-
sors...huge blocks of hewn stone" (5:29–31). The king's lavish royal
buildings are equally magnificent: the house of the Lebanon Forest,
the hall of pillars, the throne courtroom, and the royal residence, with
massive stones, mirrors, and enormous dimensions. All of these are
designed to project the grandeur and luxury befitting an emperor of
Solomon's repute.

---

13. Examples include Deuteronomy 11:14 (the second paragraph of the Shema) and
    Leviticus 26:5, 10. In the context of the blessings promised in *parashat Behukkotai*,
    which begins, "If My statutes you follow" (26:3), note 1 Kings 6:12: "if you follow
    My statutes."

THE PEOPLES OF THE EARTH WILL KNOW YOUR NAME

We have depicted a wide array of Solomon's impressive achievements. What is the purpose, the objective that drives this colossal enterprise? Why does Solomon need this empire? What is his motivation, his master plan?

Solomon articulates his aim when he dedicates the Temple. In his inaugural prayer, he says:

> If the foreigner, who is not of Your people, Israel, comes from a distant land **for the sake of Your name – for they shall hear about Your great name** and Your mighty hand... – when he comes to pray toward this house, listen in Your heavenly abode, and grant all that the foreigner asks of You; **thus, the peoples of the earth will know Your name and revere You..., and they will recognize that Your name is attached to this house that I have built.** (8:41–43)

Solomon views the Temple as open to the non-Jewish world. He seeks to create a situation in which foreigners, gentiles, will hear about God and come to find out more, to pay homage to the Almighty. Solomon repeats this point later in his prayer:

> That **all** the peoples of the world may know that the Lord alone is God; there is no other. (8:60)

A classic illustration of Solomon's program is the visit of the queen of Sheba:

> The queen of Sheba heard of Solomon's fame concerning the name of the Lord; she came to prove him with questions. She arrived in Jerusalem with a very large retinue, with camels bearing spices, a great quantity of gold, and precious stones. And when she came to Solomon, she asked him of all that she had in mind. Solomon had answers to all her questions; there was nothing that the king did not know.... When the queen of Sheba observed all of Solomon's wisdom and the palace that he had built, and the

meat of his table, and the sitting of his servants, the service and attire of his attendants, and his wine service, and the burnt offerings that he offered at the house of the Lord, she was left breathless. She said to the king, "The report that I heard in my own land about you and your wisdom was true. But I did not believe the reports until I came and saw with my own eyes that not even the half had been told to me! Your wisdom and prosperity exceed the fame that I heard. Happy are your men, happy are your servants who stand continually before you and hear your wisdom. **Praised be the Lord, your God, who delighted in you to set you on the throne of Israel; for the Lord loves Israel forever;** therefore He made you king, **to do judgment and justice.**" (10:1–10)

A powerful queen of a neighboring country has "heard" about Solomon. His reputation has spread; his power and wealth are apparent, as is his genius. People tell stories and legends about him – "The report that I heard in my own land was true ... not even the half had been told to me!" She meets with Solomon as part of a state visit, similar to the way that world leaders visit Washington today to discuss regional politics, trade, and the economy. The impressive imperial metropolis of Jerusalem is designed to appeal to tourists and intellectuals along with those who seek art, trade, and other wisdom. This queen, an exceptionally wealthy lady,[14] is dazzled. Is she overwhelmed by the beautiful architecture and streets of Jerusalem? Possibly. But upon examining her words closely, we find that she responds by praising God, by recognizing His gift of

---

14. Witness the gifts that she brings. Historians say that the area she governed in Arabia would have given her significant wealth. We have presented this visit in a spiritual vein. This is reflected, for example, in *Ex. Rabba* 27:4, in which the queen of Sheba is equated with Jethro and Rahab as expressing a passionate interest in the faith and life of the Jewish people.

Alternative approaches view this visit as having a distinctly sexual dimension. According to Rashi on 1 Kings 10:13 (in the traditional editions of his commentary), Solomon fathered a child of the queen of Sheba who was the antecedent of Nebuchadnezzar. This tradition may be found in earlier texts such as Ecclesiasticus (*Ben Sira*) and *Second Targum* on Esther 1:3. *Midrash Mishlei* 1 presents the queen's riddles as sexual.

wisdom to Solomon and his vision of "judgment and justice." Jerusalem itself reflects justice!

Solomon prays that foreigners hear about his fame and God's reputation, and that they come to seek God. This story testifies that his grand accomplishments have successfully realized his aspiration!

CONCLUSION

Solomon carefully constructs a magnificent empire. His objective is to create a national enterprise that is so impressive, so imbued with God's presence, that people will be amazed and inspired by Jerusalem and instilled with awe of God.[15] He seeks to place God at the pinnacle of his empire, so that he may galvanize global homage to Him. Accordingly, we should not be surprised by the rabbinic tradition that there was a surge in conversion to Judaism in Solomon's time.[16]

The spiritual epicenter of this imperial edifice is the Temple and its construction, to which we now direct our attention.

---

15. For more regarding this vision, see Joshua Berman, "David's Request to Build the Temple," in Nathaniel Helfgot, ed., *Yeshivat Chovevei Torah Rabbinical School Tanakh Companion to the Book of Samuel* (New Jersey: Ben Yehuda Press, 2006), 207–26.

16. Yevamot 79b; Maimonides, *Mishneh Torah*, Laws of Forbidden Relations 13:15.

1 Kings 6

The Temple: A New Era

The crowning glory of Solomon's empire is undoubtedly the Temple. Indeed, a full three chapters (6–8) detail its construction and dedication. The fact that this section occupies the center stage of the Solomon narrative testifies to its predominant status.

EXPANDED DIMENSIONS

One of the elements of the Temple that makes an immediate impression is its large dimensions. Solomon's Temple is double the length and breadth (60 cubits × 20 cubits) and triple the height (30 cubits) of its predecessor, the Tabernacle. The two main chambers of the Tabernacle – the main hall (*Heikhal*) and the Holy of Holies (*Devir*) – now have an added entrance hall (*Ulam*), extending the structure by another 10 cubits. In the times in which it was built, this was a building of sizable proportions.

The utensils, or ritual furniture, of the Tabernacle are also enlarged or multiplied in the Temple. As opposed to the single menora, table, and washbasin (*kiyor*) in the Tabernacle, Solomon's Temple contains ten menoras – five on each side of the main hall (1 Kings 7:49); ten tables

Solomon's Temple

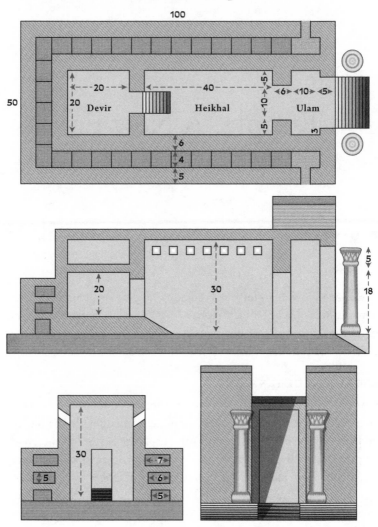

for the showbread (11 Chron. 4:8); and ten washbasins (1 Kings 7:38). How can we explain Solomon's tenfold increase?

1. *Imperial grandeur* – We have discussed how everything in Solomon's kingdom is on a larger scale, luxurious and striking. The

impressive Temple structure is built with expensive, dressed stone and paneled with the finest wood, which is carved and engraved and then overlaid with gold (7:9, 15–18, 21–22). This extravagant building amply demonstrates the shift in national fortunes and the transition from a nomadic wilderness people to a regional power broker. The ten menoras, tables, and washbasins reflect this atmosphere of abundance.

2. *Logistics* – Rabbi Meir Simḥa Hakohen of Dvinsk, author of the *Meshekh Ḥokhma* commentary on the Bible, explains the increase with a simple mathematical calculation. With the Temple's increase in size, the internal space is tenfold that of the Tabernacle. Hence, ten menoras are needed to provide the equivalent illumination produced by a single menora in the Tabernacle![1]

3. *Symbolism* – *Yalkut Shimoni* explains that the ten basins and ten tables reflect the increased needs of a more populous nation as regards rainfall (water, represented by the basin) and grain (the table held loaves of bread). The guiding principle is that the Temple is the conduit for God's grace; a larger nation requires the representation of a larger Temple. Similarly, the ten candelabras hold seventy lights, corresponding to the seventy nations of the world. The idea here is that "as long as the lights shone, [the nations] would be subjugated."[2]

This sense of expansion is not limited to the material realm, but manifests itself in other spheres. Whereas the Torah's proscription of hewn stone applies exclusively to the altar,[3] in Solomon's Temple, this law is broadened to become the standard for the entire building site!

---

1. *Meshekh Hokhma*, Exodus 27:20. The Tabernacle was 10 x 30 x 10 = 3,000 square cubits. The Temple was 20 × 60 × 30 = 36,000 square cubits, a multiple of 12!

2. *Yalkut Shimoni*, 1 Kings 185.

3. "And if you make for Me an altar of stones, do not build it of hewn stones; for by wielding your tool [lit., sword] upon them, you have profaned them" (Ex. 20:22). Rashi explains the rationale of this restriction: "R. Shimon b. Eliezer used to say that the altar was created to prolong a person's life, and iron was created to shorten a person's life; one may not wield that which shortens [life] upon that which prolongs [it]."

> When the house was built, only finished stones cut at the quarry were used, so no hammer or axe or any iron tool was heard in the house when it was being built. (1 Kings 6:7)

THE EXODUS CONNECTION

The starting date for the project of building the Temple is anchored in a reference to the Exodus:

> In the 480th year after the Israelites left the land of Egypt, in the month of Ziv – that is, the second month – in the fourth year of his reign over Israel, Solomon built the house to God. (6:1)

The standard protocol in the book of Kings calls for a significant event to be listed in reference to the years of the king's reign. Why is a reference to the Exodus suitable or at all relevant? It is notable that the Exodus is a constant presence throughout these chapters, repeatedly mentioned in the ceremonial dedication of the Temple (see 8:9, 16, 21, 51, 53, and 65). What is the nature of the linkage between the Exodus and the Temple?

Despite the length of time since the Exodus, the Temple is viewed as the culmination and completion of a long journey that commenced with the nation's leaving Egypt. In Israel's jubilant song at the Reed Sea, we read of the Jewish people's destination, the land of Canaan:

> You will bring them and plant them in Your holy mountain,
> A place for You to dwell (*makhon leshivtekha*), O Lord!
> The Temple, O Lord, which Your hands established.
> The Lord will reign **forever and ever**. (Ex. 15:17–18)

These lines reveal a national master plan – the entry to the land will culminate in the establishment of the Temple. Indeed, the phrase *makhon leshivtekha*, "a place for You to dwell," alongside the designation of "forever," is repeated by Solomon four times in his inaugural prayer at the Temple:

I have built You a stately house, a place for You to dwell **forever**.
(1 Kings 8:13)[4]

With the building of the Temple, Israel has indeed reached the "holy mountain."

The Temple constitutes a watershed in Jewish history. If the Exodus is the birth of the nation, its formative period, then the building of the Temple reflects a point at which Israel is robust and independent, having reached a mature state of adulthood.[5] It is possible that the number 480 (the number of years since the Exodus) – forty years multiplied by twelve (the tribes of Israel) – expresses the perfection of national accomplishment.[6]

A NEW CALENDAR?

Solomon, in viewing his time as the close of one era and the commencement of a new period of Jewish history, takes things a stage further – he

---

4. See also 1 Kings 8:39, 43, 49.
5. Maimonides (*Mishneh Torah*, Laws of Kings 1:1) lists three national mitzvot – to appoint a king, to eradicate Amalek, and to build the Temple. These three essentially describe a process – the establishment of an administrative system (the king), followed by the removal of an evil regime (Amalek), followed by the establishment of a focal point for national religious service (the Temple). The sense is that the Temple symbolizes a national completion of sorts, a fulfillment of our national prerequisites, and hence the nation moves into a new and more mature stage.
6. Some have seen this number as too perfect and neat, and therefore assume that it is an invention of the author of the book of Kings. Josephus (*Antiquities* 8:3) speaks of 591 years from the Exodus to the Temple, but this is probably a result of mistaken analysis of the years, including an excessive assessment of the length of the period of the Judges by putting all the historical records there end-to-end. In fact, 480 years does seem to be a correct historical approximation or estimation of this era.

 Whenever we see multiples of forty, as in the book of Judges, we may ask whether they indicate forty years precisely or simply a standardized number to express the period of a "generation." On the one hand, multiples of forty appear to be form numbers; on the other hand, is it impossible that there were forty years in the wilderness, forty days in Noah's Ark, and forty days that Moses spent on Mount Sinai? Should we challenge the lengths of David's and Solomon's reigns, both forty years?

adapts the calendar, adopting new names for the months. These are names that we do not ordinarily recognize:

The month of Ziv – that is, the second month. (6:1)

In the fourth year, the house was founded in the month of Ziv. And in the eleventh year, in the month of Bul – that is, the eighth month – the house was completed. (6:37–38)

And all of Israel were gathered to King Solomon in the month of Ethanim…that is, the seventh month. (8:2)

Three months are specified – Ziv, Bul, and Ethanim – but Solomon probably had names for all twelve months of the year. Because this episode is the sole place that these month names appear, however, it is impossible to reconstruct the names of the other nine months. The book of Kings realizes that we are unlikely to recognize these names, and therefore translates them into the traditional month numbers.[7]

Throughout the Torah, months are designated by numbers rather than names. At the time of the Exodus, Israel was instructed to begin the calendar from the month of Nisan, which thus became the "first" month (Ex. 12:1). The raw numerical ordering of unnamed months designates the month of the Exodus as the start of the year and brands the indelible mark of our miraculous national emancipation into the rhythm of time, every month bearing its imprint.[8] In a similar manner, the Hebrew days of the week are numbered rather than named. They are oriented to reflect the Creation – six days leading to Shabbat, which thus becomes the foundation of the week's structure.

Why does Solomon abandon the number system and create new names? Some scholars hear resonances of Phoenician month names, suggesting foreign influence or intent, possibly as a result of Solomon's

---

7. An identical phenomenon is found in the book of Esther, in which the Babylonian names of the months – such as Nisan, Iyar, and Adar – are translated into the classical biblical numerical system; see, for example, Esther 2:16; 3:7, 13; 8:9, 12.

8. See Nahmanides on Exodus 12:2 and 13:12.

alliance with Hiram. They hint that, much like the Tyrian influence in the Temple architecture (see 1 Kings 7:13), a new calendar was used to grant all cultures access to Israelite culture.[9] This approach, however, is unconvincing, as only the month of Ziv matches the Phoenician system. Moreover, kings like Ahab, who were far closer to Phoenician culture and even worshipped Phoenician deities, never renamed the months.

We shall suggest that these new Jewish names reflect Solomon's perspective on his era, closing the chapter of the Exodus and opening a new era of a strong nation-state and a stable monarchy.[10] As we have proposed, the Temple represents the culmination of the process of the Exodus; new names indicate a fresh historical frontier. Solomon's ambitious reframing of the months of the year (similar to his redrawing of tribal boundaries) reflects his anticipation of a new national epoch.

CHERUBIM (6:23–28)

This national coming-of-age is expressed by another feature of the Temple's architecture – namely, the huge cherubim adorning the chamber that houses the Ark of the Covenant. Solomon sculpts two wooden cherubim, overlaid with gold, which tower over the Ark and are attached to the floor.[11] Their wings – spanning ten cubits each – extend from wall to wall. Is this merely a reflection of Solomon's penchant for impressive, grand furniture, or is he making a deeper statement here?

To answer this question, we must first understand the symbolism of the cherubim. Throughout the Bible, cherubim signify God's presence. God is described as "seated on the cherubim" (Ps. 80:2, 99:1); the "presence of God [is] above the cherub" (Ezek. 10:4). Cherubim are a central feature of Ezekiel's vision of God's "chariot" (Ezek. 1).

No vessel of the Temple manifests God's presence more than the Ark:

---

9. Dr. Avigdor Horovitz, cited in O. Bustenai and M. Garsiel, *Encyclopedia of the World of the Bible, 1 Kings* (Tel Aviv: Davidson-Atai, 1994), 69 [Hebrew].

10. Similarly, Nahmanides (on Exodus 12:2) suggests that we currently use the month names of Nisan, Iyar, Sivan, etc., which are of Babylonian origin, to recall the Babylonian exile and how we returned to our land. The more recent Babylonian experience displaces the more distant Egyptian redemption.

11. See Rashi on 1 Kings 6:23.

...the Ark of God, upon which His name rests, the name of the Lord of Hosts **who dwells on the cherubim**. (ɪɪ Sam. 6:2)

The Ark stood at the epicenter of the Tabernacle in the Holy of Holies, featuring two dominant golden cherubim as the centerpiece of its cover (the *kapporet*). These cherubim demarcate the space in which God's presence is manifest when He communicates with Moses:

> I will meet with you there, and I will speak to you from above the *kapporet*, from between the two *keruvim* (cherubim) ... , all that I will command you to the children of Israel. (Ex. 25:22)

The Ark with its cherubim is God's "place," as it were. But the Ark itself does not belong in any particular location; it is designed to travel, featuring carrying rods or poles that are never to be removed (Ex. 25:15), demonstrating the portability and mobility of God's presence. The sense of movement is probably best demonstrated in the verse recited when opening our *aron kodesh*, the Ark that houses the Torah scrolls in the synagogue:

> And it was when the Ark traveled, Moses said:
> "Arise, O Lord! Scatter Your enemies; may Your foes flee before You!"
> And when [the Ark] rested, he would say:
> "Return, O Lord, to the myriads and thousands of Israel." (Num. 10:35–36)

When the Ark moves, God moves; when the Ark rests, God rests. Although the Ark serves to focus God's presence, its transient nature is an expression of God's boundlessness.

Solomon constructs and designs many furnishings and decorations for his Temple, but the Ark itself is unchangeable and irreplaceable.[12] Instead, Solomon crafts two cherubim that are immobile, fixed to the

---

12. Rashi and Nahmanides on Exodus 25:9 discuss whether the Temple utensils were required to follow the precise design and form used in the Tabernacle.

floor. This reflects the fact that God, who formerly "moved about in a tent and Tabernacle" without a permanent home,[13] now has an established address, an allocated residence, a Temple, permanent and non-transient. The fixed cherubim state that God has finally come to rest in Jerusalem. Israel's attainment of stability and permanence anchors God's presence in the city.[14]

Inward or Outward?

Which direction do the cherubim face? In Exodus, we learn that "their faces [were] **toward each other**" (25:20), but in Solomon's Temple, "**they faced the house** [Temple]" (II Chron. 3:13). The Talmud attempts to resolve the dissonance between the two images:

> When Israel acts in accordance with God's will [the cherubim turn to one another]; when Israel fails to act in accordance with God's will [they turn away from one another]. (*Bava Batra* 99a)

This tradition assumes that the cherubim were miraculous, and that both sets – in the Tabernacle and the Temple – faced each other at times and faced forward at others. This mobility on the part of the cherubim was a function of, and predicated upon, the spiritual state of Israel the Jewish people – a function of whether it worshipped God faithfully or not.[15]

An alternative, less supernatural resolution of the text is possible. The cherubim of the Tabernacle and the Temple functioned differently;

---

13. See II Samuel 7:6–7 and the entire chapter there.
14. Similarly, Solomon's Temple has a wood floor (6:15). In the Tabernacle, there was no floor, only the desert sand! This is further evidence of the shift to permanence represented by the Temple.
15. There are fascinating philosophical readings of this midrashic resolution in Rabbi Hayyim of Volozhin's *Nefesh HaHayyim* (1:8) and the Netziv's *Haamek Davar* (Ex. 25:22). This tradition of the cherubim as a spiritual barometer of the relationship between Israel and God is reflected in the following aggadic text:
    > R. Katina said: Whenever Israel came up [to the Temple] for the festival, the curtain [of the sanctuary] would be removed for them, and the cherubim, whose bodies were intertwined, were shown to them. Then [the onlookers] would be addressed thus: "Look! You are as beloved before God as the love between man and woman...." (*Yoma* 54a)

in the Tabernacle, they faced one another, while in Solomon's Temple, they faced outward. This difference in orientation may hint at a deeper shift in Solomon's Temple. The Tabernacle was internally directed, intended for service within the Jewish people. After all, in the wilderness, Israel was a detached and isolated society. In contrast, the cherubim of Solomon, the vehicles of the *Shekhina*, were oriented outward. They, like the Temple, projected to the outside world. The Temple aimed to make an impression on a wider population, to spread the name of God beyond the Jewish people.

One final architectural detail echoes this theme. These chapters abound in technical specifications and architectural jargon.[16] One particularly difficult term is *halonei shekufim atumim* (6:4). What does this phrase indicate? In ancient Hebrew, a *halon* is an open aperture in the wall.[17] The other words, however, elude any obvious interpretation.

One approach is that *shekufim* derives from the word *lehashkif*, "to look through";[18] in other words, these openings were transparent. At the same time, they were also *atumim*, sealed. In simple language, Solomon installed an unusually advanced and expensive technology in the Temple – something that we today would call a window! This reading is suggested by Abarbanel and the *Metzudot* commentaries.

However, a midrash offers a different suggestion:

> R. Ḥanina said: The Temple had windows through which light would extend to the world. As it states: "He made for the house *halonei shekufim atumim*" – they were narrow inside but wide on the outside to radiate light to the world. (*Lev. Rabba* 31:7)[19]

---

16. A comprehensive list of all the terms may be found in the appendices to *Da'at Mikra*; see vol. 2, appendix section, 77–78. The practical meaning of many of these phrases is unknown to us.

17. *Halon* is written with an accent in the *lamed*, indicating an emphasis on the letter, as if it were doubled. Thus, *halon* comes from the word *halal*, meaning a space or empty place. (In modern Hebrew, *halal* also means "outer space.")

18. See, for example, Genesis 18:16, 26:8.

19. See also *Menahot* 66b. Ralbag protests that this architectural design actually focuses light inward, not outward!

According to Ḥazal, the structure of the windows is yet another indication that the purpose of the Temple is to broadcast a message to all societies and peoples.

CONCLUSION

The themes we have discussed are intertwined. On the one hand, we have seen that Solomon's grand Temple aims to reflect the emergence of Israel from a developing tribal collective into a mature, organized, stable nation-state. On the other hand, the Temple is outward-looking, sounding its message to a broad audience, to the world community. For Solomon, these ideas are part of a single concept. Israel as a war-torn, poverty-stricken nation cannot spread its religious message; only a grand, imperial, powerful country will be able to offer its spiritual ideas to the community of nations.

1 Kings 7

Majestic Buildings

An examination of the structure and ordering of the Bible will frequently expose new dimensions of understanding. The entire Temple "unit" in 1 Kings is organized in the following manner:

6:1–10	The structure of the Temple
6:11–13	Communication from God
6:14–38	The decoration of the Temple
7:1–12	Royal buildings
7:13–51	The metalwork for the Temple
8	The dedication ceremony of the Temple

The continuity of the detailed description of the Temple architecture is punctuated by two interruptions: a communication by God to Solomon; and, more problematic, an entire section describing the king's royal complex. These digressions are an awkward intrusion into the broader theme of the Temple, especially when we consider the logically ordered flow of the topic segments:[1]

---

1. This structural paragraphing is taken from Jerome Walsh, *1 Kings* (Berit Olam Studies

Framing verse (6:1)

1   STONE CONSTRUCTION (6:2–10)
    God's communication (6:11–13)
    Framing verse (6:14)

2   WOOD CONSTRUCTION (6:15–36)
    Framing verses (6:37–38)
    The Royal Compound (7:1–12)

3   METAL CONSTRUCTION (7:13–47)
    Framing verses (7:40–47)

4   GOLD CONSTRUCTION (7:48–50)
    Framing verse (7:51)

When we view this structure in its broad categorizations, the manner in which these interpolations disturb the logical structure becomes more awkward.

THE FIRST INTERPOLATION – A WARNING AND A PROMISE

> This house that you are building – if you follow My laws and observe My judgments and faithfully keep My commandments, then I will establish all the words [promises] that I spoke to David, your father. I will reside among the children of Israel and never forsake My people, Israel. (6:12–13)

Why is God warning Solomon here? Has God identified a flaw in his religious observance? This communication is opaque and ambivalent. The first verse is ominous and cautionary; the second is optimistic. How should we assess this passage?

If the ordering of these passages is chronological, then this divine message is transmitted when the outer shell, the stone structure of the Temple, has been completed. At this stage of construction, the building

---

in Hebrew Narrative and Poetry; Collegeville, Minnesota: The Liturgical Press, 1996), 103. The "framing verses" are introductions, conclusions, or summative comments concerning the project of building or finishing the Temple.

appears complete from the outside; the builder now turns his attention to the decoration of the inside. It is at this point that the expensive wood paneling, carvings, and gold plate will be installed.

If God feels there is something wrong, He fails to specify. But the commentaries suggest that God is prompting Solomon to examine his priorities, to review the motives and goals of this project. *Metzudat David* explains the thrust of this message:

> Notwithstanding that you are building the most beautiful of structures, nonetheless, I will not rest My presence in it unless you follow My commandments, etc.

Abarbanel puts God's communication in the following way:

> Do not think, Solomon, that it [the Temple] will stand for eternity, and hence the need for such a sturdy and strong building. For its endurance is contingent upon the caveat of whether you, and those who follow you, uphold My laws. If you do, then I will fulfill My words that I spoke to [King] David, that I will dwell among the people of Israel and never abandon them.

God is guiding Solomon to concentrate more on the spiritual and less on the interior design – more on God's indwelling and less upon the luxury materials.

THE SECOND INTERPOLATION – THE ROYAL COMPOUND

This brings us directly to the construction of the royal compound, the second interpolation. These are not holy buildings, and one would expect these verses to be distinct from those regarding the Temple. Nonetheless, this section is fully integrated into the Temple narrative, with the buildings bearing identical architecture and the text utilizing uniform vocabulary regarding:

- the detailing of the dimensions of the structure
- the gems and hewn stones (5:31 and 7:9)

- the wood paneling from floor to ceiling (6:15–16 and 7:7)
- the "courtyard with three tiers of hewn stone and a row of cedar beams" (6:37 and 7:12)

Are these verses a foreign implant, a mismatch, or is this section appropriately placed and integrated? Phrased differently, what is the relationship between God's house and the king's?

A Tale of Two Houses

> In the fourth year, the house of God was founded in the month of Ziv. And in the eleventh year…the house was completed…; he built it for seven years. And Solomon built his own house for thirteen years, until he had completed his entire house. (6:37–7:1)

Seven years for the Temple, thirteen for the palace – why did Solomon spend almost twice as long on his royal compound as he spent constructing the Temple? *Pesikta Rabbati* offers an answer:

> Anyone who hears that he [Solomon] built his house for thirteen years and God's house for seven years thinks that possibly his [the king's] house was greater than that of God! That is not the case. He was slow in the construction of his own palace, whereas with God's house, he was industrious. Moreover, he prioritized God's honor over his own honor. (*Pesikta Rabbati* 6)

This midrash suggests that the disparity between the periods of construction of the palace and the Temple is to Solomon's credit: He expedites the building of the Temple, finishing it in record time, enthused to complete the project. He is less agitated to hurry the construction of his own residence and therefore builds it at a more relaxed pace. Accordingly, this is evidence that Solomon had his priorities correctly ordered.[2]

---

2. See Yehuda Kiel, *Da'at Mikra, 1 Kings*, 158 (summary of chapter 7) [Hebrew], which views the section dealing with the royal buildings as a reflection of the sanctity of the

But there is a contrary perspective, as expressed by the following aggadic story:

> When Solomon built the Temple, he wanted to bring the Ark into the Holy of Holies, but the gates cleaved to each other. Solomon recited twenty-four prayers but was not answered. He said, "Lift up your heads, O you gates, ... and the King of glory shall come in" (Ps. 24:7). The gates ran after him and sought to swallow him. They said, "Who is the King of glory?" (24:8). He answered, "God, the strong and mighty" (ibid.). (*Shabbat* 30a)

This dramatic reading of Psalms 24 is set at the inauguration of the Temple. Solomon seeks entry into the Holy of Holies to install the Ark of the Covenant, but the gates are surprisingly and mysteriously locked. He commands them to open so that "the King of glory may come in." Of course, this is a reference to God. However, the gates perceive that Solomon is referring to *himself* as the "king of glory," and they threaten to consume him. The gates then challenge him with the next line in that chapter of Psalms: "Who is the King of glory?" to which Solomon is forced to profess that God is the true King.

This powerful midrash articulates certain reservations concerning Solomon. Why is his house depicted in the same manner as the Temple? Does the fact that he builds his house for thirteen years suggest that his palace is more splendid than the Temple? How does Solomon – a king who has become an emperor – perceive himself? Most important, does he view the Temple as his house or God's? The gates accuse Solomon of perceiving himself as a god, of failing to correctly assess God's supremacy. The gates are skeptical, and we too can identify some apprehension regarding Solomon.

I believe that the perplexing structure of our chapter – interjecting the royal buildings into the fabric of the Temple – deliberately evokes this ambiguity. With Solomon's royal compound built of materials,

---

monarchy and the close ties between the palace and the Temple. Accordingly, this interjection presents no tension whatsoever. Rather, it makes a powerful statement that Solomon's reign upholds God's Kingship on earth.

pillars, and courtyards similar to those in God's house, we wonder whether the focus has been blurred somewhat.

The House of the Lebanon Forest

To illustrate the question of whether the royal establishment is competing with or eclipsing the Temple, let us examine the house of the Lebanon Forest described in 1 Kings 7:2–5.[3] This is the largest building in Jerusalem – 50 by 100 cubits with a height of 30 cubits – with a floor area three times that of the Temple. What function does this structure serve?[4] And what is the relationship between the "Lebanon Forest" and this building?

Metzudat David suggests an explanation: "The effect of the multiple pillars made it appear as a forest full of trees." Noga Hareuveni takes this idea further with a wonderfully creative and vibrant visualization. He bases his explanation upon the phrases *kerutot arazim* and *meḥeza* mentioned in the verses:

> We believe Solomon used a sophisticated gimmick to create for the visitor the illusion that he was in some kind of forest rather than a simple pillared hall. To achieve such an illusion, it would be necessary to make the pillars look like actual trees, and for the few dozen "trees" to become a "forest."
>
> The Hebrew word *kerutot*, translated as beams, is derived from the root *karot*, meaning to cut down a tree or branch.... Therefore, we can assume that these "beams" were actually ramified cedar branches still covered in needles (the "leaves" of the cedar). These branches could be bracketed horizontally into the cedar pillars and together **simulate live cedars**....
>
> We believe that this unique Hebrew word (*meḥeza*), which does not appear anywhere else in the Bible, may be rendered as

---

3. This building is mentioned centuries later in Isaiah 22:8, where it is called simply "the forest house."

4. *Targum Yonatan* translates the phrase as "the cooling house." Radak explains that kings used to build houses in the forest to cool off in the summer, but it is difficult to understand how this building would have been significantly cooler than the nearby palace.

mirror, stemming from the root *ḥazo* (see).... **The use of facing mirrors at both ends ... gave the visitor the illusion of being in a literally infinite forest – the "trees" reflected endlessly in the opposing mirrors....**

Clearly, the house of the Forest of Lebanon was most carefully planned to astound the diplomatic and trade delegations that came to Solomon from far and wide....[5]

This magnificent building dwarfs the nearby Temple! When we read about this building, whose only real purpose is to dazzle and impress, one wonders as to Solomon's need for pleasure houses of this sort.

Yet when all is said and done, these interjections within the narrative are undercurrents, or warning lights. The thrust of the story remains highly positive – Solomon is building the Temple! Let us not take away from this momentous accomplishment. The section that deals with the Temple totals 133 verses; the interjections that raise questions about Solomon's motives constitute fourteen verses in total. With that sort of ratio, we may conclude that the overwhelming textual momentum supports the king.

We have noted how Solomon's royal buildings matched the architectural style of the Temple. Perhaps we can offer a more positive perception of these royal edifices. The book of Psalms repeatedly praises the beauty of Jerusalem as acclaiming God's majesty:

> Walk around Zion; circle it,
> Count its towers.
> Take note of its ramparts,
> Go through its palaces,
> That you may recount to a future age.
> For God – He is our God forever;
> He will lead us evermore. (Ps. 48:13–15)

---

5. Israel Prize winner Noga Hareuveni made it his life's work to discover and explore the animals, plants, and landscape of the Bible. To this end, he founded Neot Kedumim (near Modiin), an agricultural park aiming to help people visualize and understand the plant life of the Bible. This passage is from his book *Tree and Shrub in Our Biblical Heritage* (Neot Kedumim, 1984), 100–04.

In this chapter of Psalms, it is the city of Jerusalem, not the Temple, that broadcasts a message of God. The royal palaces, the beauty of the city, praise the Almighty. Similarly, Psalms 122 lauds the "thrones of judgment...the thrones of the house of David" in Jerusalem. Rabbi Samson Raphael Hirsch comments:

> The purpose of the Sanctuary is served only if the Law, as symbolized in and through the Sanctuary, is made living reality also in the life of the city.[6]

If God's majesty is enhanced and highlighted through Jerusalem's magnificent royal buildings, if God's ethic is manifest in the administrational culture and moral governance of the nation, then there is no dissonance whatsoever.

NEW VESSELS

The bulk of 1 Kings 7 deals with the elaborate metalwork of the Temple. Solomon, using the most advanced mining techniques of his era, chooses to mine his own copper in the Jordan Valley.[7] Hiram, the chief craftsman, is endowed with the virtues of "wisdom, insight, and knowledge" (7:14), a reflection of the traits attributed to the famous artisan of the Tabernacle, Bezalel (Ex. 31:3).[8]

The major vessels recorded here are:

7:15–22	The two pillars, Jachin and Boaz
23–26	The reservoir
27–37	Ten bases

---

6. Rabbi Samson Raphael Hirsch, *Commentary to Psalms*, trans. Gertrude Herschler (Jerusalem/New York: Feldheim, 1978), 345.

7. *Da'at Mikra* identifies the location of this mining in the upper Jordan Valley, on the basis of the topography and archaeological evidence. See also a more recent, widely publicized suggestion: "King Solomon's Copper Mines?" *Science Daily*, 28 Oct. 2008.

8. See Nehama Leibowitz, "The Probity of Public Servants," in Leibowitz, *Studies in Shemot (The Book of Exodus)* (Jerusalem: World Zionist Organization, 1976), vol. 2, 672–78.

38–39   Ten washbasins

40–47   Summative verses

With the exception of the washbasins, these all lack a precedent or equivalent in the Tabernacle and are new additions to the landscape of the Temple.

Jachin and Boaz

Jachin and Boaz, two grand copper columns, stand at the entrance to the *Ulam*. Their dimensions are impressive: eighteen cubits tall, hollow, constructed with copper four fingerbreadths thick, and approximately four cubits in diameter.[9] The top of each column is elaborately decorated with images of lilies or pomegranates,[10] which bear a sophisticated, lattice-type decoration.

What do these columns signify? Of course, they could be nothing more than impressive architectural features, as found in many temples of the times throughout the Near East.[11] Even if this is so, what is the meaning of their names? When a pillar is given a title, that name confers meaning.[12] Radak explains:

> The pillars at the entrance to the house he named for good fortune. One was called Jachin, indicating that the house would last forever, and Boaz was indicative of strength, made up of a composite word, *bo-oz* [strength in it] – that God should grant the Temple strength and standing, as it states: "God shall give vigor to His nation."[13]

---

9. See Jeremiah 52:20–23 and II Chronicles 3:15–17, as well as our chapter, for all the dimensions. A cubit is approximately 1.5 feet.

10. There may be a connection between the imagery of Song of Songs and these pomegranates, lilies, and pillars.

11. See Prof. Nahman Avigad, "Solomon's Temple," in *Studies in the Book of Kings in the Prime Minister's Residence* (Jerusalem: Kiryat Sefer, 1985), vol. 1, 84–85 [Hebrew].

12. For names that highlight the significance of a symbolic object, see the altar called "God is my miracle/banner" by Moses (Ex. 17:15), or even the pile of stones named by Laban and Jacob (Gen. 31:47).

13. The source of Radak's opinion is *Midrash Tadsheh*, which attributes these names to Psalms 89:38 and 21:2, respectively. The context of the verse alluding to Jachin records

The pillars thus indicate themes of eternal reign as well as strength. The massive dimensions and sturdy nature of these columns certainly convey a feeling of power and permanence. The commentators offer different interpretations of whether these refer to the Temple, God, or Solomon.

The Reservoir, Washbasin, and Bases

The reservoir, washbasin, and bases are all decorative storage vats for water. The huge, circular reservoir (*yam*) is ten cubits in diameter. According to II Chronicles 4:6, its purpose is "for the washing of the priests."[14] The volume of water that it holds is "two thousand *bat*" (I Kings 7:26), but we have no clear measure of a *bat*.[15] The text also leaves us with only a vague understanding of the reservoir's precise shape. We know it is five cubits high, but are its walls straight or curved? Is it bowl-shaped or cylindrical?[16] Because of these unresolved questions, assessments of its volume vary wildly between twenty thousand and sixty-six thousand liters of water – not a very accurate picture!

---

the divine promise of an everlasting monarchy to David: "…I will not be false to David. His line shall continue forever; his throne is like the sun before Me. Like the moon, *it will be established* (*yikon* [as in Yakhin, anglicized as Jachin]) forever…" (89:36–38). The verse alluding to Boaz refers to the power of the king and his faith in God.

14. Maimonides, basing himself on the Jerusalem Talmud, states that the laws of *mikva'ot* applied to this pool, as it received a constant inflow from a reservoir that led to the Temple, and that its feet were hollow, allowing for a constant connection between the pool and a natural water source. See Maimonides, *Mishneh Torah*, Laws of Entering the Temple 5:15. There are no archaeological remnants of the First Temple, so verification of this tradition is impossible. One does wonder, however, whether it has been influenced by the images of water flowing through the First Temple in Ezekiel 47, or by the aqueduct that ran through the Second Temple, of which we have considerable archaeological evidence.

15. A further complication: II Chronicles 4:5 tells us that the volume is three thousand *bat*. The Talmud (*Eruvin* 14b) resolves this contradiction by explaining that its volume is three thousand if it is holding an overflowing pile (of some dry substance) and two thousand if it is holding liquid. Whether or not that resolution is acceptable or realistic, we can say that an accurate assessment of the dimensions of this reservoir eludes us.

16. For example, *Eruvin* 14b describes the top two cubits as spherical and the lower three as square; what this means is open to debate.

Even more mysterious are the twelve molten oxen upon which the reservoir sits. The oxen faced outward, three in each direction. Why would Solomon place these images in the Temple itself?

The ten washbasins measure four cubits in diameter and stand on decorative bases resting upon four wheels. Once again, images adorn the bases – "lions, oxen, and cherubim" (7:29).

The Divine Chariot (Merkava)

Judaism generally rejects iconography, especially in a ritual setting. The laws of the Tabernacle prescribed two golden cherubim atop the Ark and cherubim woven into rich tapestries.[17] However, even these images were restricted from the sight of anyone other than the priests.[18] Yet Solomon's Temple features images prominently. The oxen seem uncomfortably similar to a golden calf! What are we to make of this pervasive imagery?

Several commentators resolve this enigma by viewing these figures as symbolic of divine beings:

> These [images of lions, oxen, and *keruvim*] are the images seen by Ezekiel in his vision of the divine chariot, but here the image of an eagle is not mentioned. (Ralbag)

> "[The crafting of these wheels was in the form of] the wheels of the chariot" (7:33) – The holy chariot that was seen in the vision of Ezekiel, and this is how *Targum Yonatan* translated it.... Solomon in his wisdom saw that which Ezekiel son of Buzi saw in his prophecy. (Radak)

These commentators are referring to the vision of Ezekiel, in which "the heavens opened and I saw visions of God" (Ezek. 1:1); Ezekiel glimpses

---

17. See Exodus 26:1 (regarding the covering of the Tabernacle) and 26:31 (regarding the *parokhet*).
18. According to Numbers 4:5–6, the Ark was concealed when in transit. Even when the camp was stationary and the Tabernacle was functioning, the cherubim were restricted from the nation's gaze, as only a priest was permitted to enter the sanctuary. For the tension between the prohibition of images and the cherubim, see Exodus 20:19–20 and Rashi ad loc.

the "chariot" of God. The depiction of this divine spectacle in Ezekiel 1 is traditionally viewed as a mystical text, impenetrable to the uninitiated.[19] Yet even from a superficial perspective, we can identify the corollary with the Temple iconography:

> And in the center of it was also the figure of four creatures.... Each of the four had a human face,[20] the face of a **lion**..., an **ox**..., an eagle. (1:5, 10)

Furthermore, the wheels (*ofanim*) of the washbasins remind us of angelic creatures known as *ofanim*, which feature prominently in Ezekiel's vision (appearing ten times in chapter 1). All of this leads us to conclude that Solomon is drawing upon this mystical imagery, attempting to reflect the divine majesty in artistic form.[21]

Further support for this interpretation may be found in the unfortunate fate of these items. A later king of Judah, Ahaz, turns away from God and adopts the Assyrian religion. He then transforms the Temple into a pagan shrine. In his abandonment of God, we read how

> Ahaz cut the frames of the bases and removed the washbasins from them. He removed the reservoir from the copper oxen that were underneath it and placed it on the stone floor. (II Kings 16:17)

Why does Ahaz remove the water from its base, its pedestal? Why deliberately cut out these images? Apparently they are specifically Jewish symbols, recalling the divine chariot. Ahaz's removing them makes a statement of God's immobility and loss of power and status.[22]

---

19. See *Megilla* 4:10; *Ḥagiga* 2:1. For an academic treatment of the *Merkava* in later Jewish mystical tradition, see Gershom Scholem, *Major Trends in Jewish Mysticism* (New York: Schocken, 1961), ch. 2, "Merkabah Mysticism and Jewish Gnosticism," 40–79.
20. See Ezekiel 10:14, where it would appear that the human face is in fact a cherub.
21. Of course, Ezekiel postdates Solomon by three hundred years, but if this is the essence of God's mysterious "chariot," then the impressions are timeless.
22. I heard this idea from Rabbi Yaakov Medan.

Royal Decoration

However, this framing of the Temple as an expression of the imagery of the divine chariot has its opponents. One passionate and vociferous challenger is Rabbi Yosef Kara, a student and contemporary of Rashi and a staunch advocate of *peshat* readings of the Bible.[23] He expresses outrage at these interpretations:

> This view is a perversion of the truth to anyone who has the Torah of God within him! It inverts the words of the living God and leads all Israel astray in its solution. Have you seen any human who says…in regard to something he finds difficult to understand, …"Look at the heavens! What you see in the heavens, so it is on earth"? And to this we reply, "Who can ascend to the heavens and bring it down to us?" (Deut. 30:12)…. God never sought to teach future generations that which can be seen from that which is unknown and invisible. If you wish to know the correct meaning of the verse "like the construction of the wheels of honor" (*Targum Yonatan* on 7:33), go investigate the wheels of the carriages of kings, which are significantly different from those of transportation wagons in their construction. (commentary on 1 Kings 7:33)

For Rabbi Yosef Kara, these images are unrelated to the divine chariot. Abarbanel similarly has no tolerance for kabbalistic explanations of these design elements, preferring to view them as regal ornamentation.

---

23. *Peshat* is a close reading of the text bound by rules of grammar, rhetoric, and context, and in a spirit of reason and realism. Sometimes *peshat* is called the "plain," "simple," or "literal" interpretation, but these labels fail to capture the essence of a reading that is a complex process of striving for objectivity in the text as it is interpreted in a historical, linguistic, and literary context. For example, a "literal" translation of biblical poetry would distort the text and not be *peshat*. Frequently contrasted with *derash*, *peshat* values "exegetical inquiry…ahead of expounding a lesson," whereas *derash* looks to the text for "solutions to the questions of the hour," adopting more flexible rules of language and rhetoric, and frequently offering multiple meanings of the text. Quotes from Uriel Simon, "The Religious Significance of the *Peshat*," *Tradition* 23:2 (1988): 37–38.

Following this approach, these artistic masterpieces are simply part of the Temple's impressive décor.[24]

The Fate of the Temple Utensils

The Jachin and Boaz pillars and the copper reservoir remained in the Temple until its destruction. Even the twelve oxen and the decorative basins detached by King Ahaz were, it would seem, not destroyed, and they remained in the vicinity of Jerusalem. We revisit these Temple furnishings – all their details elaborately re-recorded – in the account of the Temple's destruction, as all the exquisite copper décor is removed and carted off to Babylonia by Nebuchadnezzar:

> And the copper pillars in the house of God, the bases, and the copper reservoir that were in the house of God were broken up by the Chaldees, and they took their copper to Babylonia. (II Kings 25:13)[25]

---

24. Support for this approach comes from archaeology. For example, the British Museum collection includes a bronze laver stand from Cyprus dating back to the eleventh to thirteenth centuries BCE. It has four side panels decorated with a relief of a winged sphinx, a lion, and a chariot, and it has four wheels. T.C. Mitchell suggests that these decorations and wheels parallel those of the bases. See Mitchell, *Biblical Archaeology: Documents from the British Museum* (Cambridge: Cambridge University Press, 1988), 42. In addition, there are remarkable parallels between Solomon's Temple and a structure at Ein Dara, in northern Syria, where a temple stood from 1300 to 740 BCE. See Victor Hurowitz, "Solomon's Temple in Context," *Biblical Archaeology Review* 37:2 (2011). Similarities include the three rooms of the temple and the two columns at its entrance. These sources suggest that the features are stylistic rather than reflective of uniquely Jewish concepts.

25. See also I Kings 16–17; Jeremiah 52:17–23.

1 Kings 8–9

The Dedication of the Temple

The dedication of the Temple was a fourteen-day celebration for the entire nation, with attendees hailing from Mesopotamia to Egypt. The festive throngs offered so many sacrifices, that the king had to temporarily sanctify the entire Temple courtyard for sacrificial purposes (1 Kings 8:62–66).

The story is structured in the following way:

A Narrative: gathering and dedication ceremony (8:1–11)
    B Solomon "blesses the assembly of Israel" (8:12–21)
        C Solomon's prayer (8:22–54)
    B1 Solomon "blesses the assembly of Israel" (8:55–61)
A1 Narrative: dedication ceremony and departure (8:62–9:2)
D God's response to Solomon (9:2–9)

NATION AND REVELATION

The Midrash connects the Temple dedication and two other pivotal moments in Jewish history – the dedication of Tabernacle and the revelation at Sinai:

> "Then Solomon gathered…. And all the men of Israel were gathered to Solomon…" (8:1–2) – This teaches us that the Shekhina rests only upon the entire community. Similarly [at the dedication of the Tabernacle in Lev. 9:24], "And all the people saw" (Lev. 9:24), …and at the giving of the Torah it states, "For on the third day, God will descend in view of the entire nation" (Ex. 19:11). (*Seder Olam* 15)

Whereas the Midrash draws attention to the national gathering at these three events, there is a further critical element that they share. These are each foundational national assemblies at which there is a direct experience of divine revelation. As we examine the text itself, we identify how the language creates a direct linkage:

Temple	Tabernacle
When the priests came out of the Holy, the **cloud** filled the house of God.	**The cloud** covered the Tent of Meeting, and the presence of God filled the Tabernacle.
The priests could not remain and perform the service **because of the cloud,**	And Moses could not enter the Tent of Meeting, **because the cloud** rested upon it,
for the **presence of God** filled the entire house of God. (1 Kings 8:10–11)	and the **presence of God** filled the Tabernacle. (Ex. 40:34–35)

The scenes are identical: The cloud fills the sacred space, a manifestation of God's presence, and access is restricted to those – Moses or the priests – who are to perform the service.

The description of Solomon's inauguration of the Temple in Chronicles demonstrates yet another parallelism:

Temple	Tabernacle
When Solomon completed his prayer, **fire** descended from heaven and **consumed** the burnt offerings and sacrifices….	**Fire** came forth from before God and **consumed** the burnt offering and the fat on the altar,
All the children of Israel saw as the fire descended…, and they bowed their **faces to the ground**, praising God, "For He is good, for His kindness is eternal." (II Chron. 7:1, 3)	and **all the people saw** and shouted and **fell on their faces**. (Lev. 9:24)

Both at the Temple and in the Tabernacle, God's fire dramatically descends to consume the sacrifices on the altar. The people respond to this divine sign by bowing and shouting praises to God. These symmetrical depictions highlight how God's tangible presence in Solomon's Temple was equivalent to that in the Tabernacle.[1]

One further parallel is particularly poignant. On the eighth day, the culmination of the Tabernacle dedication,[2] Aaron blessed the nation immediately after completing the complex sacrificial service. Solomon's blessing echoes that moment:

Temple	Tabernacle
And when Solomon finished his prayer to God…he arose from before the **altar**, from kneeling with **his hands outstretched** to heaven.	Aaron **lifted up his hands** toward the people and blessed them, and he descended [from the altar,] from performing the sin offering, the burnt offering, and the peace offering.
He stood and **blessed the entire community of Israel**…. (I Kings 8:54–55)	Moses and Aaron entered the Tent of Meeting; they emerged and **blessed the people**. (Lev. 9:22–23)

---

1. Verses such as I Kings 8:9 underscore the similarity between Moses' Tabernacle and Solomon's Temple.
2. It is highly probable that Solomon's celebration specifically for seven days (and then an eighth; see I Chronicles 7:9) is built upon the pattern set by the *miluim*, the seven-day dedication of the Tabernacle described in Exodus 29 and Leviticus 8 (followed by an eighth day; see Leviticus 9).

In both stories, leaders stand with hands extended at the altar,[3] concluding the ceremony by bestowing God's blessing on the nation.

The antecedent of both the Temple and Tabernacle inaugura-
tions is the revelation at Sinai. At Sinai, Israel's ascent to the mountain is
restricted due to God's presence. There too, the nation witnesses God's
tangible presence in cloud and fire:

> "Let them be ready for the third day, for on the third day the Lord
> will come down, in the sight of all the people, on Mount Sinai.
> **Beware of going up the mountain.**" ... And Mount Sinai was all
> in smoke, for the Lord had come down upon it in fire.... **And all
> the people saw** the thunder and lightning and the sound of the
> shofar... and stood at a distance. (Ex. 19:10, 18; 20:15)[4]

Nahmanides draws upon this connection, asserting that the Tabernacle perpetuates the living experience of God and the centrality of His
Torah.[5] The Tabernacle enables the Sinai revelation to continue. In our
context, this three-way parallel[6] frames the inauguration of the Temple

---

3. Solomon prays on his knees, with his hands outstretched (1 Kings 8:54). This posture,
   unusual from a contemporary perspective, may have been standard in ancient times.
   See the identical posture in Nehemiah 9:5 and in combining Isaiah 1:15 and 45:23.
   One wonders whether the arms were fully outstretched or just the palms extended,
   as Muslims pray. For a discussion of changes in Jewish prayer posture as a response
   to Islam and Christianity, see Prof. Daniel Sperber, *Jewish Customs*, vol. 3 (Jerusalem:
   Mossad Harav Kook, 1994), 88–91 [Hebrew].
4. Exodus 24's description of the giving of the Torah is also starkly reflected in Exodus
   40, describing the Tabernacle (as well as in the verses we quoted from Chronicles):
   "And Moses ascended the mountain.... And God's presence rested upon Mount Sinai,
   and the cloud enveloped it for six days, and He called to Moses on the seventh day
   from the cloud.... And Moses entered the cloud and ascended the mountain..." (Ex.
   24:15–18). However, these verses deal with Moses personally, not with the nation in
   its entirety.
5. Nahmanides on Exodus 25:1.
6. Two tannaitic midrashim further the linkages between these three events. Both are
   based on Song of Songs 3:11, which refers to Solomon:
   > Linking Sinai and the Temple: "'On the day of his wedding' – that is the giving
   > of the Torah; 'on the day of his bliss' – that is the day of the building of the
   > Temple." (*Taanit* 4:8)

not merely as a royal spectacle, but as a sacred moment in which the *Shekhina* is evident to all.[7]

WILL GOD RESIDE UPON EARTH?

Does God reside in the Temple? One of the most striking statements of Solomon's prayer addresses this question:

> But will God really reside upon earth? Even the heavens to their uttermost reaches cannot contain You, how much less this house that I have built! Yet turn, O Lord, my God, to the prayer and supplication of Your servant, and hear the cry and prayer that your servant offers before You this day. May Your eyes be open day and night toward this house, toward the place of which You have said, "My Name shall abide there," to listen to the prayer that Your servant will pray toward this place. (I Kings 8:27–29)

Solomon takes a clear theological stand that God is not contained by the Temple; it is not His residence. At the very most, it is a place where "My Name shall abide," a place that represents God but does not enclose or confine Him.[8]

Linking the Tabernacle and Temple: "'On the day of his wedding' – that is the seven days of the miluim [dedication of the Tabernacle]; 'on the day of his bliss' – that is the day of the building of the Temple." (*Seder Olam* 15)

7. *Da'at Mikra* develops the theme of Covenant as a central feature of this chapter. See Yehuda Kiel, *Da'at Mikra*, I Kings, 197–98 [Hebrew].

8. Earlier, Solomon seems to make the opposite statement: "I have built a stately house for You, a place where You may dwell forever" (I Kings 8:13). Yet the dominant thrust of his prayer is that God listens from the Temple but does not reside there. Interestingly, King David's refers to the Temple as "the footstool of God" (I Chron. 28:2). Does this imply that the Temple is God's residence, or that it is merely representative of God?

The two names for the Tabernacle may represent these dialectical perspectives. "Tabernacle" (*Mishkan*) designates the residence of God; "Tent of Meeting" (*Ohel Moed*) indicates that it is a rendezvous point with God but not His home. Similarly, our *Kedushah* prayer oscillates between God's not having a place ("His honor fills the whole earth!") and His having a place ("Blessed is the honor of God from His place… when will You reign in Zion").

Earlier, God has appeared to Solomon and assured him, "I will abide among the children of Israel" (6:13). If this is not God's residence, then how does God reside within Israel? How does the Temple function? Here we come to Solomon's second point. **The Temple is, first and foremost, a house of prayer**; it is the portal through which our prayers find God and through which He hears our prayers. God dwells "in the heavens," but His "eyes and ears" are focused upon this spot.

Solomon articulates these principles in the theological preamble to his prayer, quoted above. However, in the body of the prayer itself, these ideas are restated in a deliberate and well-ordered list, organized in a refrain of sorts, a recursive formula. Solomon presents a sevenfold menu of scenarios that necessitate prayer. He outlines a paradigm of prayer: the appeal by the petitioner, followed by God's response – God hearing Israel's prayers and issuing forgiveness. This section (8:31–53) follows a pattern:

> **A** When X happens [a curse/military defeat/drought/plague/ the visit of a foreigner/war/exile][9]
> **B** And they offer prayer and supplication to You in this house
> **C** O Hear in Your heavenly abode
> **D** And forgive Your people[10]
> **E** And take action

As we have said, the implications are significant: God dwells not in the Temple, but "on high," and the primary function of the Temple is prayer. All Israel Turns Its Hearts to a Single Place

---

9. The fact that a sovereign ruler entertains the prospect of exile is quite remarkable. Solomon's entire prayer is replete with the language of Deuteronomy, and reflects its predictions and threats nonchalantly. Parallels include (1) "In the heavens above and the earth below" (1 Kings 8:23 and Deut. 4:39, 5:7); (2) the notion of a house for God's "name to be there" (1 Kings 8:16, 29, and Deut. 12:11; 14:23; 16:2, 6); (3) the phraseology of exile (1 Kings 8:46–48 and Deut. 4:29, 30:1–4); and (4) the usage of the phrase "proverb and byword (*mashal ushenina*)" (1 Kings 9:7, evoking the *tokhaha*, the grim rebuke of Deuteronomy 28:37).

10. This conclusion is not relevant for scenario 1 (a curse) or 5 (the foreigner).

One ramification of this philosophy is the centrality of Jerusalem and the Temple as the conduit for all prayer, from near or far. This is further expressed in the halakhic directive regarding the orientation of prayer:[11]

> If one is standing outside Eretz Yisrael, he should focus his mind (*yekhaven libo*) toward Eretz Yisrael. As it says, "and they pray unto You toward their land" (I Kings 8:48).
>
> If he is standing in Eretz Yisrael, he should focus his mind toward Jerusalem. As it says, "**and they pray unto the Lord, toward the city that You have chosen**" (8:44).
>
> If he is standing in Jerusalem, he should focus his mind toward the Temple. As it says, "**and they pray toward this place**" (II Chron. 6:26).
>
> If he is standing in the Temple, he should focus his mind toward the Holy of Holies. As it says, "**and they pray toward this place**" (I Kings 8:35).
>
> …Consequently, if he is in the east, he should turn his face to the west; if in the west, he should turn his face to the east; if in the south, he should turn his face to the north; if in the north, he should turn his face to the south. **In this way, all Israel will be turning its hearts toward one place.**
>
> R. Avin, and others say R. Avina, said: What is the meaning of the verse "Your neck is as the tower of David, built like Talpiyot…" (Song 4:4)?[12] It means a hill (tel) toward which all mouths (piyot) turn. (*Berakhot* 30a)

---

11. For a halakhic discussion of this topic, see Rabbi David Brofsky, *Hilchot Tefilla* (Jersey City: Ktav, 2010), 152–55.

12. The word "*Talpiyot*" has no parallel outside of Song of Songs, and its precise meaning has eluded both traditional interpretation and modern translation. According to the midrash, "*talpiyot*," which is associated with the tower of David (that is, Jerusalem), figuratively depicts "a hill toward which all mouths turn." In other words, the Temple is the focus of all our prayers.

Parenthetically, the tower of David spoken of in Song of Songs has no relationship

All the biblical proof texts in this passage originate in the inauguration of the Temple, and Solomon's prayer in particular. When we pray toward Jerusalem, we are invoking the concept articulated by Solomon. The result is a beautiful expression of global unity: "all Israel turning their hearts to one place."

THE FOREIGNER

A third important principle featured in Solomon's prayer is the statement that the Temple is accessible to and oriented toward the non-Jewish world:

> If the foreigner, who is not of Your people, Israel, comes from a distant land for the sake of Your name – for they shall hear about Your great name and Your mighty hand ... ." (1 Kings 8:41)

Solomon envisions that gentiles will hear about God and come to discover more, enthused to pay homage to the Almighty. Solomon repeats this point later in his prayer as well:

> That *all* the peoples of the world may know that the Lord alone is God; there is no other. (8:60)

Solomon is certainly not alone in this vision of the house of God. This universal message is found in the words of several other prophets as well, especially in reference to the messianic era:

> As for the foreigners who attach themselves to the Lord to be His servants ... and hold fast to My covenant: I will bring them to My holy mountain and let them rejoice in My house of prayer; their burnt offerings and sacrifices shall be welcome on My altar, for My house shall be called a house of prayer for all peoples. (Is. 56:6–7)

---

to the structure bearing that name today. That structure, built on the remains of Herod's magnificent palace, is a crusader fortress. It is highly unlikely that David had any connection whatsoever with that site, since his city was about a kilometer away.

...all the nations...shall make a pilgrimage year by year to bow down to the King, Lord of Hosts, and to observe the Sukkot festival. (Zech. 14:16)

Solomon, however, appears to be the first figure in the Bible to so explicitly extend an invitation toward gentiles, welcoming them to join Israel in the service of God.

IN CONCLUSION

We have reached the apex of the Solomonic era. The Torah mandated the building of a Temple some five hundred years previously; only now, in a state of national stability, is this central institution established.

Though God has already expressed His acceptance of the Temple by means of His revelation in a cloud, He now responds to Solomon's prayer in a prophetic dream:

> I have heard the prayer and supplication that you have offered to Me.
> I consecrate this house that you have built.
> I set My name there forever.
> My eyes and heart shall ever be there. (1 Kings 8:2–3)

God affirms His sanctification and approval of the Temple.

And yet, as we shall see, the book of Kings now adjusts its focus to more troubling dimensions of Solomon's reign.

1 Kings 9–10

Wealth and Opulence

The Solomon chapters bear a double reading. Upon first acquaintance, the reader is impressed and overwhelmed by the power and accomplishments of this king, by his wealth and wisdom. But as one revisits these chapters a second time, especially with the awareness of Solomon's failures at the end of his reign, one appreciates that he did not fail overnight; darker strands and shadows are revealed, indicating the deep flaws that threatened the impressive national enterprise. We shall demonstrate how chapters 9 and 10 of 1 Kings exemplify this literary ambivalence, as the biblical text increasingly accentuates the negative aspects of Solomon's reign.

A GOLD EXCHANGE

> It came about at the end of twenty years in which Solomon had built the two houses, the house of God and the king's house. Hiram, king of Tyre, had supplied Solomon with cedar and cypress timber and gold according to all his desire; then King Solomon gave Hiram twenty cities in the land of Galilee. So Hiram came out of Tyre to see the cities that Solomon had given him,

and they did not please him. He said, "What are these cities that you have given me, my brother?" So they named the land Kabul ... Hiram sent the king 120 talents of gold. (9:10–14)

This episode transpires twenty years after Solomon begins the construction of the Temple, and we are thus in the twenty-fourth year of his reign.

The text presents a tense conversation, as Hiram expresses his dissatisfaction with the trade agreement signed with King Solomon, protesting the quality of the land he has received. The details of the problem are unspecified,[1] but we sense that Solomon is failing to honor his commitments. What has happened to his wealth and prestige? It is worthwhile to compare this text with an earlier, parallel passage:

> Hiram provided Solomon with all the cedar and cypress wood that he required. And Solomon delivered to Hiram twenty thousand measures of wheat, provision for his household, and twenty measures of finely pressed oil – thus Solomon gave Hiram annually. (5:24–25)

Twenty years earlier, the country produced excess wheat and oil, financing the imports of cedar and cypress timber. Now, Solomon is in such deficit that he has to trade away segments of the land of Israel! What has changed?

One shift is that the kingdom is importing not only timber; Hiram supplies Solomon with "gold according to all his desire." The national agricultural surplus, sufficient for timber, cannot cover the expense of the gold, and the king therefore must relinquish territory. [2] But why does Solomon need so much gold?

---

1. The term Kabul is difficult to understand. The Talmud (*Shabbat* 54a) suggests that it means infertile. Josephus notes that in Phoenician it means "dissatisfaction." Others think it is phonetically related to the Hebrew word *gevul*, border, and therefore signifies borderlands.

2. Many commentators view this arrangement with Hiram differently. In light of II Chronicles 8:2, which describes Hiram's giving twenty cities to Solomon, Ralbag and Radak explain that this was more of a land exchange, "for it is inconceivable for a king to diminish the size of the land of Israel" (Ralbag). Likewise, see Yehuda

It seems that the increased demand for gold is representative of a wider shift in national lifestyle and priorities. The Talmud picks up on this change in the standard of living:

> What is the land of Kabul? R. Huna said: The residents were tied up with silver and gold. Rava replied: ... Since they were wealthy and spoiled, they did not engage in manual labor [so the land deteriorated]. (*Shabbat* 54a)

The country has undergone a significant socioeconomic shift. When Solomon rose to power, the nation was made up primarily of farmers, earning their living from the land itself. The gross national product was enormous and consumption was relatively modest, resulting in a huge national surplus. But now, the people have become affluent; they are "wealthy and spoiled," with no desire to get their hands dirty in the field. If this Talmudic passage is correct, the problem is not so much the import of gold, but the fact that Israel has abandoned agriculture for "higher" pursuits, such as commerce and national planning and administration (see 9:22–23).[3] With declining national production and increasing domestic consumption, the country suffers from a deficit, and Solomon eventually has to surrender land in order to pay off the national debt!

This is just one example of a significant transformation in the lifestyle of the kingdom. Chapters 9 and 10 use an intertextual technique to depict this shift. These chapters revisit most of the topics already addressed in chapters 3–5; by a method of "compare and contrast," the reader can take note of the national transitions.[4]

In expressing the overwhelming opulence and excessive luxury that now characterize Israelite culture, chapters 9 and 10 feature a *leitwort*, a recurrent word: "gold," which appears seventeen times in this

---

Kiel, *Da'at Mikra, 1 Kings* [Hebrew]. Abarbanel asserts that no land was handed over. Rather, the area in question was an Israelite-populated tax zone, whose tax tribute went to Hiram.

3. See Oded Bustenai's comments in Bustenai and M. Garsiel, eds., *Encyclopedia of the World of the Bible, 1 Kings* (Tel Aviv: Davidson-Atai, 1994), commentary ad loc. [Hebrew].

4. I heard this analysis from Rabbi Mordechai Sabato.

section. In contrast, chapters 3–5 fail to refer to gold even once.[5] Thus we discern a palpable emphasis upon material extravagance and over-indulgence. Something is wrong in Solomon's kingdom.

Taxes, Forced Labor, and Royal Buildings

Chapter 5, reflecting the early days of Solomon, depicts how he imposed a labor tax in order to cut timber in Lebanon with which to build the Temple:

> And King Solomon raised **a levy out of all Israel**, and the levy was thirty thousand men. And he sent them to Lebanon, ten thousand a month by courses. A month they were in Lebanon, and two months at home; and Adoniram was over the levy. (5:28–30)

Here, the Israelites perform the physical labor themselves; the levy is used to construct the Temple. The impression given in chapter 5 is of a nation willing to engage in national service for the sake of the Temple. However, 9:15–25 records a different "levy." Here, the manual labor is performed by foreign workers:

> All the people who were left of the Amorites, the Hittites, the Perizzites, the Hivites, and the Jebusites, who were not of the children of Israel, …of them did Solomon raise a **levy of bond-servants** (*mas oved*) unto this day. **But of the children of Israel Solomon made no bondservants;** but they were the men of war, and his servants, and his princes, and his captains, and rulers of his chariots and of his horsemen. (9:20–22)

This levy is one of forced labor. What is the purpose of this tax? It is used to build the Temple, but there is also an extensive list of other royal and military projects:

---

5. Even in the description of the Temple, in which gold features prominently, the section dealing with copper takes up thirty-four verses, whereas the vessels of gold take up a mere three verses tacked on to the end of the Temple chapters. This is a stark contrast even to the chapters that describe the Tabernacle in Exodus.

...his own palace, the Millo, the wall of Jerusalem, Hazor, Megiddo, and Gezer... And all of Solomon's storage towns (*arei miskenot*), chariot towns and cavalry towns – and the pleasure building that Solomon set his heart on building.... (9:15, 19)

The phrase *arei miskenot* recalls Israel's experience of slavery in Egypt (Ex. 1:11), but Solomon is the slave master! It is one thing to impose a labor tax in order to build the Temple; it is another for Solomon to enslave other nations for his pleasure buildings, military projects, and palaces.

Collaboration with Hiram

In chapter 5, Hiram and Solomon collaborate to build the Temple. Now, they join forces to set up a navy whose sole purpose is to sail to Africa to procure luxuries: gold, rare woods, precious stones (1 Kings 10:11–12), exotic animals, and birds (10:22).

Gold and Other Luxuries

The excess gold (10:10, 14–17) is fashioned into six hundred decorative shields. These are placed not in the Temple, but in the house of the Lebanon Forest. We read of Solomon's extravagant throne,[6] and of his ostentatious tableware:

---

6. Solomon's throne is famous for the colorful midrashic stories describing its supernatural powers. One example is *Lev. Rabba* 20:1: "Pharaoh Necho...sought to sit upon the throne of Solomon. He did not know its workings, so a lion struck him and maimed him." Louis Ginzberg draws a composite based on these midrashim:

   On each of its six steps were two golden lions and two golden eagles, a lion and eagle to the left and a lion and eagle to the right.... The royal seat was at the top, which was round.... On the first step leading to the seat crouched an ox, and opposite him a lion; on the second a wolf and a lamb, on the third a leopard and a goat, on the fourth perched an eagle and a peacock, on the fifth a falcon and a cock; and on the sixth a hawk and a sparrow – all made of gold. At the very top rested a dove, her claws upon a hawk, to betoken that the time would come when all peoples and nations [would] be delivered into the hands of Israel.... When Solomon set foot upon the first step to ascend to his seat, its machinery was put into motion. The golden ox arose and led him to the second

> All of King Solomon's drinking cups were gold, and all the tableware of the Lebanon Forest house was pure gold; there was no silver; it counted for nothing in Solomon's days. (10:21)

The Purpose of Wisdom

The earlier chapters presented God's gift of wisdom with the noble objective articulated by Solomon, "to judge Your people, to distinguish between good and bad" (3:9). In these later chapters, however, Solomon's wisdom functions merely a source of revenue:

> All the world came to pay homage to Solomon and listen to the wisdom with which God had endowed him. And each one would bring his tribute – silver and gold objects, robes, weapons, spices, horses and mules.... (10:24–25)

This eclipsing of the spiritual power of Solomon's wisdom is expressed using another literary feature as well. God has informed Solomon that his wisdom will be unprecedented and never superseded – "There has **never** been anyone like you before, nor will anyone like you arise **again**" (3:12). This designation of historic uniqueness is now applied to other contexts:

> Queen of Sheba: "**Never again** did such a vast quantity of spices arrive...." (10:11)

---

step and there passed him over to the care of the beasts guarding it, and so he was conducted from step to step to step to the sixth, where the eagles received him and placed him upon his seat. As soon as he was seated, a great eagle set the royal crown upon his head. Thereupon, a huge snake rolled itself against the machinery, forcing the lions and eagles upward until they encircled the head of the king. A golden dove flew down from a pillar, took the sacred scroll out of a casket, and gave it to the king, so that he might obey the injunction of the Scriptures, to have the law with him and read therein all the days of his life.

See Ginzberg, *Legends of the Jews*, vol. 4 (Philadelphia: Jewish Publication Society of America, 1941), 157–60.

Almog wood: "Such a quantity of almog wood has **never** arrived or been seen **again** to this day." (10:12)

Solomon's throne: "**Never again** was such throne ever made for any other kingdom." (10:20)

By this simple technique, we gain a vivid sense of Solomon's spiritual decline, as luxury woods and elegant spices make more of an impression than the king's capacity to bring justice to the nation.

Horses from Egypt

Horses are described in chapter 5 as a legitimate need of the military. In chapter 10, in contrast, Solomon becomes the central trader of Egyptian horses:

Solomon's horses were procured from Egypt and Kue. The king's dealers would buy them from Kue at a fixed price. ... and these in turn were exported by them to all the kings of the Hittites and the Arameans. (10:28–29)

THE JEWISH KING

Reading about Solomon's horses and the heightened focus upon gold reminds us of the series of restrictions that are incumbent upon the Jewish king:

He may not amass **horses** for himself and send the people back to Egypt to add to his horses, since the Lord has warned you, "You must not go back that way again." And he may not amass **wives** for himself, lest his heart go astray; nor may he amass **silver and gold** to excess for himself. (Deut. 17:16–17)

The king is denied excessive indulgence in three areas: horses, wives, and wealth. The objective of these restrictions is to ensure that he "not raise his heart above his brothers" and "not deviate from Torah, neither to the right nor to the left" (17:20). As we have seen, Solomon fundamentally violates this code: he has kept many horses, buying them precisely from Egypt; he has accumulated much wealth; and, as we will see in chapter 11, he has married a thousand women.[7]

How does Solomon come to disregard the Torah so flagrantly? The Talmud articulates his overconfidence:

> R. Yitzḥak said: Why were the reasons for biblical laws not revealed? Because in two verses, reasons were revealed, and they caused the greatest in the world [Solomon] to stumble. It is written: "he may not amass wives [lest his heart go astray]." **Solomon said, "I will amass and not let my heart stray."** Yet we read, "When Solomon was old, his wives turned away his heart" (1 Kings 11:4). Again it is written: "He may not amass horses [and send the people back to Egypt to add to his horses]. **Solomon said, "I will amass and not cause [Israel] to return [to Egypt]."** Yet we read, "And a chariot came up and went out of Egypt for six hundred shekels of silver" (10:29). (*Sanhedrin* 21b)

Solomon ignores the warnings of the Torah, miscalculating his personal resilience. He considers himself immune to temptation, insisting that he can control his impulses and instincts – but the wisdom of the Torah exceeds his own.

The Bible actively contrasts the early Solomon with the Solomon of the later years.[8] His modest beginnings give way to an empire with a very different tone. The wealth, the horses, the rise in the standard of living, and the trappings of grandeur become an end in and

---

7. The Jerusalem Talmud outlines this offense explicitly:
    R. Aha said: Solomon said: Three things I violated, for which I was punished: [I violated] "he may not amass wives," for it says, "King Solomon loved many foreign women" (1 Kings 11:1) .... "He may not amass horses," for it says, "King Solomon had four thousand stalls for horses and chariots, and twelve thousand horsemen" (11 Chron. 9:25) .... "Nor may he amass silver and gold to excess," for it says, "The king made silver as plentiful in Jerusalem as stones" (1 Kings 10:27). (*Sanhedrin* 2:6)
8. In this section, we have spoken about at least two distinct periods in Solomon's life. The Midrash (*Song Rabba* 1:10) also describes his developing biography: R. Yonatan

of themselves, rather than a means to higher things. Solomon has gone astray from his original orientation and goals.[9]

IN CONCLUSION

Solomon builds an empire, and he seeks to build a Temple as the jewel in the crown of a most impressive kingdom. The imperial grandeur is a platform from which he can spread the name of God near and far. But the empire has a momentum of its own. It consumes Solomon, as the center of gravity spins out of control.

In this regard, Solomon is reminiscent of the businessman who is determined to achieve financial security and a good life for his family. To that end, he establishes a business and dedicates himself to it, so that it will guarantee him leisure time with his wife and children. And yet, as the business grows and his responsibilities expand, they dominate his time and attention, and only too late does he realize how he never sees his wife and children at all. In the words of Ecclesiastes (traditionally ascribed to Solomon):

> I multiplied my possessions; I built myself houses; I planted myself vineyards. I made myself gardens and groves in which I planted every kind of fruit tree. I constructed pools of water, enough to irrigate a forest. I bought male and female slaves...; herds and flocks, more than all who were before me in Jerusalem. I further amassed silver and gold, and treasures of kings and

---

suggests that Solomon wrote Song of Songs in the exuberance of his youth, Proverbs in his mature middle age, and the somber Ecclesiastes when he was elderly. The Talmud also records a decline in Solomon's power:

Resh Lakish said: At first, Solomon reigned over the higher beings, as it is written, "Then Solomon sat on the throne of the Lord as king" (1 Chron. 29:23); afterward, [having sinned,] he reigned [only] over the lower beings.... So did he reign over the whole world. But eventually his reign was restricted to Israel.... Later, his reign was confined to Jerusalem alone.... And still later he reigned only over his bed.... And finally, he reigned only over his staff (scepter?). (*Sanhedrin* 20b)

9. Prof. Avraham Grossman articulates this beautifully in his article, "1 Kings Chapter 11: The Sins of Solomon," http://www.daat.ac.il/daat/tanach/rishonim/grossman3. htm [Hebrew].

provinces.... I gained more wealth than anyone before me in Jerusalem; in addition, my wisdom remained with me. I denied myself no enjoyment. Then my thoughts turned to all the fortune my hands had built up, to the wealth I had acquired and won – and behold, it was futile and a pursuit of wind, and there was no real value under the sun. (Eccl. 2:4–11)

Nothing exemplifies this shift more than Solomon's two dreams:

In the inaugural dream, God offers him everything – wealth, military prowess. But Solomon wants only wisdom. His modesty and spiritual priorities are self-evident.

God's second dream to Solomon (9:1–10) is dark and cautionary, filled with ominous warnings. Both the king and the nation are exhorted to remain loyal to God's commands, as explicit images of exile and destruction are revealed in His words. One gains the impression in this second prophetic dream that the process of deterioration has already begun, that this prophecy is meant as a wake-up call encouraging Solomon to reorient his kingdom.[10] Unfortunately, chapters 9 and 10 indicate that the materialism only accelerates.

In the next chapter, we encounter Solomon's most severe offenses, resulting in God's decision to fragment his kingdom.

---

10. The second dream (1 Kings 9:2) is explicitly linked to the earlier prophecy at Gibeon (3:5–14).

1 Kings 10

Solomon's Sins

Solomon's downfall is painfully detailed. Up to this point, his fundamental religious faithfulness has been uncontestable, much like the regional hegemony of his kingdom. Chapter 11 overturns this impression as it charts Solomon's demise. We now read of his idolatry and become aware of military and political opposition to his rule. God issues a devastating condemnation proclaiming the split of Solomon's kingdom, and we meet Jeroboam son of Nebat, whose political insurgency will tear the kingdom into two.

The chapter begins by introducing Solomon's one thousand wives. At first glance, we sense that the text notes this plethora of women as a contravention of the second of the biblical restrictions incumbent upon a Jewish monarch – those of horses, wives, and wealth.[1] However, Solomon's foreign wives engender a more severe religious offense, as the king turns to idolatry. In a chilling reversal, the man who built the Temple now constructs pagan shrines:

> And in Solomon's old age, his wives caused his heart to stray after
> other gods, and he was not wholeheartedly devoted to the Lord,

---

1. See Deuteronomy 17:16–17.

his God, as his father, David, had been. Solomon followed Ashtoreth, god of Phoenicia, and Milcom, the abomination of the Ammonites. Solomon did evil in the eyes of God and did not remain loyal to God like his father, David. At that time, Solomon built a shrine to Chemosh, the abomination of Moav, on the hill near Jerusalem, and one to Molech, the abomination of Ammon. He did the same for all his foreign wives, who offered and sacrificed to their gods. (11:4–8)

The reader digests this information with a sense of bewilderment. Solomon is, after all, the wisest of men. He is the author of the book of Proverbs, in which he repeatedly warns about the dangers of straying after other deities, foreign cultures, and worldly attractions, which he refers to as "foreign women":

> Why be infatuated, my son, with an outside woman,
> And embrace the breast of a foreigner?
> For a man's ways are before the eyes of God...
> The wicked man will be trapped in his iniquities. (Prov. 5:20–21)[2]

How could Solomon himself fall into their trap? Would the person who wrote so passionately of the love of God and Israel in Song of Songs turn his back on his beloved God?

RABBINIC READINGS

The Talmudic sages debated Solomon's motivation in entering into his disturbing marriages:

> "And King Solomon loved foreign women" (1 Kings 11:1) –
> R. Shimon bar Yoḥai said: "Loved" literally; his motivation was sexual.

---

2. See also Proverbs 2:16, 6:24, 7:7–8:6. Proverbs is attributed to Solomon in its opening line.

Hanania...said: He transgressed "You shall not marry them" (Deut. 7:3).
R. Yose said: He sought to attract them with words of Torah and draw them close to the divine presence. (Jerusalem Talmud, *Sanhedrin* 2:6)

In this fascinating debate, R. Shimon bar Yohai views Solomon's foreign wives as symbolic of his hedonistic personality, his sensual indulgence. Others share this negative view; the Talmud records an opinion that includes Solomon in the infamous list of the condemned who forfeited their place in the World to Come (*Sanhedrin* 104b)! Hanania perceives Solomon neutrally, as transgressing the technical prohibition of inter-marriage.[3] In contrast, R. Yose views Solomon's motivation favorably. He asserts that Solomon's intent was to convert these foreign women, his only desire being a passion to spread Judaism to foreign cultures and civilizations.

The Talmud records a rabbinic debate as to the legitimacy of the sacred books attributed to Solomon, some arguing that Song of Songs and Ecclesiastes should be banned from the Bible (*Shabbat* 30b). The fact that these books were ultimately included reflects the enduring rabbinic view of Solomon as positive. R. Akiva declared Song of Songs the "holy of holies" – interpreting it as descriptive of God's love for Israel, rather than illicit love of women – thereby giving a stamp of approval to Solomon's literary legacy and affirming his positive spiritual orientation.[4] Along these same lines, the Talmud, in a famous aggadic passage, claims that Solomon never served idolatry; only his wives did:

R. Shmuel b. Nahmani says in the name of R. Yonatan: **Whoever says that Solomon sinned is mistaken**, as it states: "...he was

---

3. The end of the verse quoted by R. Hanania is, "For they will turn your children away from Me to worship other gods" (Deut. 7:3). In that sense, there may be a connection between Solomon's marriages and his "turning away" from God.
4. The banning of Solomon's literary works is also discussed in *Yadayim* 3:5. *Avot DeRabbi Natan* 1:4 describes how the Men of the Great Assembly revealed or rein-terpreted Solomon's writings to accord with the spiritual principles of Judaism.

> not wholeheartedly devoted to the Lord, his God, as his father,
> David, had been" (1 Kings 11:4) – not as devoted as David, but
> nonetheless he did not sin! (*Shabbat* 56b)

How does the Talmud presume to explain the verses explicitly stating
that Solomon built altars to other deities and served them?

> Because he should have protested his wives' acts, and he failed
> to do so, he is treated as if he served [idolatry] himself. (ibid.)

The text speaks as if Solomon had practiced idolatry, but in truth, he is
taken to task for failing to stop his wives from doing so.

Some object to this approach as an exercise in rabbinic apologet-
ics and character whitewashing. Indeed, this is part of an entire series of
statements by a single Talmudic sage – R. Shmuel b. Naḥmani – which
seek to exonerate several of the Bible's most prominent transgressors.[5]
Yet in Solomon's case, this reading is adopted by the great medieval commentators, Rashi, Ralbag, and Radak, and by the modern commentary
Da'at Mikra. In other words, traditional commentary refuses to view
Solomon as an idolater.

There are some textual supports for this approach. God's direct
accusation of Solomon (1 Kings 11:11–13) omits any sin of idolatry. In
addition, there is the point raised by the Talmud itself – if Solomon were
genuinely guilty of the cardinal transgression of idolatry, it would seem
like a rather absurd understatement to say that "he was not wholeheartedly devoted to the Lord, his God, as his father, David, had been" (11:4).[6]

---

5. The characters discussed are Reuben, the sons of Eli, David, Solomon, and Josiah.
   The opinions are all attributed to R. Shmuel b. Nahmani in the name of R. Yonatan,
   and all involve the rereading of the biblical account in a non-literal manner in order
   to recast explicit sins as legitimate acts. As regards the motive of the rabbis, when
   the Talmud quotes a statement by Rebbi (R. Judah the Prince) seeking to exonerate King David, a later opinion suggests that he is motivated to defend his personal
   lineage, because he himself was descended from him. In other words, some of these
   approaches – so inconsonant with the plain meaning of the text – might be driven
   by an ulterior motive.
6. See Ralbag on 1 Kings 11:4–9.

Even if we succeed in exonerating Solomon of the formal indictment of idolatry, his record is far from cleared. After all, the Talmud
informs us that Solomon bears responsibility for his wives' sacrificial
altars and that his guilt is sufficient to cost him his kingdom. How did
Solomon make such a dire error? What can explain his actions?

Solomon had one thousand wives from a panoply of nations.
One imagines that this huge collection of women was part of a foreign
policy strategy, with Solomon seeking to forge political alliances through
marriage. Reflecting the view of R. Yose, we may propose that Solomon
had an additional goal of drawing these nations closer to monotheism.
But to what degree were these women genuinely integrated into Jewish
ideas, practice, and belief? Even if his wives were formally converted,[7]
they never absorbed a Jewish value system. Culturally, they remained
affiliated with their native kingdoms. The more powerful among them
likely gained royal permission and funding to build their own shrines
on the outskirts of the city, where they could worship their gods: Chemosh, Milcom, and Molech. These temples would have been built under
royal command, by the king's construction teams, and they would have
been emblazoned with Solomon's royal insignia. Did Solomon actually
build these temples? Well…yes! In the same manner in which we could
say that he built anything, we could correctly say that "Solomon built a
shrine to X, Y, and Z." After all, he signed the checks.

Imagine the surprise and confusion of the visitor to Jerusalem,
arriving in the world's leading monotheistic city and intending to worship the one true God at the Temple. The discovery of government-
sponsored pagan shrines scattered around the city would most certainly
appear drastically discordant.[8]

The Torah has zero tolerance for idolatry; no wavering is permitted when it comes to pagan worship. Solomon's lackadaisical attitude

---

7. See Radak on 3:1, who grapples with this issue on the basis of a discussion in *Yevamot*
   76a.
8. See Rabbi Yitzchak Levi's article, "Shelomo's Monarchy in Jerusalem (v) – The
   Fall," The Virtual Beit Midrash, http://vbm-torah.org/archive/yeru2/15yeru.htm,
   in which he discusses the location of these shrines in Jerusalem and their contrast
   to the Temple.

toward his wives' idolatry brought down the entire enterprise that he sought to build; he was complicit in their acts.

THE DAUGHTER OF PHARAOH

In addressing the theme of foreign wives, one wife in particular is highlighted from the very outset of Solomon's reign:

> Solomon allied himself with Pharaoh king of Egypt, and he took the daughter of Pharaoh as his wife, bringing her to the city of David until he had completed his house and God's house.... And Solomon loved God.... (3:1–3)

This marriage is the opening detail about Solomon following his initial struggle for the throne and the defeat of his rivals. It is an ambivalent description. At this early stage, the verses emphasize Solomon's love of God, informing us that his religious orientation is extremely positive. Yet the prominent marriage to Pharaoh's daughter seems ominous. From this point on, she interjects into the storyline regularly:

> And the throne room in which he judged, the court of justice, ... Solomon made a house for the daughter of Pharaoh, whom he took [as a wife],.... (7:7–8)

> Pharaoh, king of Egypt, arose and captured Gezer and burnt the city and killed all the Canaanites who lived there, and he gave it as a gift to his daughter, wife of Solomon. (9:16)

> ...the daughter of Pharaoh ascended from the city of David to her house that [Solomon] had built her; that was the building of the Millo. (9:24)

> And King Solomon loved many foreign women in addition to Pharaoh's daughter.... (11:1)

In hindsight, the tight intertwining of Solomon with Pharaoh's daughter serves as a grim and deeply troubling refrain in his story. By making their marriage the opening (3:1) and closing (11:1) note of the Solomon narrative, the Bible is tainting Solomon from start to finish.[9]

In its uniquely creative style, the Midrash proposes that the day of the dedication of the Temple was in fact the day of Solomon's wedding to Pharaoh's daughter:[10]

> R. Yudan said: All seven years of building the Temple, Solomon never drank wine. When he built it and married the daughter of Pharaoh, that night he drank wine. And there were two dances: One was the celebration of the building of the Temple, and the other was the celebration of Pharaoh's daughter. God said: "Whose should I find acceptable, these or those?" At that moment, He considered destroying Jerusalem....[11]
>
> R. Ḥonia said: Pharaoh's daughter danced eighty dances that night, and Solomon slept until the fourth hour. The keys to the Temple were under his head. This is the instance about which [the rabbis] taught that the daily sacrifice was brought [as late as] the fourth hour. His mother came in to rebuke him, and some say it was Jeroboam who came in to rebuke him. (*Lev. Rabba* 12:1)

Did Solomon's wedding in fact coincide with the opening of the Temple? I believe that the Midrash brilliantly unifies the timing to tell a tale of Solomon's two conflicting loves – that of the Temple and that of Pharaoh's daughter – distilling this dual attraction into a single event. It depicts the two celebrations as taking place in tandem, bearing equal weight. Indeed, God also expresses His frustration and "confusion" at

---

9. See 1 Kings 11:27, which ties the Jeroboam rebellion to the daughter of Pharaoh.
10. The text indicates that these two events were separate. *Seder Olam* 15 states that Solomon married Pharaoh's daughter in the fourth year of his reign. The Temple dedication was much later, in the eleventh or even twenty-fourth year of his reign.
11. The rabbis drew a causal link between Solomon's marriage to the daughter of Pharaoh and the destruction of the Temple, as if the former made the latter inevitable:
    R. Yitzhak said: At the moment Solomon married Pharaoh's daughter, the angel Gabriel came down [to earth] and stuck a cane into the sea. It gathered a sandbank around it, and there the great city of Rome was built. (*Shabbat* 56b)
    In the midrashic imagination, Rome, the destroyer of the Second Temple, originated in this terrible moment!

this hybrid of discordant festivities: "Whose should I find acceptable, these or those?"

The Midrash depicts Solomon prior to his marriage as a paragon of self-control, a man who never slept late and never indulged in wine. From the advent of his marriage, his control slips, as he oversleeps, unable to tear himself away from his one love, his wife, to go to his other love and loyalty, the Temple service. In the end, his wife prevails, and Solomon's oversleeping threatens the Temple service on its inaugural day. The king's attraction to Pharaoh's daughter undermines the Temple and its integrity.

Developing this idea further, the Midrash adds some colorful elements:

> The rabbis said: The daughter of Pharaoh introduced one thousand songs, and everyone was commanded before Solomon that night to listen to them. She would say to Solomon: "This is the song for this idol; that is the tune for that idol...." (*Num. Rabba* 10:4)

With her one thousand songs, Pharaoh's daughter personifies all one thousand of Solomon's wives. Each song is dedicated to a particular deity; Solomon's wives bring an equivalent number of foreign gods, swamping the kingdom. Moreover, her singing affects the entire audience, which has been instructed to attend.

It is unlikely that Solomon's wedding actually coincided with the Temple dedication, but by superimposing one upon the other, the Midrash vividly expresses Solomon's two-mindedness. Similarly, in recording the marriage to Pharaoh's daughter at the very outset of the Solomon narrative, the book of Kings asserts that these competing loves contend for his heart from the earliest moment. Solomon seeks to balance the two, but he does not know which dance to dance, which party to attend.

Solomon is caught between clashing forces. Seeking to influence the world, he instigates a benevolent foreign policy, extending a hand in partnership to each country of his empire. The daughter of Pharaoh represents Egypt, Solomon's most powerful ally, symbolizing the power, trade, and international influence that appeal to his imperial mind. However, the world around Solomon is not neutral; it is pagan. He seeks to export monotheism, but he soon discovers that there is a cultural two-way street. His wives import a devastating idolatrous culture, which in time, "in his old age," overwhelms him.

As we noted in the introduction, the book of Kings examines history from the vantage point of the Temple's demise, probing the causes of its destruction. The Midrash depicts God as contemplating the Temple's destruction from its very beginnings, as if to label the Temple fundamentally flawed. Solomon's marriages further threaten his greatest achievement.

1 Kings 11

Punishment

God responds to Solomon's sins by issuing the ultimate punishment: the disintegration of his kingdom. This fate is first proclaimed by God to Solomon directly and later restated in greater detail by the prophet Ahijah at the end of the chapter 11. The repetition creates a literary envelope:

1–10	Solomon's sin of idolatry	
11–13	Declaration of punishment	
14–28	Political adversaries	
	Hadad (14–22)	
	Rezon (23–25)	
	Jeroboam (26–28)	
29–40	Ahijah the Shilonite's restatement of Solomon's punishment	
41–43	Summative verses of Solomon's reign	

In between these two proclamations is a detailed series of political adversaries, denoted by the word *satan*. This unusual language is deliberate, having featured earlier, in Solomon's own words:

> Now the Lord, my God, has given me respite all around; there
> is no adversary (*satan*) and no mischance. (5:18)

In an inverse parallelism, while Solomon's commitment to God induced
a national era of peace, without any *satan*, his waywardness generates
political turbulence and trouble, with many *satanim*.[1]

ALL THE DAYS OF SOLOMON?

The three insurgents listed – Rezon, Hadad, and Jeroboam – all pose
some manner of rebellion against King Solomon, rejecting his sovereignty. There are many unanswered questions about these political dissidents, however.

The first *satan*, Hadad, from the Edomite royal family, escaped
as a baby during King David's six-month campaign against that nation
(11:14–15).[2] He took refuge in Egypt until King Solomon's rise to power,
and we read about his son's marriage to Egyptian royalty. At a certain
point, Hadad returned to Edom to lead a resistance movement against
King Solomon. How do we pinpoint the historical timing of this rebellion? Solomon rules for forty years; at what stage of his reign does Hadad
become a national threat?

And is he a national threat? We have no account of Hadad's significantly challenging or harming the Israelite kingdom. We can confidently say that Solomon fully controls the lands of Edom, managing a
fully functional Israelite port at Ezion-Geber (9:26).[3] We have read of

---

1. *Satan* frequently denotes an opposing force. See, for example, the story of Balaam
   (Num. 22:22); I Samuel 29:4; Zechariah 3:1–2. For a full treatment of this topic, see
   The Biblical Encyclopedia (Jerusalem: Bialik Institute, 1982), vol. 8, s.v. *satan*, cols.
   277–83 [Hebrew].
2. See II Samuel 8:13–14.
3. Evidence in the Bible regarding relations between Israel and Edom does not give
   a comprehensive historical picture. II Samuel 8:13–14 and I Kings 22:48 mention
   Israelite dominance over Edom. Many scholars suggest uninterrupted Israelite
   control of Edom throughout the period of David and until after Jehoshaphat. In
   fact, Edom joins Judah and Israel as an ally in war in II Kings 3. Only in 8:22 do we
   see the Edomites gain independence from Judah. Later in the Bible, Edom is an
   aggressor, especially in the context of the destruction of the Temple; see Psalms
   137:7, Lamentations 4:21–22, and the book of Obadiah.

the exotic merchandise he has obtained on his sea voyages to Africa. If Edom was giving him border trouble, attacking convoys traveling from the port to Jerusalem, Solomon would certainly have retaliated – but there is no record of any such military campaign waged by the king.

The second *satan* – Rezon of Syria (Tzova) – is described as "an aggressor to Israel **throughout the days of Solomon**" (11:25), and other verses seem to indicate that Aram gained independence during this period.[4] Yet chapter 5 states quite explicitly that Solomon "controlled the entire region west of the Euphrates... and had peace on all his borders roundabout. **All the days of Solomon...**" (5:4). Was Rezon a threat of any significance during Solomon's long reign?

Radak addresses this problem:

> It is referring to the period after Solomon grew old – then these political dissidents arose, at the same juncture that his heart turned away from God. (11:23)

In other words, Radak sees the verses that express Solomon's full regional hegemony as representing the accurate historical picture. He therefore concludes that the statements placing this political opposition "throughout the days of Solomon" need some reinterpretation. He resolves this difficulty by suggesting that the aggressors began causing trouble only in Solomon's latter years – after he capitulated to idolatry. Clearly, the former is the result of the latter.

If these *satanim* are far from serious threats to Solomon's hegemony, why is I Kings interested in presenting them as if they oppose

---

4. I Kings 11:25 is very confusing. After talking about Rezon, it reintroduces Hadad into the picture: "He was an aggressor to Israel all the days of Solomon, adding to the trouble caused by Hadad; he rejected the rule of Israel, and he ruled over Aram." Who ruled over Aram – Rezon or Hadad? On the one hand, Rezon is the subject of the verse. He comes from Syria, making his rule in Aram quite anticipated. On the other hand, the name Hadad, or Benhadad, is the standard name for the king of Aram/Syria. On this basis, is it likely that Rezon would be the ruler of Aram? For this reason, Ralbag assumes that it is Hadad who becomes king in Aram! In contrast, the Septuagint changes Aram to Edom – exchanging the letter *resh* for a *dalet* – assuming that Hadad from Edom becomes king in Edom.

the king throughout his reign? We might suggest that these characters and the freedom movements they instigate represent the first cracks in Solomon's empire, small beginnings that ferment and grow, generating future catastrophe. Egypt's nurturing of dissidents such as Hadad and Jeroboam is a harbinger of the invasion by Pharaoh Shishak (14:25–26 and 1 Chron. 12:9–11), which devastates Jerusalem just five years after Solomon's death, as Egypt "carried off the treasures of the house of God," stripping the capital of the wealth and finery of the Solomonic era. Evidently, Shishak was planning this attack for a generation.

Of all the political adversaries harbored by Pharaoh, none will prove more destructive that the third *satan* – Jeroboam – who destroys Judah from within.

An Allegorical Reading

Prof. Amos Frisch offers a fascinating allegorical reading of the personality of Hadad by noting several significant comparisons to the biblical portrayal of Moses.[5] Both Hadad and Moses are born against the backdrop of the killing of the males of their nations. Saved as a young child, each grows up in Pharaoh's house as royalty. They each escape to Midian and marry the daughter of their protector in the land to which they have fled (Jethro/Pharaoh). And in each case, upon the death of a despotic ruler (Pharaoh/David), they request leave of their father-in-law to return to their oppressed brethren and lead the opposition to the oppressive regime.[6]

If we follow this allusion to its logical conclusion, Hadad is a surrogate for Moses, and Solomon is identified with Pharaoh! This comparison is even more poignant if we recall Solomon's forced labor, the building of *arei miskenot* (1 Kings 9:18), and his son Rehoboam's

---

5. Amos Frisch, "The Exodus Motif in 1 Kings 1–14," *Journal for the Study of the Old Testament* 87 (2000): 3–21. See also Avigdor Shinan and Yair Zakovitch, *That's Not What the Good Book Says* (Tel Aviv: Miskal–Yedioth Ahronoth and Chemed, 2004), 195–201 [Hebrew], which treats this story from a critical perspective.

6. Regarding Moses, see Exodus 1:22; 2:2–3, 10, 21, 23; 4:18. Regarding Hadad, see 1 Kings 11:14–22.

depiction of him as "whipping" the nation (12:14).[7] In this novel interpretation, the *satanim* are literary foils intended to brand Solomon as a Pharaoh-like tyrant. This reading is exceptionally harsh, but it helps explain the lengthy digression regarding adversaries who seem to do only minor damage.

TEARING THE KINGDOM – ABSOLUTELY?

Let us return to God's declaration of Solomon's punishment, which is expressed in an intriguing way. First, there is a categorical pronouncement:

> I will tear the kingdom away from you and give it to one of your servants. (11:11)

The initial impression from this verse is that Solomon will be ousted from the throne, and replaced by one of his subjects or courtiers. The phrasing of this decree reflects the language of the book of Samuel, where Saul is condemned to the untimely termination of his monarchy:

> The Lord has this day **torn the kingship** of Israel away from you and **given it to another** who is worthier than you. (I Sam. 15:28)

Similarly, Ahijah's ripping of the robe into twelve pieces recalls Saul's ripping of Samuel's robe (15:27);[8] these are graphic dramatizations of the severing of Saul's and Solomon's rule.

---

7. Cf. Exodus 1:18; 5:14, 16.
8. Ḥazal discuss whether it was Saul's robe or Samuel's that was ripped; see *Midrash Shmuel* 18:5. Further similarities connect Saul and Solomon beyond the pronouncements made about them and the acts of tearing. In both characters' stories, the contender for the throne (David or Jeroboam) finds himself under threat of death, inducing him to defect from the country and take refuge with foreign aggressors of Israel (David with the Philistine king Achish [1 Sam. 27] and Jeroboam with Shishak of Egypt). The phrase "and the two of them [Ahijah and Jeroboam] were alone in the field" (1 Kings 11:29) is reminiscent of Saul's appointment; see 1 Samuel 9:26, 10:1.

Initially, then, we would anticipate an absolute termination of Solomon's royal line, akin to the fate of Saul. However, Solomon's punishment, expressed at first in absolute terms, is promptly limited – and one might even say mitigated – in two dimensions:

1. "I will not do it [tear the kingdom] in your lifetime; I will tear it away from your son" (1 Kings 11:12). Why? "For the sake of your father, David" (ibid.).
2. "I will not tear away the whole kingdom; I will give your son one tribe" (11:13). Why? "For the sake of My servant David, and for the sake of Jerusalem, which I have chosen" (ibid.).

In other words, the punishment is delayed – it will occur after Solomon's lifetime – and it is limited in scope. Despite the rupture of his kingdom, his royal line will endure and retain Jerusalem. Ten tribes will secede from the kingdom, but the house of David will reign intact in Jerusalem.

This is quite surprising. If Solomon's actions warrant severe punishment, why does God commute his sentence? How does the memory of David or Jerusalem serve to postpone and diminish the decree?

For the Sake of David

The statement that the kingdom will not be torn from David's descendants first appears here (11:12, 13, 32, 34), but recurs throughout the book of Kings as an argument to ignore misdemeanor and delay punishment: "The Lord refrained from destroying Judah for the sake of His servant David" (15:4; II Kings 8:19, 19:34, 20:6). In each instance, the dismal spiritual situation warrants a total termination of the royal line, but each time, God acquiesces "for the sake of David." Why is the memory of David a reason to preserve his lineage?

The answer is found in God's statement to David after his request to build the Temple:

> ... the Lord declares to you that the Lord will establish a house for you. When your days are done, and you lie with your fathers, I will raise your offspring after you ... and establish his kingship. He shall build a house for My name, **and I will establish his royal throne**

forever. ... when he does wrong, I will chastise him with the rod of men and the affliction of mortals. **But I will never withdraw My favor from him as I withdrew it from Saul.... You and your house shall be secure before you forever; your throne shall be established forever.** (II Sam. 7:11–16)

David has requested to build a house for God, to construct a Temple. In this momentous prophecy, God states that He will preserve a royal house of David. In practical terms, this means that David's heir – his son – will succeed him and continue his sovereignty after him. In a second beautiful expression of reciprocity, God promises that specifically David's son, who represents the royal line, will be granted the opportunity to build the Temple.

But a second point here is more radical: God pledges **never** to treat David's line as he treated the house of Saul. He issues a divine assurance that David's throne will stand for eternity.

This promise goes some way to explain why Solomon lives out his reign unharmed. God has pledged to establish Solomon's kingship. Of course, if he sins, "I will chastise him with the rod of men and the affliction of mortals" – precisely the challenge posed by the political adversaries described in our chapter.[9] However, the royal line of David reigns forever, as promised.

For the Sake of Jerusalem

But what of "for the sake of Jerusalem, which I have chosen?" What is the source of the eternal connection between the house of David and Jerusalem? The book of Psalms offers a possible solution:

A Song of Ascents. Lord, remember unto David all his affliction; **How he swore unto the Lord** and vowed unto the Mighty One of Jacob:
"I will not enter my house, nor will I mount my bed;
I will not give sleep to my eyes, or slumber to my eyelids;

---

9. See Rashi on I Kings 11:23 and Ralbag on 11:40.

Until I find a place for the Lord, an abode for the Mighty One
of Jacob."
… **The Lord swore to David** a firm oath that He will not renounce:
"One of your issue I will set upon your throne.
If your sons keep My covenant and My decrees that I teach them,
Then their sons also, to the end of time, shall sit upon your throne."
For the Lord has chosen Zion;
He has desired it for His seat:
"This is My resting place for all time;
Here I will dwell, for I desire it." (Ps. 132:1–5, 11–14)

David swears not to rest until God has a resting place. In response, God
promises that as long as his descendants follow the Torah, they shall sit
on his throne. In addition, David cites God's eternal selection of Jerusalem as His dwelling place! These promises cannot be abrogated.[10] Even if

---

10. The question of the abrogation of the promise to David arises in Jeremiah 33:20–21
and Psalms 89. In the latter, the promise to David is restated:
> … I have exalted one chosen out of the people.
> I have found David My servant; with My holy oil have I anointed him;
> … Forever will I keep for him My mercy, and My covenant shall stand fast with
> him.
> His seed also will I make to endure forever, and his throne as the days of heaven.
> If his children forsake My law, and walk not in My ordinances;
> If they profane My statutes and observe not My commandments;
> Then will I visit their transgression with the rod, and their iniquity with strokes.
> But My mercy will I not break off from him, nor will I be false to My faithfulness.
> My covenant will I not profane, nor will I alter that which is gone out of My lips.
> Once have I sworn by My holiness: Surely I will not be false unto David;
> His seed shall endure forever, and his throne shall be as the sun before Me.
> It shall be established forever as the moon; and be steadfast as the witness in
> the sky. (Ps. 89:20–21, 29–38)

The author of this psalm, who apparently lived after the Temple's destruction, protests
that despite this pledge, the Davidic line has been rejected:
> Yet You have rejected and spurned and become enraged with Your anointed.
> You have repudiated the covenant of Your servant; You hast profaned his crown
> even to the ground.
> … You have brought his strongholds to ruin.
> All that pass by the way spoil him; he is become a taunt to his neighbors….
> You have made his brightness to cease, and cast his throne down to the ground. …

Solomon violates God's covenant, the promise of Jerusalem to David's heir remains intact. For this reason, even today, we pray for the restoration of *tzemah David* – the sprout of David.[11] Our tradition anticipates the Messiah as a descendant of David – *ben David* – in fulfillment of this promise.[12] God does not renege on His promises, and hence an eternally chosen Jerusalem still awaits the Davidic heir.

How long, O Lord, will You hide Yourself forever? How long shall Your wrath burn like fire? (89:39–42, 45, 47)

This psalm challenges God as to how He could have broken His promise of eternal sovereignty to David. Ibn Ezra notes: "There was a great scholar in Spain – wise and pious – and he found this chapter [of Psalms] too [theologically] difficult, so much that he would not read it or hear it, because the author [of the psalm] speaks so harshly against God."

11. For the notion of the "sprout of David" and the promise of Israel's restoration, see Isaiah 11:1; Jeremiah 23:5–6, 33:14–16; Zechariah 3:8, 6:12.
12. The word *mashiah* (Messiah) simply means "anointed" and refers to the king; see, for example, I Samuel 24:6; 26:16, 23; II Samuel 1:14, 16; 19:22.

Jeroboam

Jeroboam is the man who dares oppose the imperial king, Solomon, and he becomes the rebel leader who eventually splits the kingdom. In the next few chapters, we will attempt to understand what drives this man and how we should assess him.

On the one hand, the Mishna groups Jeroboam among the evil personalities of the Bible who are condemned to eternal perdition:

> Three kings and four commoners have no portion in the World to Come: Three kings – Jeroboam, Ahab, and Manasseh. (*Sanhedrin* 10:2)[1]

Jeroboam earns this reputation due to the images and altars he sets up in Bethel and Dan.

On the other hand, Ḥazal highlight positive aspects of Jeroboam's biography, celebrating him as a leading Torah scholar[2] and commending him for his defiant stand against the king:

---

1. See also *Rosh Hashana* 17a.
2. "Just as the new robe was flawless, so was Jeroboam's Torah…. They [Jeroboam

> Why did Jeroboam deserve to be king? Because he denounced
> Solomon. (*Sanhedrin* 101b)

It is evident that Jeroboam is a nuanced and complex character; a composite of virtues and flaws, successes and failures.

POLITICAL OPPOSITION

> Jeroboam son of Nebat, an Ephraimite of Zereda, the son of
> a widow whose name was Zeruah, was in Solomon's service;
> he raised his hand against the king. The circumstances under
> which he raised his hand against the king were as follows: Solo-
> mon built the Millo, repairing the breach of the city of David his
> father. Jeroboam was an able man,[3] and when Solomon saw that
> the young man was a capable worker, he appointed him [as tax
> collector] over all the province of the house of Joseph. (1 Kings
> 11:26–28)

The order of these verses makes them difficult to decipher. Several commentators reorganize them to tell the following story:[4] Jeroboam, a man

---

and Ahijah] innovated [Torah] the likes of which had never been heard before….
All the scholars of the generation were like the grass of the field compared to them"
(*Sanhedrin* 102a). The text of the book of Kings bears no evidence of Jeroboam's
Torah scholarship, however. The Talmud similarly presents King David as a *talmid
hakham* ruling on halakhic topics: "David said to the Holy One Blessed Be He: Am I
not a righteous man? For all the kings of east and west sit around [basking] in glory,
while I dirty my hands with blood, amniotic fluid, and placentas in order to [issue
the halakhic rulings that] make a woman permissible to her husband" (*Berakhot* 4a).

3. This is the NJPS translation of the Hebrew *gibbor hayil*. We do not find Jeroboam
   serving in a military capacity – unlike David (1 Sam. 18) or Naaman (11 Kings 5:1),
   who also carry this appellation – although he may have. The other biblical figure
   who functions in a civilian context and shares this title is Boaz (Ruth 2:1). Perhaps
   gibbor hayil represents some form of social status, as we see in 11 Kings 15:19–20,
   where Menahem son of Gadi requires all *gibborei hayil* to pay one thousand talents
   of silver. In that context, the term refers to people of higher class or financial means.
   Importantly, other potential kings – both Saul (1 Sam. 9:1) and David (16:18) – are
   introduced with this title.
4. See Rashi, Radak, and Ralbag.

of humble beginnings, exhibits outstanding management and leadership skills. His impressive qualities lead Solomon to appoint him head of the administrative region of Joseph, collecting the taxes used to finance the palace.[5] In this capacity, and possibly due to his upbringing as an orphan, Jeroboam is highly aware of the heavy financial burden weighing upon the common folk.

Amid the burgeoning expenses of an extravagant government, Jeroboam voices his opposition to Solomon's taxation policy. The text describes this act in an extreme way: "he raised his hand against the king" (11:26), indicative of confrontation, defiance, and even mutiny. We can surmise that Jeroboam's critique is expressed publicly and that Solomon views it as a provocation, an act of betrayal.[6] We know the result:

> Solomon tried to kill Jeroboam, but Jeroboam fled to Egypt, to Shishak the king, and stayed there until Solomon's death. (11:40)

A king does not seek to eliminate a political opponent unless he views the protagonist as a significant threat.

Jeroboam's activism in tax-related issues resurfaces in chapter 12, where he is invited to lead the northern tribes in their challenge to Solomon's son Rehoboam, the new king. They demand that the king lower taxes. Jeroboam is the obvious leadership choice, as he has already championed their cause and protested against the government on behalf of the working class.

THE MILLO

The specific event that angers Jeroboam is the Millo building project. The first we hear about the Millo is that "...the daughter of Pharaoh

---

5. See I Kings 4:7: "And Solomon had twelve officers over all Israel, who provided for the king and his household; each man had to make provision for a month in the year."

6. Abarbanel notes: "There is no doubt that this rebuke was not one of public critique rooted in 'hidden love'; there was hatred and vulgarity. If not for that, Solomon would not have sought to have him killed." The Talmud (*Sanhedrin* 101b) faults Jeroboam for publicizing his differences with Solomon, but it is difficult to assess how these issues could have been resolved behind closed doors.

ascended from the city of David to her house that [Solomon] had built her; that was the building of the Millo" (9:24). Jeroboam's protest concerns the appropriation of public land for the construction of a palace for Pharaoh's daughter.

The second relevant detail regarding the Millo is that it "repaired the breach of the city of David" (11:27). What exactly is the Millo? Where is it? And how does it repair the "breach," or gap, in the city of David?

Archaeologists and traditional commentaries offer an array of suggestions regarding the nature of the Millo. There are three basic options:[7]

1. It is a fortress. This is the translation of the Septuagint.[8]
2. It is a fortification of the slopes and outer wall surrounding Jerusalem. Walls were constructed and filled with dirt (a landfill, "Millo" deriving from the Hebrew word *malei*, "full"), creating reinforced terraces and a steep gradient with which to defend the city. Archaeologists have found evidence of structures such as this on the eastern flank of the city of David.

According to these two explanations, the Millo is a specialized war fortification. This definition fits well with several other biblical references to the Millo in a military context.[9]

---

7. The book of Kings speaks of "the Millo and the walls of Jerusalem" (9:15), indicating a connection between the two. Rashi explains: "A low wall filled in with earth, the high point of the mound being in the middle and sloping in all directions – this is called Millo. Upon it, David constructed buildings, and that Millo surrounded the stronghold" (commentary on II Samuel 5:9). For a good summary of biblical references and archaeological perspectives on the topic, see O. Bustenai and M. Garsiel, eds., *Encyclopedia of the World of the Bible, I Kings* (Tel Aviv: Davidson-Atai, 1994), commentary on 9:16 [Hebrew]. Rabbi Yitzchak Levi has also written a very useful article on the Millo; see "Shelomo's Monarchy in Jerusalem (VI) – The Millo," The Virtual Beit Midrash, http://vbm-torah.org/archive/yeru2/16yeru.htm.
8. This may be the meaning of the phrase "house of Millo" in Judges 9:20. That story takes place in Shechem, which demonstrates that the term is not limited to Jerusalem.
9. See II Samuel 5:9; II Chronicles 32:5.

3. It is a tract of land that connected the city of David to the Temple Mount. Solomon's Temple was situated on a hillock hundreds of meters from the populated area of David's City. Prior to the construction of the Temple, this had been agricultural land outside the city limits. But with the Temple standing, the Millo was an empty expanse in the middle of the city. In that sense, the construction of the Millo "repaired the breach of the city of David." Some have even suggested that there was a need for heavy earthworks or landfill (again, *malei* meaning "full") to connect the two hills – hence the term Millo. Accordingly, when Psalms lauds "Jerusalem built up, a city joined together" (122:3), it is referring to a city that joins the Temple with the palace, the sacred with the mundane. This "joint" is the Millo!

What was controversial about the development of this vacant city space?

[Jeroboam said to Solomon:] Your father, David, created passageways (*peratzot*) in the walls [of Jerusalem] to facilitate access to the Temple for the pilgrimage to the Temple. How could you seal the passageways to make a building, built by tax labor, for Pharaoh's daughter? (*Sanhedrin* 101b)

David ... had left an open space for all of Israel, a place to gather and seek God in the presence of the Ark. [Solomon] closed it, cordoning it off for Pharaoh's daughter. (Rabbi Yosef Kara)

He closed the passage in the wall of the city of David: There was a place for people to approach the king freely and easily in order to complain or to offer their arguments for adjudication. (Ralbag)

Three explanations of the "breach" are offered here:

1. It facilitates access from the city to the Temple.
2. It is a space for national assembly alongside the Temple.
3. It grants access to the king, so that he may act as an appeals commission and a judge.

This space, designated for the nation and its spiritual pursuits, has now been requisitioned and cordoned off for royal purposes. And this is no ordinary royal commission; this national space is being allocated to house a foreign queen![10]

Considering the above, we can better understand Jeroboam's political and financial advocacy on behalf of the people. Seeing the central public space of Jerusalem rezoned as a royal precinct, he protests the expansion of the crown at the expense of the citizenry, whose land has been misappropriated. The Talmud adds a religious dimension – Jeroboam campaigns for open access or passage to the Temple (and its courts of law), which has been closed off due to the construction of this royal compound. Jeroboam can justifiably protest that religious priorities have been eclipsed by imperial indulgences.[11]

JEROBOAM'S DIVINE MANDATE

This strident political criticism of Solomon receives divine sanction in Jeroboam's encounter with Ahijah the Shilonite:[12]

---

10. We now appreciate how Solomon's marriage to Pharaoh's daughter constitutes both the catalyst for his religious infractions and the seeds of his political downfall.

11. In our discussion of I Kings 12, we will discuss how these elements – the democratic and religious perspectives – find their way into Jeroboam's religious reforms.

12. When does the prophet Ahijah communicate his prophecy? There are two options: (1) After Jeroboam denounces the king and publicly expresses his opposition. On his way out of Jerusalem, fleeing the wrath of Solomon, Jeroboam is confronted by the prophet, who presents him with this approving image of his actions, boosting his rebellion. Jeroboam then defects from the country (11:40). This approach follows the order of the verses and is adopted by Yehuda Kiel, *Da'at Mikra, I Kings* [Hebrew]. (2) Radak and other commentaries suggest that this prophecy is relayed at the start of Jeroboam's career, when he is appointed to high office. Radak writes: "'At that time' – Before he had rebelled against the king, Ahijah found him and gave him the news of his kingship." *Metzudat David* states: "'At that time' – When he was newly appointed and left Jerusalem to begin the process of collecting taxes." The biblical phrase "at that time" frequently indicates a disruption in the historical flow, pointing to an earlier event (see, for example, Deut. 1:9; 10:1, 8). These commentators propose that the encounter with Ahijah precedes Jeroboam's insurrection and possibly takes place on the very day of his appointment to a government position.

In this context, the designation of the ripped garment as a "new robe" is intriguing. *Ḥazal* debate whether this was Ahijah's robe or Jeroboam's. We might suggest that

> At that time, Jeroboam went out of Jerusalem, and the prophet
> Ahijah the Shilonite met him on the way; he had put on a new
> robe; and the two of them were alone in the field. Ahijah took
> hold of the new robe he was wearing and tore it into twelve pieces.
> "Take ten pieces," he said to Jeroboam, "for so says the Lord, God
> of Israel: I am about to tear the kingdom out of Solomon's hands,
> and I will give you ten tribes." (11:29–31)

The dramatic image of Ahijah tearing the new robe into twelve shreds
is deliberately traumatic; rending of clothes always indicates shock
or tragedy.[13] Interestingly, the Hebrew term for "robe" here is the relatively unusual *salma*. With different vowels, this word reads "Shlomo" –
Solomon! This play on Solomon's name is designed to illustrate the
ripping apart of the king himself.

Jeroboam represents fierce opposition to Solomon's style of government and national priorities. This renegade is expelled, forced to
abandon the kingdom under threat of death. Ahijah's speech to Jeroboam,
however, assures him that his revolt bears divine approval.

---

the new robe symbolizes Jeroboam's new appointment as governor of the province
of Joseph. (Obvious examples of royal appointments marked with special clothing
are Joseph's [Gen. 41:42] and Mordecai's [Esther 8:15].)

Reconstructing the scene according to this second approach, the story takes place
on the day of Jeroboam's installation in his new position. He travels to Jerusalem,
probably with family and friends, for a ceremony filled with pomp and solemnity,
wearing his elegant new robe of office. Possibly, he attends his first cabinet meeting,
making the acquaintance of fellow government officials. Perhaps he celebrates with
his inner circle, maybe even offering a sacrifice in the Temple. Filled with dignity and
elation, he leaves Jerusalem – only to encounter Ahijah, who tears his robe and indicates that he will tear the kingdom apart! One can only imagine Jeroboam's confusion.

If we read the story this way, it seems that Ahijah's prophecy has a Machiavellian
influence upon later events, instigating Jeroboam to flex his political muscle and
publicly oppose Solomon.

13. Just a few of numerous examples: Reuben tears his coat when he realizes Joseph is
gone (Gen. 37:29); Caleb and Joshua tear their clothing in response to the report
of the spies (Num. 14:6); Jephthah tears his clothing upon understanding that he
has vowed to kill his daughter (Judges 11:35); and in a crisis, the king of Israel tears
his clothing (II Kings 5:7), as do Josiah (22:11) and Mordecai (Esther 4:1).

1 Kings 12

Revolution

Although the seeds of revolt have been sown in the days of Solomon, it is not readily apparent at the time. The revolution does not erupt until after the king's death and the succession of his son, Rehoboam. This is the story of the splitting of the kingdom, a rift that leaves the nation divided until Israel's exile from the land.

SHECHEM

> Rehoboam went to Shechem, for all of Israel had gone there to make him king. When Jeroboam son of Nebat heard this (and he was still in Egypt, where he had fled from King Solomon, and he dwelt in Egypt), they sent for him [Jeroboam], and Jeroboam and the whole assembly of Israel came and spoke to Rehoboam, saying: "Your father put a heavy yoke on us, but now lighten the harsh labor and the heavy yoke he put on us, and we will serve you." He [Rehoboam] answered, "Go away for three days, and then come back to me"; so the people went away. (1 Kings 12:1–5)

Why does Rehoboam stage his coronation at a location so remote from the capital? This seems to be a strange choice. The verses tell us that "Israel had gone" to Shechem; in other words, it is the people who decide where the coronation will be held! In its demand for a tax cut, it is evident that the nation is issuing terms and conditions for its support of Rehoboam's sovereignty. Moreover, it is at this point that the people recall the exiled Jeroboam[1] – an old rival of the house of David – to represent them. Without broad public backing, Rehoboam cannot be crowned. This fact makes a strong statement about the power of the common people in ancient Israelite society.[2] Rehoboam makes a gesture toward the disgruntled nation, stepping outside his capital city, his "safe zone," to meet the people. However, one may argue that far from being perceived as a generous gesture, this move is viewed as a sign of weakness, inviting further political pressure.[3]

---

1. Jeroboam translates as "he will fight for the people" and is highly evocative, representing with great precision this figure's central political identity. Some have proposed that the name Jeroboam is a play on the name of his rival, Rehoboam, and was taken on as a gesture of opposition to the house of David. Rehoboam's name is also significant; it means "wide nation," probably representing the expansiveness of Solomon's era (*Tiferet Yisrael* (Boaz) commentary on *Shekalim* 6:1). In retrospect it resonates with a certain irony, as Rehoboam's reign saw the secession of the vast majority of his nation.

    The phenomenon of *midrash shemot* – connecting biblical figures' names and biographies – is widespread in the Bible. Good examples are Noah (Gen. 5:29, 6:8), Jacob (Gen. 25:26, 27:26), Peretz (Gen. 28:29), Naomi (Ruth 1:20–21), and Nabal (1 Sam. 25:25); a verse explicitly articulates the meaning of each name. Although Abraham ibn Ezra comments (on Gen. 46:8) that one should not analyze names other than those explicitly derived in the Bible, the Midrash does so extensively. See *Berakhot* 7b for the concept of *hashem gorem*, names that influence biography. Modern literary analysis has similarly focused on the names of biblical characters. See Moshe Garsiel, *Biblical Names: A Literary Study of Midrashic Derivations and Puns* (Ramat Gan: Bar-Ilan University Press, 1991).

2. Though this is a traditional monarchy, we should recall that even after King Saul is anointed, he does not effectively function as king until he has won the people's confidence (see I Sam. 10–11). Similarly, despite David's designation by God as the future king, only when all the tribes of Israel proclaim him as such (5:1–4) can he function as the national monarch. God can designate the king, but broad national support is an indispensable element of royal succession.

3. See Yehuda Kiel, *Da'at Mikra, 1 Kings* [Hebrew].

Why is Shechem selected in particular? First, its infrastructure must have been optimal for facilitating national gatherings.[4] Shechem is the site of the national covenant ceremony – the blessings and curses – when Israel enters the land.[5] Similarly, Joshua's final address to the nation also takes place there.[6] Furthermore, its central location at the crossroads of the north-south and east-west highways makes it an accessible city.[7] It has enormous national-strategic importance as a first stop for travelers entering the country from Mesopotamia.[8]

But second, Shechem is the most prominent city in the tribal region of Joseph. If we have identified tension between the sovereign from Judah and the popular leadership of Joseph, then in this inaugural act, King Rehoboam is venturing out of his natural constituency to the heartland of the tribes of Joseph.

AN ANCIENT RIVALRY: JUDAH AND JOSEPH

> A *tanna* taught a teaching of R. Yose: Shechem is a place prone to tragedy.... There Joseph was sold; there the kingdom of David was divided. (*Sanhedrin* 102a)[9]

---

4. On the acoustics of Shechem and the "natural amphitheater" created by the topography of the mountains, see http://blog.bibleplaces.com/2008/12/acoustics-of-mounts-gerizim-and-ebal.html; http://bibleandtech.blogspot.com/2008/12/using-digital-mapping-tools-mount-ebal.html.
5. See Deuteronomy 11:26–32, 27; Joshua 8.
6. Joshua 24.
7. Its central location is certainly the reason Shechem was one of the cities of refuge (Josh. 20:6).
8. As seen in the stories of Abraham (Gen. 12:7) and Jacob (33:18).
9. Genesis 37:13 tells us that Shechem is the place to which Joseph traveled when sent by his father to seek out his brothers. When he failed to locate them, he progressed to Dotan (37:17), and there the brothers cast him into the pit, and from Dotan he was sold into slavery. In the Talmudic passage quoted above, R. Yose adds another tragedy to Shechem's history, namely the rape of Dinah. Of course, as mentioned, Shechem is not associated exclusively with negative biblical events – a number of positive covenantal events took place there. But the geographical linkage between Joseph's sale, instigated by Judah, and its corollary, the rejection of Judah by the tribes of Joseph, is striking.

The splitting of the kingdom is a story with deep roots, a resurgence of the pan-historic rivalry between the sons of Jacob, Joseph, and Judah. The tension between these two brothers begins in the friction between their mothers, Rachel and Leah. Joseph, the firstborn of Rachel, and Judah, the leading son of Leah, both contend for the family and national leadership.[10] The fiercest manifestation of their feud is the terrible sale of Joseph to Egypt, instigated by Judah.

Centuries after Israel has founded a nation-state, the rift between Judah and Joseph persists nonetheless[11] – as evidenced in the period of Saul, when Judah is still viewed as separate from the other tribes:

> He [Saul] numbered them in Bezek; and the children of **Israel** were 300,000, and the men of **Judah** 30,000. (1 Sam. 11:8)

> So Saul summoned the men and counted them at Telaim – 200,000 foot soldiers and 10,000 men from **Judah**. (15:4)[12]

Later, after the death of Saul, the kingdom splits in two for seven and a half years, as civil war rages. Judah is led by King David, but all the other tribes follow Saul's son Ishbosheth (II Sam. 2:10), who is from the tribe of Benjamin, a descendant of the "Rachel faction." David eventually unites the kingdom, but the seam between Judah and the other tribes is prone to unraveling. Moments of national tension, such as the Absalom revolt, invite charlatans to stir up intertribal friction. One such character, Sheba son of Bichri, manipulates an apparent insult to the tribe of Benjamin and attempts to once again split the nation (see II Sam. 19). His battle cry:

---

10. See I Chronicles 5:1–3.
11. Rabbi Yaakov Medan offers a comprehensive picture of this pan-historic divide. See Y. Medan, "Yosef and Yehuda," The Virtual Beit Midrash, http://vbm-torah. org/archive/parsha65/11-65vayigash.htm. Recent thinkers have attempted to sketch typological studies of Judah as opposed to Joseph. See Rabbi Abraham Isaac Kook, "The Eulogy in Jerusalem," in *Maamarei HaRa'ayah* [*Essays of Rabbi Abraham Isaac Hakohen* (Kook)] (Jerusalem: n.p., 1984), 94–98 [Hebrew]; and Adin Steinsaltz, *Biblical Images* (Jerusalem: Maggid, 2010), in the chapters on Rachel and Leah.
12. See also II Samuel 24:9.

We have no portion in David, and no inheritance in the son of
Jesse! Every man to his tent, O Israel! (20:1)

This history is significant, because that same phrase returns as the ral-
lying call of our chapter:

When all [the people of] Israel saw that the king did not listen
to them, the people answered the king, saying, **"What portion
do we have in David? We have no inheritance in the son of
Jesse! To your tent, O Israel!** Now look after your own house,
David!" (1 Kings 12:16)

Jeroboam's public rejection of the rule of the house of David resuscitates a secessionist statement declared more than a generation earlier.

We have discussed how Jeroboam represents the tribes of Joseph
in opposition to Solomon's leadership, which favors Judah. This rebellion, then, is the latest chapter in the historical rivalry. This division
of the nation into two separate states prevails until the demise of the
northern kingdom and the exile of the ten tribes. It constitutes a fault
line so deeply embedded in the national psyche that only in messianic
times can the prophet Ezekiel foresee a unification, a healing of this rift:

The word of God came to me to say: You, son of man,[13] take one
piece of wood and write on it, "For Judah and the children of
Israel, his friends," and one piece of wood and write on it, "For
Joseph, the wood of Ephraim and the entire house of Israel, his
friends." Bring them together, each to the other, to become one
piece of wood, and they will become one in your hands. When
they say to you, your people, "What does this mean?" tell them,
"So says God: Behold, I will take the tree of Joseph, which is in
the hand of Ephraim and the tribes of Israel, his friends, and I
will put on them the tree of Judah and make them one tree, and
they will become one in My hand. (Ezek. 37:15–20)

---

13. This is the way God addresses Ezekiel throughout his prophecies.

What does this symbolism mean? God explains:

> I will take the Israelite people from among the nations that they
> have gone to, and gather them from every quarter, and bring
> them to their own land. I will make them **one nation** in the land
> on the hills of Israel, and **one king** shall be king over them all.
> Never again shall they be two nations, and never again shall they
> be divided into two kingdoms. (37:21–23)[14]

THE WISDOM OF THE CHILDREN

As we proposed earlier, Rehoboam's understanding that internecine
trouble is brewing leads him to acquiesce in staging his coronation at
Shechem, thereby extending respect and prestige to the tribes of Joseph.
At this point, we witness his first mistake. When the people make a rather
reasonable and modest request – a tax break – Rehoboam suggests a
three-day hiatus to reflect and seek advice. This act of consultation, which
ordinarily might appear commendable, proves disastrous. The three-day
wait intensifies the malcontents and the opposition, letting the unrest
fester.[15] By the time he returns with an answer, things have reached a
fever pitch, as we can see from the stoning of Adoram, the reviled tax
minister (1 Kings 12:18).

Rehoboam's second mistake is his choice of advisers. He abandons Solomon's sage consultants for the "children with whom he had
grown up" (12:8),[16] and their advice proves incendiary. One rabbinic
voice condemns any reliance upon inexperienced young advisers:

> If elders say, "Destroy," and children say, "Build," destroy and do
> not build. For the destruction of elders constitutes an act of con-
> struction, and the building of youths constitutes an act of destruc-

---

14. See also Isaiah 11:13.
15. King David, facing a similar tribal revolt, gave the army three days to mobilize against
    the opposition. He knew the flames of political unrest had to be doused fast. See
    II Samuel 20:4.
16. Obviously, these were not children or even teenagers, but young adults. I believe
    the text calls them "children" to emphasize their foolishness and juvenile "wisdom."

tion. The exemplar of this principle is the story of Rehoboam son of Solomon. (*Megilla* 31b)

According to this approach, as a rule, one should prefer the mature wisdom of the elder to the unripe, inexperienced word of the youth, which lacks perspective. This biting critique of youth, which sounds rather crotchety to the modern ear, deems all advice of the young destructive.

A further characterization of these children, indicated by the phrase "with whom he had grown up," offers a different critique of Jeroboam's advisers. This phrase denotes a group of youngsters whose entire life experience has been framed by the wealth and luxury of the Solomonic era. They are the palace crowd, the wealthy and privileged who have never known a day of hardship in their lives. Their disastrous advice is not merely a function of their age, but a matter of upbringing. They contemptuously make their recommendations, dismissing the burden of the hardworking peasantry:

> ... say to them, "My little finger is thicker than my father's loins. My father imposed a heavy yoke on you; I will add to your yoke; my father flogged you with whips; but I will flog you with scorpions!" (1 Kings 12:10–11)

This response is thick with smugness, evincing a detached "Let them eat cake" attitude. We should not be surprised, then, by the ensuing revolution.

REHOBOAM – A POSITIVE PERSPECTIVE (12:20–24)

Based upon our perspective of Rehoboam thus far, we might view him as a wholly negative figure. But this king clearly has his virtues. This episode reveals his tremendous reverence for prophecy and his remarkable restraint. As the northern tribes renounce his authority and withdraw from the kingdom, any normal king would muster his army and enforce full control. Indeed, Rehoboam mobilizes 180,000 troops to restore order. But when the prophet Shemaiah informs him that this uprising is God's decree and warns him not to engage in a civil war, Rehoboam listens to him and calls off his military action. Imagine – the king is in the process of losing ninety percent of his country, and he simply obeys God's command! He backs down and lets it happen! We should not minimize the formidable religious faith that must have gripped Rehoboam in order to adhere to this prophecy.

1 Kings 12

New Kingdom, New Religion

Jeroboam has now become king over the northern kingdom. Up to this point in the story, he has been depicted as the hero, but at this juncture, we witness Jeroboam's deterioration, and the process that earns him his infamous reputation. It all begins with a specific concern:

> Jeroboam said to himself, "Now the kingdom may well return to the house of David. If this nation goes up to offer sacrifices at the house of God in Jerusalem, the heart of this nation will turn back to [its] master, King Rehoboam of Judah...." (1 Kings 12:26–27)

Jeroboam's worry should not be minimized. In the ancient world, there was a close affinity between the king and the Temple.[1] If Jerusalem was designated as the religious center, it would be only natural for the people to associate it with national government as well. With the kings of

---

1. See Amos 7:13, in which the Temple is termed *mikdash melekh* and is directly under royal authority.

Judah presiding over the Temple proceedings, Jeroboam fears that he will find himself discredited.[2]

Jeroboam's solution is to offer an alternative to Jerusalem,[3] creating two new religious centers – at Bethel and Dan – and instituting an entire array of new religious practices. His religious reforms include:

1. shrines at Dan and Bethel (12:29–31)
2. golden calves (12:27–28)
3. allowing the general public to function as priests (12:31)
4. changing the date of Sukkot (12:32)
5. the king functioning as a priest and performing the sacrificial service on the altar (12:22–13:1)

Let us carefully examine and expand upon these points.

SHRINES AT DAN AND BETHEL

These two sites represent the northern and southern extremities of Jeroboam's kingdom, so it is natural for him to establish royal and religious gathering points at here. But this is not the sole reason these locations are selected; each has a rich religious past.

Bethel was the site of Jacob's prophetic dream, in which he saw a ladder linking heaven and earth. He awoke and proclaimed:

> God was in this place and I didn't know? …how awesome this place is! This is none other than the house of God, and this is the gateway to the heavens! (Gen. 28:16–17)

---

2. The traditional commentators (Rashi, Radak, etc.) all quote Ḥazal to the effect that only royal descendants of David were allowed to be seated in the Temple. In that case, Rehoboam would sit and Jeroboam would have to remain standing. This halakhic language effectively articulates Jeroboam's concern of delegitimization.

3. Note the interesting verb *vayivaatz*, describing Jeroboam's taking counsel. This word featured in connection with Rehoboam's unsuccessful act of consultation with his young advisers. Now it reappears as Jeroboam consults his (anonymous) advisers and emerges with his foolhardy religious reforms.

The very name Bethel – "house of God" – attests to a long history as a religious site, possibly predating Abraham. Even in Saul's time, Bethel functioned as an Israelite center of worship (1 Sam. 10:3). In fact, if one relies solely on the Torah text, Bethel's historic credentials are explicit, whereas Jerusalem is never mentioned outright as a site of revelation. While there is a rabbinic tradition that both the *Akeida* (the binding of Isaac) and Jacob's dream took place in Jerusalem,[4] Jeroboam probably maintained that the city's history of revelation was nothing but a fabrication of the house of David, whereas the true house of God was in Bethel.

Dan, too, has a rich history of worship.[5] The book of Judges narrates the story of the idol of Micah and the syncretic house of worship that existed there:

> The tribe of Dan set up the molten image, and Jonathan son of Gershom son of Manasseh and his sons were priests...until the day of the exile of the land[6]...all the days of the house of God in Shiloh. (18:30–31)

Thus, Dan was an "alternate" site of divine worship throughout the Shiloh period. It was always controversial, with its illicit mix of worship of God with a molten image, but the people probably viewed it

---

4. See Rashi on Genesis 28:17: "Jacob called Jerusalem 'Bethel.'" According to tradition, the Temple Mount is on Mount Moriah, where the *Akeida* took place. See also Maimonides, *Mishneh Torah*, Laws of the Temple 1:3. Some association here is linguistic: The site of the *Akeida* is described as *hamakom* (the place), and the Temple site – later revealed as Jerusalem – is always called *hamakom asher yivhar Hashem* (the place that the Lord will choose). However, Bethel is also called *hamakom*; see Genesis 28:11, 16 –17. One fascinating intertextual connection linking the *Akeida* to the site of the Temple in Jerusalem may be found in II Samuel 24:16–25, where the language and storyline are highly reminiscent of the *Akeida*. The chapter ends with David purchasing the land for the Temple.

5. Tel Dan has been excavated by Avraham Biran, who discovered the city gate and an altar site there. In 1993, at this incredibly rich archaeological site, scholars unearthed an inscription from the ninth century BCE, citing the "house of David."

6. The "exile of the land" in this context indicates the destruction of Shiloh and the loss of the Ark, as described in I Samuel 4.

as a legitimate place to serve the Lord; they were unbothered by the contradictory religious elements.

From a contemporary perspective, with our knowledge of the importance ascribed by the Torah to a single, central place of worship, and the centrality of the site of the Temple in Jerusalem throughout Jewish history, we might be surprised that the people accepted the new religious centers of Dan and Bethel. In those times, however, there were regular fluctuations as to the permissibility of *bamot*, local sacrificial altars. We should presume that there was a great deal of confusion regarding these matters on the popular level. Thus, when the king officially launches two new religious sites, it does not engender the outrage that we might expect. Local altars were religiously appropriate prior to Solomon; maybe after him, they were permitted yet again! Moreover, Jerusalem was a comparatively new venue for national service of God. One supposes that followers of Jeroboam were waiting for the opportunity to restore the site of sacrifices to the tribes of Joseph.

THE GOLDEN CALVES: AARON AND JEROBOAM

Jeroboam's two golden calves arouse our curiosity. Are they idols? The installation of these calves is all the more enigmatic as we identify a series of sophisticated parallels between this story and the sin of the golden calf in the wilderness:

1. In both stories, the object of worship is a molten gold figure of a calf.
2. Jeroboam's pronouncement:
    > Enough of your going up to Jerusalem! This is your God, O Israel, who brought you up from the land of Egypt! (1 Kings 12:28)

    This statement mirrors precisely the people's proclamation regarding the original golden calf:
    > These are your gods, O Israel, who brought you up from the land of Egypt! (Ex. 32:4)

    That calf also had an altar associated with it (32:5), just like each of Jeroboam's calves.

3. In the wilderness, Aaron was the key figure who created the calf. Two of his sons were named Nadab and Abihu; Jeroboam's sons are Nadab (1 Kings 14:20) and Abijah (14:1)!

4. After the sin of the golden calf, Aaron was appointed as high priest. In our chapter, Jeroboam functions as a priest at the altar (13:1).

What should we conclude from these similarities? It seems that Jeroboam deliberately perpetrates a recurrence of the golden calf, casting himself as a second Aaron of sorts. But don't the people know that worshipping the original calf was a severe sin? Why would Jeroboam base his rituals on such an atrocity?

Once again, it seems that Jeroboam successfully rereads the Bible. He portrays Aaron as a hero, a *tzaddik*, whose golden calf was clearly not that terrible a crime. After all, the Torah records that God forgave the nation and that Aaron, the instigator and builder of the calf, was "promoted" to the position of high priest! If Aaron had perpetrated idolatry, why wasn't he executed? Radak articulates these arguments:

> His [Jeroboam's] rhetoric convinced them: "Don't you know that the kingdom has been split by God's desire, as transmitted by Ahijah the Shilonite? Therefore, God has rejected the rule of the house of David and also Jerusalem..., so we need an alternative place to worship." And why a calf? He said: "When Moses was absent and they sought an alternative, didn't Aaron create a calf upon which to rest God's presence? Now, in the absence of Jerusalem, let us make a calf to receive the *Shekhina*." (Radak, 12:28)

Further factors lent legitimacy to Jeroboam's new cultic centers. Solomon's Temple featured twelve oxen and a host of other animal figures, and he also installed two huge cherubim.[7] And of course, at the instigation of Solomon's wives, full-fledged pagan shrines stood in Jerusalem itself! The book of Kings is aghast at Jeroboam's new religious centers,

---

7. For the relationship between the symbolism of a calf and the cherubim, note that a comparison between Ezekiel 1:10 and 10:14 reveals that the two images, the cherub

but the king has ample room to claim that his sites are just as legitimate as Jerusalem itself. Furthermore, he has seized power by divine sanction. What better approval than this?

PRIESTS FROM ALL THE PEOPLE

> ...he [Jeroboam] appointed priests from the ranks of the people, who were not of Levite descent. (12:31)

We have already drawn attention to Jeroboam's ideological stance as the leader of an anti-elitist, people-based movement. With this opening of the priestly service to all Israelites, he can take up his people's cause and grant access to religion for all.[8]

Interestingly, furthering our golden calf parallel, we should recall that the tribe of Levi in particular opposed its worship (Ex. 32:26). It is possible that Jeroboam steered clear of Levi for this very reason, or

---

and calf (or ox), may be seen as interchangeable. On this basis, Rabbi Amnon Bazak suggests that Jeroboam's calves were designed to function in a manner similar to the Temple cherubs. He states:

> A profound ideological intention underlies Yeravam's act. The nation has already become accustomed to the fact that God rests between two *keruvim*. For this reason Yeravam does not suffice with one calf-*keruv*, but rather fashions two. The significance of placing these *keruvim* at the borders of Israel is an expansion of the area in which the Divine Presence is manifest. Instead of the Divine Presence dwelling between the two *keruvim* in the Temple, it will henceforth rest between the two calves in the north and in the south – i.e., throughout the borders of Israel.

See A. Bazak, "The Ideological Foundations of the Sin of the Golden Calf," The Virtual Beit Midrash, http://www.vbm-torah.org/archive/parsha65/21-65ki%20 tisa.htm. We may add that the notion of God resting throughout the land would suitably amplify Jeroboam's democratic message.

8. The phrase *rav lakhem* (lit., enough for you) in 1 Kings 12:28 is a direct parallel to the phrases used in Numbers 16 in the context of the Korah rebellion. Like Jeroboam, Korah sought to legitimize non-priests as candidates for the Temple service, and he challenged the established authorities. And just as Jeroboam offered incense at his forbidden altar (*lehaktir* – 1 Kings 13:1), Korah led his faction in an illicit offering of *ketoret* (incense).

perhaps the priests refused to comply with his religious reforms. Whatever the reason, II Chronicles (11:13–14) records a huge influx of priests and Levites to the southern kingdom of Judah. In response to Jeroboam's rejection of the tribe of Levi, its members migrated to the only place in which they could serve God properly – the Temple.

CHANGING THE CALENDAR

Jeroboam's initial problem is the *aliyah laregel*, the mass pilgrimage to Jerusalem. If the people flock to the city, his entire plan will collapse.[9] To circumvent this problem, Jeroboam formulates an ingenious strategy:

> And Jeroboam established a festival on the fifteenth day of the eighth month – the month he contrived of his own mind to establish a festival. (I Kings 12:32–33)

If the festival is to be celebrated in the eighth month, a month after Sukkot, how does this help? People will still travel to the Temple for Sukkot in the seventh month. How will the institution of a new holiday deter people from *aliyah laregel*? Furthermore, what is "the month he contrived of in his own mind"?

The simplest and most elegant solution is that Jeroboam adds a month to the calendar, declaring a leap year of sorts; Abarbanel explains that this is the "month he contrived of." As a result, the calendar in the north runs a month later than in the southern kingdom, so that the sixth month in the north coincides with the seventh month in the south. Thus, when the northerners begin considering going to Jerusalem for Sukkot (in what they think is the seventh month), they are surprised to discover that the holiday has already been celebrated there a month previously! With the addition of an extra month, the "seventh month" is, in fact, the "eighth month"; Sukkot is over in Jerusalem! With no recourse, the people are forced to celebrate in the northern kingdom. Hence, the addition of a month prevents them from celebrating in Jerusalem.

---

9. Ḥazal state (*Bava Batra* 121b) that Jeroboam stationed sentries on the way to Jerusalem to prevent *olei regel* (pilgrims) from reaching the city. The text here fails to record this detail and seems to indicate more subtle techniques.

This extensive assortment of religious changes assures Jeroboam that his subjects will not drift toward Jerusalem. However, these actions clearly represent a drastic departure from legitimate practice.

DID JEROBOAM INSTITUTE IDOLATRY?

One question that occupies all the commentators is the degree to which Jeroboam's calves and altars constituted idolatry.[10] On the one hand, his calves are viewed by the Bible with great severity; the book of Kings consistently refers to Jeroboam's sins as "other gods and images," which enrage God. These acts bring punishment and destruction upon the house of Jeroboam and are a catalyst in the eventual national exile.[11] Furthermore, added to the golden calves is the sin of the *asherim* (14:15), the idolatrous trees banned in the Torah.[12] This would thus appear to be an open-and-shut case.

Yet many traditional commentaries question whether these calves were truly perceived as idolatry. What evidence suggests that they weren't?

1. In chapter 13, when the "man of God" arrives in Bethel to denounce Jeroboam's religious deviance, the prophet addresses his reproach to the king's **altar** but fails to mention the calf there. Surely molten images are worse than an altar. Why does the calf go unmentioned?
2. Religious campaigns aimed at eradicating idolatry in the times of Elijah, Jehu, and Hezekiah target Baal as a national problem.

---

10. We have already addressed the interesting parallels with the original golden calf, regarding which there is a similar discussion about whether it constituted idolatry. See, for example, Nehama Leibowitz, "The Golden Calf," in Leibowitz, *Studies in Shemot (The Book of Exodus)* (Jerusalem: World Zionist Organization, 1976), vol. 2, 549–57. For a different Bible-based approach mitigating the idolatrous aspect of the sin, see the article by Rabbi Menachem Leibtag, Parashat Ki Tissa, at the Tanach Study Center, http://tanach.org/shmot/kitisa.txt. Both Jeroboam's calves and the golden calf in the wilderness are given the title "the great sin." See Exodus 32:31 and II Kings 17:21.
11. See in particular I Kings 13:33–34; 14:7–11, 14–15; 15:30, 16:26; II Kings 17:21–23.
12. See Exodus 34:13; Deuteronomy 7:5, 12:3, 16:21.

The golden calves are never removed! If they were idolatry, why weren't they destroyed?

3. After the exile of the northern tribes, the Assyrians settle a non-Jewish population in place of the ousted Israelites. These non-Jews experience a mysterious attack of lions, which is perceived as a sign that God is furious with their alien worship, their idolatry. The solution to the problem is that an exiled Israelite teaches these foreigners how to worship: "So one of the priests who was exiled from Samaria came and settled in Bethel and taught them how to worship the Lord" (11 Kings 17:28). If the religion of Bethel and Dan was idolatry, how does this Samarian priest offer a solution that will remove the threat of the lions?

For these reasons, many commentators suggest that the calves were forbidden images but not idols:

> In truth, a major distinction must be made between Jeroboam's worship [of golden calves] and Ahab's worship [of Baal]. **Only the Baal worshippers are idolaters**, and it is in reference to this group that Elijah said, "If you are for the Lord, our God, then follow Him, and if you are for Baal, then follow him" (1 Kings 18:21)…. And it was against the Baal worship that Elijah made his call of "I am zealous for the Lord, the God of Israel" (19:10). But he never called out against [the calves of] Jeroboam. **The men of Jeroboam's group were "for the Lord, the God of Israel," in all their deeds, and their prophets were the prophets of God**, whereas Ahab's prophets were the prophets of Baal. God sent Jehu to wipe out the memory of Ahab…, but he did not destroy the calves [of Jeroboam].
>
> The worshippers of the golden calf [in the wilderness] and **the altars of Jeroboam and the idol of Micah** (Judges 17–18) **sought only to serve the God of Israel.** Nonetheless, they transgressed a commandment that carries a death penalty. They can be compared to a person who marries his sister… but observes all the halakhic restrictions of marriage, or to someone who eats pork but meticulously slaughters [the pig] according to the strictures

of *sheḥita,* and drains the blood, and observes all other *kashrut* restrictions. (*Kuzari* 4:13)

Obviously, eating pork after *sheḥita* and the draining of the blood does not make a strictly kosher meal! These commentators are far from legitimizing Jeroboam, but they make a significant and fundamental distinction. There are two basic forms of idolatry.[13] In one form, a person worships another god; he abandons service of God and replaces Him with a different deity. In the other form, one worships God through an improper and illicit medium. This transgresses the second of the Ten Commandments, as it involves images and physical likenesses, but it does not constitute the rejection of God and the adoption of a foreign deity; it is merely worship of God through incorrect means. Jeroboam's altars and calves were directed at serving the God of Israel, not repudiating Him.

Abarbanel is even more generous, claiming that the calves were not intended for any manner of worship:

> The calves were not for the purpose of idolatry and not for any type of worship – for sacrifice or bowing down – as was the calf in the wilderness.... **Their purpose was that just as Solomon had built two pillars, placing them at the entrance to the sanctuary of the house of God as a sign of David and Solomon,**[14] **similarly, he [Jeroboam] decided to make a symbol for his rule.** Because he was from the tribe of Joseph..., whom Moses had blessed: "Like the firstling bull in his majesty, his horns are the horns of an ox..." (Deut. 33:17), Jeroboam decided to use the symbol of the calf as his family insignia...made of gold, which designates eternity and the splendor of royalty, ...and this calf was at the entrance to his temple at Bethel, where the *bamot* stood, just like the pillars in the Temple.[15]

---

13. I have discussed this distinction in greater depth in a *shiur* on *parashat Va'ethanan.* See A. Israel, "Idolatry," The Virtual Beit Midrash, http://vbm-torah.org/ parsha.62/40vaet.htm.

14. Abarbanel's view is that Jachin and Boaz symbolized the power of the monarchy.

15. Abarbanel on 1 Kings 12, p. 557 in the standard edition.

According to this understanding, these calves are in fact royal insignia, emblematic figures that reflect the strength of the royal house of Jeroboam, and not representative of gods in any way. Interestingly, Abarbanel suggests that the Temple in Jerusalem – strongly associated with the monarchy – was Jeroboam's prototype. His calves – reflecting the ox in the blessings of Joseph – connect the tribal symbol with his new temple.

1 Kings 13

Confrontation at Bethel

After learning about Jeroboam's cultic temples, we read that God issues a prophet to censure him and his new worship. In a colorful chapter, the visiting prophet paralyzes the king's arm, an altar miraculously cracks apart, and an otherwise placid lion kills a guilty seer. This is a mysterious and sometimes confusing story, but we will attempt to unveil its powerful message.[1]

The chapter opens with an anonymous prophet from Judah, designated as *ish Elokim* (a man of God), arriving in Bethel to deliver a terrifying prophecy:

> And behold, there came a man of God from Judah by the word of God to Bethel; and Jeroboam stood upon the altar to present

---

1. The following excellent articles explore this chapter in greater depth: Elchanan Samet, "Sanctification of God's Name Is Greater than Desecration of God's Name," *Megadim* 6 (1988): 55–85 [Hebrew]; and the superb response by Tamar Verdiger, "You Shall Come to See the Difference between the Righteous and the Wicked," *Megadim* 8 (1989): 97–104 [Hebrew], which assumes the approach that we have taken. See also Uriel Simon, *Reading Prophetic Narratives* (Bloomington: Indiana University Press, 1997), 130–54.

the offering. And he [the man of God] cried against the altar by the word of God, and said: "Altar, O altar! Thus says the Lord: Behold a child shall be born to the house of David, Josiah by name, and he shall slaughter upon you the priests of the shrines who bring offerings upon you; and human bones shall be burned upon you." He gave a sign that day, saying, "Here is the sign that the Lord has decreed: This altar shall break apart, and the ashes on it shall be spilled." (1 Kings 13:1–3)

Jeroboam is worshipping, functioning as high priest at his altar in Bethel and offering a festive sacrifice.[2] If we follow the flow of the text from 12:33 to 13:1,[3] we may surmise that this occasion is the dedication of the shrine at Bethel, which is timed and staged to take place on Sukkot with the king presiding, in the style of Solomon's Temple dedication in Jerusalem (8:1–2). This is thus the perfect place and time for the *ish Elokim* to admonish Jeroboam and decry his new altar. In classic prophetic style,[4] this man of God dramatically confronts Jeroboam in the midst of his crime.

Interestingly, the *ish Elokim* addresses the altar, not the king. Why? Moreover, he does not critique the new sacrificial service directly, but offers a more oblique statement – that the bones of the priests will be burned upon the altar – as well as a sign, the breaking apart of the altar. It is possible that this is a deliberate snub of the king. Addressing the altar means Jeroboam is ignored and hence publicly shamed. However,

---

2. The biblical verb *lehaktir*, which seems to indicate the offering of *ketoret* (incense), is also a generic term referring to the bringing of sacrifices. See, for example, Leviticus 1:9, 13, 15; 1 Samuel 2:15. Hence Jeroboam, who has deregulated the sacrificial service, is described and condemned with this verb. On the other hand, the use of this verb in particular may indicate that Jeroboam offered *ketoret*, which is associated with the priesthood (see Num. 16) and is viewed as a test of worthiness (as in the cases of Nadab and Abihu [Lev. 10], Korah [Num. 16], and King Uzziah [11 Kings 15]).

3. The opening word of 1 Kings 13:1, *ve-hinei* ("and behold") invites us to view Jeroboam's service upon the altar as a continuation of the previous scene.

4. For example, Samuel catches Saul red-handed, with the sheep of Amalek bleating behind him and Agag alive (1 Sam. 15), and Elijah meets King Ahab in the field of Naboth, whom he had killed (1 Kings 21:19).

we sense that this message has been choreographed to be delivered to the people rather than the king. Its frightful prediction of the burning of the priests' bones upon the altar issues a direct deterrent to the freshly appointed priests. Furthermore, it visually communicates the illicit nature of this altar to the throngs participating in the festivities. The king is impervious to the message of the prophet, but perhaps the people will heed God's word.

If the audience doubts the *ish Elokim's* authenticity, suspecting him to be a political heckler sent by Rehoboam's regime, then his performance of a *mofet* – a miraculous act – clearly demonstrates the truth of his mission.[5] When Jeroboam attempts to have the man arrested, the king's arm freezes, and he must implore the *ish Elokim* to appeal to God on his behalf. Jeroboam thereby unwittingly authenticates this mysterious and unsettling visitor.

EATING, DRINKING, AND RETURNING

Unable to overpower his prophetic antagonist, Jeroboam quickly adopts a tone of honor, deference, and appeasement, inviting the prophet to his palace to feast with him and offering him gifts. But the *ish Elokim* refuses, intoning that God has restricted his eating and drinking and forbidden him to return the same way he came.

Many commentaries view the restrictions on eating and drinking as a means of avoiding any contact with idolatry:

> One is forbidden to enter a city of idolatry other than to warn or prevent them [the inhabitants] or to speak God's word. He [the prophet] was restricted from eating or drinking there so the people would see that he had gone there only to deliver his prophecy. (Radak)

---

5. See Simon, *Prophetic Narratives*, 138–39, who dwells upon the difference between an *ot* and a *mofet*; an *ot* is an illustration and reminder, whereas a *mofet* establishes credibility. See the usage of the latter word in Exodus 7:9 and, for our purposes, regarding the veracity of a prophet in Deuteronomy 13:3.

God commanded this to convey the message that there was no benefit or purpose to the place and that they [its inhabitants] would all be destroyed. (Ralbag)

In other words, the restrictions signify absolute severance from Bethel and all that it represents. This approach certainly rings true.

But there is another dimension of "eating bread" with prophets.[6] Many years after this event, another prophet confronts a king and high priest in Bethel. In this scene, the prophet Amos has prophesied against the king and is expelled from the sanctuary:

> And Amaziah [the high priest] said to Amos, "Seer, go, run away to the land of Judah, and **eat bread there** and prophesy there. But do not continue to prophesy in Bethel, for it is the sanctuary of a king and the capital of the kingdom." And Amos replied and said to Amaziah, "I am neither a prophet nor the son of a prophet, but I am a cattle herder and an inspector of sycamores. And the Lord took me from following the flock, and He said to me: 'Go, prophesy to My people, Israel.'" (Amos 7:12–15)

Amaziah tells Amos to "eat bread" in Judah. What does he mean? And why does Amos reply by detailing his professional background? This passage gives us a perspective on the place of the prophet in biblical society. Kings hired bands of "prophets" to bolster the royal regime and gain religious leverage. Thus, we read that hundreds of prophets of Baal "eat at Jezebel's table" (1 Kings 18:19),[7] boosting her religious and political standing. When Amaziah suggests that Amos "eat bread" in Judah, he is assuming that the prophet's financial support comes from the king. Amaziah tells him: In this temple, you must prophesy in line with royal policy. If you are looking for a paycheck, either go to Judah – "Eat bread there, and there you can prophesy" – or change your tune!

---

6. See Nili Samet, "Between 'Thou Shalt Eat Bread There' and 'Thou Shalt Not Eat Bread,'" *Massechet* 2 (2004): 167–181 [Hebrew].

7. See 1 Kings 18:19; see also ch. 22, where we see the prophets simply chanting the message that the king wants to hear.

Amos responds that he doesn't need anyone's money, and he explains to Amaziah what it really means to be a prophet. Amos is a prophet because God called upon him to deliver a terrible but vital message. Unlike the many career prophets – "prophets, sons of a prophet" – in ancient Israel, telling kings precisely what they desired to hear, Amos does not deliver government-sponsored prophecy; he does not "eat bread" at anyone's table. Only under these independent conditions may the voice of God emerge, criticizing the ruling powers when they sin.

Using Amos as our guide, we suggest that the *ish Elokim* in our story has been banned from eating with the king **in particular**. God will not allow any compromise, any sense that this prophet can be "bought" or his opinions sold to the highest bidder. One who bears the word of God does not eat or drink at the king's table.

The Way He Came

The insistence on taking a different route home is also symbolic. Prof. Uriel Simon explains:

> We must clarify how the biblical worldview understands *route* or *way*, both as an experience and as a concept. For our starting point, we may cite the injunction against returning to Egypt to buy horses, because "the Lord has told you that you must not go back that way again" (Deut. 17:16). Commentators, both ancient and modern, have had difficulty explaining this rationale; evidently, we should understand it in the light of the punishment that concludes the list of retributive catastrophes.... "The Lord will send you back to Egypt in ships, by a route for which I told you that you should not see again. There you shall offer yourselves for sale to your enemies as male and female slaves but none will buy" (Deut. 28:68). Returning to Egypt is the harshest of punishments because it cancels out the Exodus.... The fact that this conception of returning to one's starting place as the cancellation of the original journey appears as part of the legal proscription indicates that this was the real mental attitude of those who retraced their steps, willingly or otherwise, and not merely rhetoric.

Moreover, just as returning to one's point of departure may be regarded a cancelling out the journey, retracing one's footsteps can be regarded as negating one's mission and abandoning its goal.[8]

In other words, the prophet may not retrace his steps, lest he appear to be metaphorically retracting his mission and the decree he has pronounced. It must be clear to all that his prophecy is non-negotiable and irrevocable.

THE ELDERLY PROPHET

At this point, we meet the *navi zaken*, the other prophetic figure of this story, who lives in Bethel. He tricks the *ish Elokim* with a fabricated prophecy, inducing him to abrogate his God-given restrictions and essentially causing his death. Who is this elderly prophet? Due to the man's duplicity and its pernicious effects, most traditional commentaries follow *Targum Yonatan* in viewing him as a false prophet. On this basis, what would be the *navi zaken*'s motive in misleading God's prophet? We could suggest that this elder is one of Jeroboam's backers and therefore seeks to harm the *ish Elokim*. But can we be sure this man is a fraud? Certainly, the *navi zaken* does not emerge as a particularly worthy character, and he definitely misleads the *ish Elokim*, but he appears to have received an authentic divine message (13:21–22). Can we be sure he is indeed a false prophet?

We will adopt the approach of Abarbanel, however, who sees the *navi zaken* as a genuine prophet, even as he deceives the *ish Elokim*. We will attempt to understand this man's background by making a number of observations:

1. The *navi zaken* hears about the dramatic incident with the *ish Elokim* from his own sons (13:11), who presumably attended the inauguration of Jeroboam's altar. Why did this elder fail to attend

---

8. Simon, *Prophetic Narratives*, 140. A similar approach is suggested by both Rabbi Yoel bin Nun, "By Way of the Land of the Philistines," *Megadim* 3 (1987): 25–31 [Hebrew]; and Rabbi Yaakov Medan, "Weeping for the Moment, Weeping for Generations," *Megadim* 10 (1990): 34–37 [Hebrew].

the event himself? If he is a false prophet and one of Jeroboam's supporters, why was he absent from the great celebration? If he deliberately stayed away, perhaps he has his own doubts about Jeroboam's new religious practices. (We cannot argue that he was old and therefore housebound, as he has no trouble traveling later in the story.)

2. The *navi zaken* owns a burial plot in Bethel, as indicated by 13:28–30 and II Kings 23:16–19. He has evidently been living in the town for some time and therefore is not a new prophet imported by Jeroboam to staff his shrine.

3. The *navi zaken* is clearly a genuine prophet in that he receives God's word! In 13:20–22, he receives a direct divine communication regarding the dreadful fate of the *ish Elokim*. Moreover, when he tells an untruth in the story, it is explicitly noted by the text (13:18), indicating that he is generally trustworthy.

Thus, we propose that the *navi zaken* has authentically prophesied in the past; he is a true prophet of God.[9] If so, we have to explain his duplicity.

Jeroboam has transformed Bethel into a sacrificial site. The prophet is not sure what to make of that. On the one hand, Jerusalem has been chosen eternally, and therefore sacrificial altars outside the city are outlawed. On the other hand, Jeroboam has been divinely mandated to establish his own monarchy. Perhaps these altars and calves have been granted special legitimacy?

Because of his dilemma regarding Jeroboam's religious initiatives, the *navi zaken* boycotts the opening ceremony of the king's shrine. But when he hears about the visiting prophet, the *ish Elokim* from Judah, and the miracles he performs, paralyzing Jeroboam's arm and then restoring it, the *navi zaken* recognizes that this man is the key to understanding whether the king's new religion is legitimate or reprehensible. After all, God has delivered a message to this prophet.

---

9. Others see the *navi zaken* as wholly pernicious; see Elchanan Samet, "Sanctification of God's Name"; and Simon, *Prophetic Narratives*. Some suggest that this elder schemes to annul the prophecy of the *ish Elokim* by enticing him to return. In this view, the prophecy can be undone by "rewinding" the journey of the prophet.

The *navi zaken*'s lie to the *ish Elokim* is a test of sorts. He imagines that if this "man of God" backtracks upon his own words, then he is an imposter, a political agitator. If, however, he persists with his defiance regarding "eating, drinking, and returning," then the *navi zaken* will have to investigate the source of his message.

When he meets the *ish Elokim*, who is taking shade under a tree, the *navi zaken* invites him home with him. The *Ish Elokim* refuses, restating his divine restriction and reinforcing his authenticity. Then the elderly prophet fabricates his own contradictory "prophecy":

> He said to him, "I am also a prophet as you are, and an angel spoke to me by the world of the Lord, saying: Bring him back with you into your house, that he may eat bread and drink water".... (13:18)

We readers are confused; has God contradicted His own explicit command? The text does not leave us with this uncertainty for long, however:

> ...but he lied. (ibid.).

The *ish Elokim*, possibly a young novice prophet, is fooled by the older man. Only when they are dining together does God's word emerge loud and clear (with an unusual mid-verse break, implying a trauma of sorts):[10] The *Ish Elokim* has contravened God's word and therefore will die a premature death. On the prophet's homeward journey, during which he is killed, the symmetry is striking: Just as the *navi zaken* "found him" (*vayimtza'ehu*), luring him and seducing him into defying God's word, a lion "finds him" (*va-yimtza'ehu*) and kills him as punishment for his abrogation of that word. This supernatural spectacle demonstrates to all that the prophet's death is a divine sign; God has killed the *ish Elokim* for violating the terms of his mission.

THE MORAL OF THE STORY

The uncertainty we have depicted as motivating the *navi zaken*, which resurfaces at various points in the story, reflects the confusion about

---

10. See Genesis 35:22 and II Samuel 12:13.

Jeroboam that must have gripped the entire nation. The people are unsure whether the king's shrines, calves, and altars are legitimate. On the one hand, he has been appointed by God; on the other hand, his actions seem to defy God's word.

This story is about the *ish Elokim*, a man who is issued clear instructions by God. When he disobeys God's law, he must pay the price. The prophet has good reason to contravene God's word; after all, he was tricked! Yet when God defines your mission, if you fail to comply, you lose your divine legitimacy. Your demise will verify the truths you failed to affirm in your lifetime.

The same goes for Jeroboam. He may have been appointed by God, but his actions betray that election. He has contravened the dictates of the Torah and exceeded the mandate of his rule, so he will be removed from the monarchy.

A Call to Jeroboam – Return!

A striking wordplay, recurring fifteen times throughout this episode, involves the Hebrew root *sh-v*, meaning to return or restore, and also to repent. Essentially, this is a story about whether it is possible to "return." Jeroboam asks that his arm be "restored" to him, and it is. Yet the *ish Elokim* is forbidden to "return" along the same path, and when he does, he is not granted a second chance.

What of Jeroboam? Can the ritual centrality of Jerusalem be "restored" once he has flagrantly violated it? Can he "repent"? I would suggest that, unlike the *ish Elokim*, the king retains the possibility of "returning" by abandoning, reversing, and annulling his forbidden acts, just as his arm is restored to him. This chapter is a wake-up call to him, his final warning. But he chooses to ignores it; he fails to return.

We detect that this is a call to repent from the final lines of the chapter:

> **Even after this incident,** Jeroboam **did not turn back** (*shav*) from his evil ways, but continued (*vayashav*) appointing priests from the ranks of the people for the *bamot*.... Thereby, the house of Jeroboam incurred guilt, to its utter annihilation from the face of the earth. (13:33–34)

UNITY?

This story, then, expresses the confusion into which Jeroboam's new religious centers thrust the nation. The chapter states unequivocally that even a leader designated by God may not abrogate God's word.

What were Jeroboam's options? He knew that the Torah mandated a single place of worship (see Deut. 12); his *bamot* clearly violated this law. Jeroboam had been designated by God to establish a new administration for the nation, but Jerusalem and the Temple could have remained the religious focal point. Indeed, certain northern and southern kings cooperated with one another (Ahab and Jehoshaphat, for example). Had Jeroboam collaborated with Rehoboam, had he had not allowed his resentment of the house of David to dominate, then the Jewish people might have remained a single nation with two states, two administrative centers – one in Shechem and one in Jerusalem. In the final reckoning, Jeroboam's absolute severing of the two kingdoms weakened the nation religiously and politically.

> R. Abba said: ... The Holy One Blessed Be He seized Jeroboam by his garment and urged him, "Repent! Then I, you, and the son of Jesse [i.e., David] will walk in the Garden of Eden." He [Jeroboam] inquired: "And who shall be at the head?" [God answered:] "The son of Jesse shall be at the head." "If so," [he replied,] "I do not desire [it]." (*Sanhedrin* 102b)

1 Kings 14

Jeroboam Condemned

Faced with the life-threatening sickness of his son and heir, Jeroboam sends his wife in disguise to consult with the blind prophet, Ahijah:

> Go disguise yourself, that you not be recognized as the wife of Jeroboam; then go to Shiloh; Ahijah the prophet is there – the one who told me I would be king over this people. Take ten loaves of bread with you, some cakes, and a jar of honey, and go to him; he will tell you what will happen to the boy. (1 Kings 14:2–3)

Jeroboam seeks counsel with Ahijah because he is the prophet "who told me I would be king over this people." Jeroboam knows that Ahijah speaks the truth. Ironically, Ahijah will now prophesy Jeroboam's son's death and the demise of his royal dynasty.

The verses mock Jeroboam's wife's masquerade as pointless: "Ahijah could not see, for his eyes had become sightless with old age" (14:4). Ahijah cannot see those who seek his counsel; his vision transcends his eyesight.

Nonetheless, what is the purpose of this disguise? And why can Jeroboam not visit Ahijah personally? Malbim suggests that it is a matter of public relations:

> He [Jeroboam] was concerned that people would say he was inquiring of the prophets of God, rather than the prophets of his [golden] calves.

However, Radak sees Jeroboam as having damaged his relationship with the prophet, anticipating an expression of Ahijah's ire towards him:

> He [Jeroboam] knew Ahijah hated him, for he had removed himself from the way of God. He said to himself: If Ahijah knows it is my wife, he will prophesy nothing but bad tidings.

Jeroboam is convinced that if Ahijah identifies his visitor as the king's wife, he will pronounce a curse rather than a blessing. So the king resorts to subterfuge, imagining that he can fool the prophet:

> When a prophet inquires [of God] regarding a given matter, he inquires regarding that issue specifically…. If he [Ahijah] did not know that this was Jeroboam's wife, he would inquire only as to whether the sick child would live, and maybe he would pray for him. But if he knew that it was Jeroboam's wife, then he would prepare to inquire of God regarding all matters of the house of Jeroboam, for this is a public matter. (Malbim)

Jeroboam thinks he will gain greater assistance and a better chance for his son if he is treated merely as a random individual with a gravely ill infant.

EVADING GOD

The Bible contains many stories in which people dress in costume in an attempt to conceal their identity. In these incidents, the objective is not merely misrepresentation but to perpetrate an act of deception.[1] In

---

1. In some Bible stories, the aim of a masquerade is to gain access to someone without

this regard, the story of Jeroboam's wife and the blind Ahijah recalls the scene of the biblical Jacob seeking a blessing from the blind Isaac. In both cases, the protagonist imagines that if he can trick the purveyor of the blessing, he may emerge with a blessing rather than a curse.

However, another biblical story – that of Adam and Eve hiding in the Garden of Eden – may provide a more poignant comparison. In that episode, the act of concealment is an attempt to outwit the all-knowing God rather than to deceive man. Prof. Yair Zakovitch comments:

> The greatest paradox transpires when mere mortals, whose vision is a human, flesh-and-blood perspective, attempt to deceive Heaven…. He who hopes to evade God under the disguise of a mask is animated by either naivety or desperation…. The paradox is readily apparent: At the very moment of hiding from God, the road leads to Him. Even the blindness of the prophet will not help the scheming king.[2]

Here, too, Jeroboam seeks to hide from the prophet and circumvent God; however, it is God who guides the prophet.[3] Thus, no matter how Jeroboam's wife conceals her identity, and no matter how blind the prophet may be, God will send His inexorable word to His prophet and deliver His pronouncement.

---

being discovered. In these cases, the objective is to deliver a message that would otherwise be rejected. Instances include the prophet who condemns Ahab (1 Kings 20:35–41) and the woman from Tekoa sent by Joab to pressure David to reconcile with his estranged son, Absalom (II Sam. 15).

2. Yair Zakovitch, "Man Sees with the Eyes, and God Sees to the Heart: Camouflage in the Flight from God," in *A Range of Views on Faces, Masks, and Masquerade in Our Literary Heritage*, ed. Dror Kerem (Tel Aviv: Israel Ministry of Education, 1996), 15–27 [Hebrew].

3. Does a prophet possess an independent power to curse or bless? This theme deserves deeper analysis. After all, Abraham is told, "Those who bless you, I will bless" (Gen. 12:3), indicating that the power of blessing is his. The prophet Elisha curses some mocking youths, and they are instantaneously mauled by wild bears (II Kings 2:23–25); treated well by the Shunammite woman, he blesses her with a child (ibid. 4). Elisha seems to possess the power of blessings and curses. Generally, however, the prophet simply relays God's word.

In a cruel reversal, the messenger sent by the king to bring about the child's recovery becomes an agent of God bearing a message of death:

> As for you, arise, go to your house; when you enter the city, the child will die. (14:12)

Jeroboam's wife is forced to endure an excruciating journey home, fully cognizant that her return will bring about her son's demise. In a sinister echo of the *mofet*, the prophetic sign of the previous chapter (13:3), the very death of her child verifies Ahijah's prophecy. Indeed, had Jeroboam heeded the first sign, the second would not have been necessary.

The prophet instructs Jeroboam's wife, "Arise, go to your **house**" (14:12), and the child dies "when she came to the **threshold of her house**" (14:17). There is a deliberate interplay here between Jeroboam's physical house or home and his royal "house" (14:10, 13).[4] The death of the child at the moment of entry into the house signifies the "death" of Jeroboam's royal dynasty.[5]

ECHOES OF SAUL

The scene here touches upon some clear parallels to the Saul-Samuel relationship:

1. Before consulting Ahijah, a gift is offered: "Take ten loaves of bread with you, some cakes, and a jar of honey, and go to him..." (14:3). We read of a similar gift before Saul's early encounter with Samuel:

    > Saul said to his servant, "If we go, what can we give the man? ...We have no gift to take to the man of God; what do we have?" The servant answered Saul again: "Look," he said, "I

---

4. In II Samuel 7, there is a similar overlap between the notion of the home (God's and David's) and the royal house of David.
5. See Jerome Walsh, *1 Kings* (Collegeville, Minnesota: The Liturgical Press, 1996), 197–99. Walsh takes this idea further, suggesting a pun of sorts – the *saf habayit* (threshold) of the palace echoing *sof habayit*, the end of Jeroboam's dynasty. I think the pun, while tempting, is unsubstantiated by the text.

have a quarter of a shekel of silver; I will give it to the man of God, that he may tell us which way to take." (1 Sam. 9: 7–8)

2. In both cases, God informs the prophet of the arrival of the guest in advance:

> God had told Ahijah: "Jeroboam's wife is coming to ask you about her son...." (1 Kings 14:5)
>
> Now the day before Saul came, the Lord had revealed to Samuel: "About this time tomorrow, I will send you a man from the land of Benjamin; anoint him leader...." (1 Sam. 9:15–16)

3. The most evocative connection is the disguise. Just as Jeroboam's wife disguises herself, Saul, in a famous episode at Endor, disguises himself to illegitimately contact the prophet:

> Saul disguised himself, putting on other clothes, and at night he and two men went to the woman. "Consult a spirit for me," he said, "and bring up for me the one I name." ...Then the woman asked, "Whom shall I bring up for you?" "Bring up Samuel to me," he said. (1 Sam. 28:8, 11)

4. In both cases, the petitioner solicits the prophet in desperation, as life hangs in the balance. In each instance, the prophet responds with a simple question:

> "Come in, Jeroboam's wife. Why are you disguised?" (1 Kings 14:6)
>
> "Why did you anger me to raise me?" (1 Sam. 28:15)

With this terse greeting, the prophet instantaneously dashes his petitioner's hopes as the encounter becomes filled with foreboding. Instead of the reassurance and assistance the visitor seeks, the prophet gloomily dispenses death.

5. In both cases, the prophet who appoints the king later announces his rejection.[6] Furthermore, each prophet pronounces the

---

6. We sense that these kings are each accompanied by a particular prophet. Saul's destiny is closely tied to that of Samuel (see 1 Sam. 1:20, 27–28), who mourns the king's failure greatly (see 1 Sam. 16:1–2 and Abarbanel ad loc.). After their respective sins, both Saul and Jeroboam break off contact with their prophets; Saul does so after Samuel announces God's rejection of his rule, and Jeroboam similarly keeps his distance from Ahijah. Estranged from their spiritual benefactors, these kings are nonetheless forced to turn to them when their very survival hangs in the balance.

demise of the king, the death of his son (or sons), and the defeat of all Israel (1 Kings 14:15 and 1 Sam. 28:19). Of course, these parallels are augmented by the other similarities between Saul and Jeroboam that we have noted in previous chapters.[7]

The similarity between Jeroboam and Saul is that they both face the absolute termination of their royal lines. Whereas David's line is awarded perpetuity (II Sam. 7:13–15), the royal houses of Saul and Jeroboam are discontinued.

THE PROCLAMATION

Ahijah's condemnation is divided into two parts:

1. 14:6–14   Jeroboam's punishment
2. 14:15–16   National punishment[8]

Jeroboam "has acted worse than all who preceded him" (14:9), and his punishment is expressed in furious and crude terminology. The coarse references to "he who urinates against the wall" and "dung" (14:10), ancient expressions of crass street language, reflect God's disgust at Jeroboam's sins and His determination to eliminate all his descendants. Indeed, in reporting the death of Jeroboam's son, Nadab, the book of Kings invokes the divine judgment: "he [Baasha] did not spare a single soul of the house of Jeroboam ... in accordance with the word of God by the hand of Ahijah the Shilonite" (1 Kings 15:29).

The vocabulary of this speech becomes a recurrent feature of the book of Kings, proclaiming the absolute destruction of dynasty after dynasty and addressed to each of the errant royal houses of the northern kingdom.[9]

---

7. These include the tearing of the coat, the rendezvous between the prophet and the prospective king in the open countryside, and the use of similar language.

8. These punishments are indeed carried out: Jeroboam in 15:29–30, and Israel much later, in 11 Kings 17:21–23. God articulates Jeroboam's guilt with the same phrases used in Ahijah's initial prophecy to him; cf. 1 Kings 11:38 and 14:8.

9. See 1 Kings 16:1–2, 11; 21:20–25; 1 Samuel 25:22; 11 Kings 9:8. The prediction regarding Jeroboam's descendants, that "he who dies in the city shall be devoured by dogs, and anyone who dies in the field will be eaten by the birds" (1 Kings 14:11), recalls

Efes Atzur Ve'Efes Azuv

One expression in Ahijah's indictment has particularly deep roots: "I will cut off from Jeroboam ... *atzur ve'azuv* (bondsman and freeman)" (14:10).[10] This cryptic phrase relates to a verse in *Haazinu*:

> For the Lord will vindicate His people
> And take revenge for His servants
> When He sees that their might is gone,
> And neither bondsman nor freeman (*efes atzur ve-efes azuv*) remains. (Deut. 32:37)

Haazinu foresees Israel's ups and downs, the turbulence of sin and punishment.[11] In this poem, the decimation of all the population, "bondsman and freeman," illustrates the nation's lowest point, on the one hand, but also indicates a national revival, as God mercifully restores the national fortunes from ruin to repair.

Thus, when we hear this phrase, we should understand its implications: First, it is indicative of the greatest national misfortune. Second, despite the violence and chaos ahead, better times will come. Third, the events described here in the book of Kings should not surprise us; they were already prophesied in the Torah.

---

the ranting of Goliath (1 Sam. 17:44) and hence is most probably ancient rhetoric of carnage and violent decimation. (See Yehuda Kiel, *Da'at Mikra*, *1 Kings*, 301 [Hebrew], regarding its roots in the *tokhaha*; see Deuteronomy 28:26.) Only in the case of the evil Ahab and Jezebel do we see these words carried out literally; see 1 Kings 22:37 and 11 Kings 9:35.

As for cutting off "he who urinates against the wall," Radak offers various interpretations: (1) Even the dogs will be wiped out; (2) the male line of the family will be destroyed; (3) people of intelligence and discernment will cease to be. This third option also appears in *Targum* and Rashi.

10. Due to the unusual vocabulary here, as in much of biblical poetry, this phrase is a challenge to translate. The traditional commentaries offer a wide range of explanations. We have adopted Rashi's reading.

11. For a good structural analysis of *Haazinu*, see Rabbi Elchanan Samet, "Song of the Future or Song of the Present," The Virtual Beit Midrash, http://vbm-torah.org/parsha.60/51haazin.htm.

SHECHEM TO TIRZAH

Before concluding with the death of Jeroboam and the succession of his son, Nadab, we are told quite incidentally that Jeroboam's palace is located in a town called Tirzah (14:17). We have not been informed that a new capital city has been built in Tirzah, just a few miles north of Jeroboam's initial center in Shechem (12:25). Tirzah functions as the royal capital (16:9, 15–18) until the reign of Omri, when the northern capital moves to Samaria (16:24).

1 Kings 14

Rehoboam

A t this point, the tone of the book of Kings changes. Thus far, we have been reading a flowing narrative: the struggle for leadership, the life achievements and downfall of Solomon, Jeroboam and the split of the kingdom. Now the rhythm alters sharply, as the next two chapters narrate succinct, formulaic accounts of kings. These passages lack the dramatic energy of the Solomon and Jeroboam stories.

In our introduction, we established that the book of Kings uses these accounts of kings to generate a sense of continuity from the establishment of the Temple to its destruction. And yet, notwithstanding the telegraphic language of these paragraphs, and possibly due precisely to their economy of phrase, a close reading will demonstrate how enormously effective they are in conveying both information and meaning. A classic illustration is found in the opening lines of the story of Rehoboam:

> Rehoboam was forty-one years old when he became king, and he reigned seventeen years in Jerusalem, **the city the Lord had chosen out of all the tribes of Israel to establish His name there;** his mother's name was Naamah. (14:21)

At the outset, this verse seems to follow the form language for all kings, listing the king's age, length of reign, mother's name, etc. However, the exposition of Rehoboam deviates from the norm in that it records Jerusalem's unique association with God's name. Why? Rehoboam's historical context offers an obvious answer. Jeroboam's shrines have contested Jerusalem's supremacy. The text responds by adjusting the formula to convey that from God's vantage point, Jerusalem remains the sole site of the *Shekhina*.

THE ACCOUNT IN THE BOOK OF KINGS

The account of Rehoboam's reign in the book of Kings is exceedingly compact, consisting of only three topics:

1. the idolatry of Judah
2. the invasion by Shishak, king of Egypt, in Rehoboam's fifth year
3. the bronze shields

Rehoboam's story begins with a disturbing depiction of widespread idolatrous practices:

> And Judah[1] did evil in the sight of God and angered Him more than their fathers had done by the sins that they committed. They too[2] built *bamot*, pillars, and *asherim* on every high hill and under every leafy tree; there was also sacred prostitution (*kadesh*) in the land. Judah imitated all the abhorrent practices of the nations that God had dispossessed before the Israelites. (14:22–24)

All these elements – pagan altars, idolatrous pillars and trees, and cultic sexual perversion – indicate a terrible descent into local pagan norms.[3] The portrayal of Israel's worship "on every high hill and under every

---

1. The use of the term "Judah" is interesting here. Does it denote the people of Judah or, as indicated by *Targum Yonatan*, the house of Judah, i.e., Rehoboam himself?
2. "They too" suggests that Judah followed in the footsteps of Israel, which had engaged in illicit worship (Rashi).
3. Ralbag sees these practices as syncretic worship of God –through illicit means – rather than attachment to a foreign god.

leafy tree"[4] directs our attention to the selfsame phrase in Deuteronomy depicting the Canaanite religion, with its manifold worship at sites that exhibit the strength and vitality of the natural world (Deut. 12:2–3). In the Deuteronomic passage, two laws are legislated: the obligation to eradicate *avoda zara* from the land, and its corollary – the institution of a single place of worship. This intertextual reference, then, both censures the adoption of Canaanite religious mores, as well as the affront to the supremacy of the Temple. The ominous reference to the Canaanites as "the nations that God had dispossessed before the Israelites" warns that Israel is placing itself on shaky ground.

Against this idolatrous backdrop, we read of Shishak's devastating attack on Jerusalem and his plunder of its royal buildings and the Temple treasury. The causal link of crime and punishment – of Judah's idolatry followed by Egypt's offensive – is never stated outright but is very much in tune with the central thesis of the book of Kings.

The Egyptians rampaged throughout the southern kingdom before reaching Jerusalem. An ancient inscription found upon the walls of the impressive temple of Amon in Karnak, Egypt,[5] documents the heavy military blow dealt by Shishak to dozens of cities in both the southern and northern kingdoms, listing each place by name. However, instead of a comprehensive inventory of the enemy's conquests, Kings illustrates the breadth of the national ruin with a subtle but poignant anecdote:

> King Shishak of Egypt marched against Jerusalem. ...he carried off everything; **he even carried off all the golden shields that Solomon had made.** King Rehoboam had bronze shields made instead.... Whenever the king went into the house of the Lord, the guards would carry them and then bring them back to the armory of the guards. (14:25–28)

---

4. See also Jeremiah 2:20, 3:6; Ezekiel 6:13.

5. This inscription details an extensive campaign in the north, whereas the Bible mentions nothing of the kind. For a resolution, see Yehuda Elitzur, *Israel and the Bible: Studies in Geography, History and Biblical Thought*, ed. Yoel Elitzur and Amos Frisch (Ramat Gan: Bar-Ilan University Press, 1999), 152–56 [Hebrew].

These golden shields deliberately allude to Solomon. They remind us of the hefty gold-tax revenues flowing into the royal treasury (10:16–17) and used to finance Solomon's indulgences. These shields symbolize the splendor of the Solomonic era.[6] Shishak is depicted as stripping away the accumulated grandeur of a generation a mere five years after Solomon's death. One senses a cynicism of sorts as the text details twice that the replacement bronze shields were carefully stored in the armory. It would seem that these ceremonial accessories were handled cautiously and stored fastidiously. The disparity between the carefree luxury of Solomon and Rehoboam's cheap replicas encapsulates the sharp fall of the kingdom. Moreover, through this succinct detail we realize that this military conquest is punishment for Solomon's idolatry even more than for Rehoboam's.

THE ACCOUNT IN CHRONICLES

Whereas the account of Rehoboam in the book of Kings is streamlined and relatively straightforward, the parallel text in II Chronicles (11–12) is filled with new details and gives a dramatically different impression. The disparities between the two are significant:

Chronicles opens with Rehoboam's preparations for war. We read of impressive and extensive defensive construction and national fortification. Anticipating Shishak's siege, Rehoboam stores grain, wine, and oil, and he stockpiles weaponry. He and the nation "follow the path of David and Solomon" (11:17) for three years. Following this we are told of the king's eighteen wives and sixty concubines, echoing his father, Solomon. And then:

> When the kingship of Rehoboam was firmly established, and **he grew strong, he abandoned God's Torah**, he and all of Israel with him. (12:1)

At this point we read of Shishak's invasion (12:2–4). In God's name, Shemaiah the prophet tells the king and his cabinet: "You have aban-

---

6. I think that this is what Ḥazal mean when they read the phrase "he carried off *everything*" (1 Kings 14:26) as a reference to Solomon's grand throne.

doned Me; so I am abandoning you to Shishak" (12:5). They "humbly" concede: "God is the Righteous One!" (12:6). The prophet informs them of God's response to their submission: "My wrath will not be poured out over Jerusalem" (12:7).

This incident is followed by the story of the bronze shields and the following conclusion:

> After he had humbled himself, God's anger was averted … and good things were found in Judah. King Rehoboam grew strong in Jerusalem and exercised kingship…. (12:12–13)

The depiction in Chronicles is markedly different from that in the book of Kings:

1. Chronicles describes Rehoboam as a strong, successful king, loyal to God except for a brief aberration in the fourth and fifth years of his reign.
2. Only Chronicles notes Rehoboam's many marriages.
3. In Kings, Rehoboam's sin is idolatry. In Chronicles, it is a general sense of pride – his "strength" and a vague "abandonment of Torah." Moreover, Rehoboam's subsequent responsiveness to God saves Jerusalem.
4. In the book of Kings, the invasion of Shishak and the episode of the shields provide a snapshot of national humiliation. In Chronicles, they constitute a reprieve.
5. Chronicles explicitly links Rehoboam's abandonment of the Torah (12:1) and the advance of Shishak (12:2). In Kings, the text fails to connect the two; any such connection may be inferred only contextually, if at all.
6. The book of Kings omits the interaction with Shemaiah.

How might we resolve the discrepancies between the two accounts? How can we gain a true, accurate perspective on the reign of Rehoboam?

On the one hand, it is possible to read the two texts as complementary, each filling in the lacunae of the other despite the disparities between the two books. Rehoboam indeed boasted significant building achievements and valiantly defended the country from Shishak's attack. The idolatry in 1 Kings is depicted by Chronicles as a general abandonment of God, but it is difficult to know its scope – did it affect the ruling class, the peasantry, or both? The book of Kings too presents a somewhat ambivalent portrayal of Rehoboam, depicting him as highly responsive to the prophet Shemaiah immediately following his coronation (12:22–24). It is plausible that the king interacted with Shemaiah subsequently and responded positively to his guidance on a regular basis, as implied by Chronicles.

On the other hand, the significant divergence between the two accounts leads us to probe why each book would describe Rehoboam so differently. This is a fundamental methodological question that we must address. If we are dealing with a single event or era, why do two books paint such vastly diverse portraits of the same reality, the identical king?

TWO BOOKS, TWO PERSPECTIVES

To explain this phenomenon, let us refer to our introduction and the distinct authorship and texture of each book. Any book narrates its story with a particular objective in mind. The selection of relevant facts and historical details tells the story in a unique way. The books of Kings and Chronicles are no exception to this rule. And they each communicate a different message. In the words of historian Prof. Avraham Grossman:[7]

> The depiction in the book of Kings is ahistorical, as if it deliberately omits the great military events and puts the entire emphasis upon the Temple. The most reasonable explanation...is that the purpose of the transmission of the story is not to report historical events, however important they may be, but to teach religious lessons.

Prof. Grossman is saying that the Bible does not record objective historical data. Instead it crafts the story, selecting and choosing the facts

---

7. Prof. A. Grossman, "1 Kings, Chapter 14:25–28, Shishak's Campaign," http://www.daat.ac.il/daat/tanach/rishonim/grosman4.htm [Hebrew].

and their presentation, as it is driven by an educational-spiritual agenda rather than an objective-historical one.

In resolving the discrepancies between the texts, we may suggest the following: The sin that occupies the book of Kings is **idolatry**. This account focuses on the widespread national worship involving the *bamot*, *asherim*, and *kadesh*. The resultant damage or punishment is described as affecting Jerusalem, the Temple, and the royal treasury.

In Chronicles, however, the sin is dramatically different; it is broader and less specific. Here, the sin is one of excessive pride, self-reliance accompanied by an abandonment of God. Rehoboam's military fortifications are proven worthless by Shishak, and must be replaced by faith in and reliance upon God. In the resultant war, Jerusalem is spared rather than ravished, because the king is highly responsive to a prophet who mentors him to repentance.

Each book tells Rehoboam's story from its vantage point. The book of Kings concentrates on the sin of idolatry and seeks to explain the tragic destruction of the Temple. The responsibility is that of the king. Hence, Rehoboam is viewed through the prism of rampant national idolatry. Moreover, the focus on Solomon's shields expresses the idea that Rehoboam is also suffering for his father's sins.

Chronicles, however, is grappling with different issues. The challenge of the early Second Temple period – *Shivat Tziyon* – was the rebuilding of the country. The nation severely lacked confidence, with most believing Jerusalem could never regain its grandeur. The people struggled not with idolatry, but with broader religious commitments, such as observing Shabbat and fighting intermarriage. Moreover, Chronicles views the Davidic kings as fundamentally righteous.

Hence, Chronicles highlights the achievements of this ambivalent king but teaches that a slip in faith engenders a national calamity. Against the backdrop of grand national endeavors, it pushes for a broad commitment to Torah and its laws, and encourages repentance. These are the key elements stressed in this story.

Is one book more accurate than the other? I think we have demonstrated that the same historical narrative can be presented effectively in various ways. There is no single authoritative style of relating an event or era. How one tells a story reflects the message of the historical events for his own times.

1 Kings 15

Civil War

THE PERSPECTIVE OF THE SOUTHERN KINGDOM OF JUDAH

After Solomon, the southern kingdom experiences religious decline, internal political instability, and conflict with the northern kingdom. We have already described the turbulence of Jeroboam's revolution, which splintered the nation into two kingdoms, and the attack five years later by Pharaoh Shishak. However, a quick survey of the kings of Judah reveals the religious contours of this era and the vehement hostility between Judah and Israel.

From a religious vantage point, the kings of Judah chart an interesting journey:

- **Rehoboam** reigns for seventeen years. Idolatry prevails.
- **Abijah (Abijam)**, son of Rehoboam, reigns for three years. Idolatry continues unabated.
- **Asa** reigns for forty-one years. He purges the kingdom of idolatry, and restores and maintains correct religious standards.

Thus, after a steep decline in religious loyalty following Solomon, King Asa represents a return to the proper Jewish orientation.

Judah				Israel			
King	Years	Good/Bad	Military	King	Years	Good/Bad	Military
Rehoboam	17	Bad	Egyptian invasion + civil conflict	Jeroboam	22	Bad	Civil conflict
Abijam	3	Bad	Civil conflict				
Asa	41	Good	Civil war: Asa pays Aram to attack Baasha	Nadab	2	Bad	Civil conflict
				Baasha	24	Bad	Civil war + invasion
				Elah	2	Bad	
				Zimri	7 days	Bad	
				Omri	12	Very bad	

Dotted lines indicate assassination and/or revolution

Another vector charted by these chapters is the internecine tension or civil war between north and south:

There was continual war between **Rehoboam** and Jeroboam. (14:30)

There was war between **Abijam** and Jeroboam. (15:7)

There was war between **Asa** and King Baasha of Israel all their days. (15:16)

The enmity between the kingdoms escalates into full-fledged military campaigns inflicting devastating casualties. At its peak, the northern king, Baasha, constructs a colossal wall obstructing passage between north and south and effectively severing the two kingdoms.

In Judah, then, we have two stories to follow. The first is the spiritual slump and the recovery therefrom; the second is the civil war that reaches its climax and conclusion under King Asa.

ABIJAH, KING OF JUDAH

In the book of Kings, the reign of Abijah[1] is narrated in telegraphic style:

> He reigned three years in Jerusalem; his mother was Maachah daughter of Abishalom. He continued in all the sins of his father before him.... Yet for the sake of David, the Lord, his God, gave him a lamp in Jerusalem, by raising up his descendant after him and by preserving Jerusalem.... There was war between Rehoboam and Jeroboam.... (15:2–4, 6)

Abijah is a king who facilitates *avoda zara*. The reader anticipates his removal from the throne. In response, the text emphasizes God's special relationship with David and his royal line as an assurance of Abijah's continued reign, notwithstanding his personal failings.

Whereas the book of Kings offers no details regarding the war between Abijah and Jeroboam,[2] Chronicles describes a huge battle, with 400,000 soldiers under Abijah and 800,000 under Jeroboam! The war begins with a rousing ideological speech by Abijah:

> Listen to me, Jeroboam and all Israel: Do you not know that the Lord, God of Israel, gave the rule over Israel to David and his sons forever by a covenant of salt?[3] Yet Jeroboam son of Nebat, the servant of Solomon son of David, rose up and rebelled against his master. And worthless men gathered about

---

1. The book of Kings 15 refers to him as Abijam; in II Chronicles 13, he is Abijah.
2. The book of Kings actually refers to a war between *Rehoboam* and Jeroboam, though this verse appears in a paragraph dedicated to Abijah(m). See Ralbag and Yehuda Kiel, *Da'at Mikra, I Kings* [Hebrew], who explain that Abijam fought alongside his father against Jeroboam.
3. The phrase "covenant of salt" appears twice in the Torah (Lev. 2:13; Num. 18:19)

him, scoundrels, who proved too strong for Rehoboam son of Solomon, when he was young and timid and could not hold his own against them. Now you intend to resist the kingdom of the Lord through the sons of David, being a great multitude and having with you the golden calves that Jeroboam made as gods for you. Have you not driven out the priests of the Lord, the sons of Aaron and the Levites, and made for yourselves priests like the peoples of other lands? ... But as for us, the Lord is our God, and we have not forsaken Him; and the sons of Aaron are ministering to the Lord as priests, and the Levites attend to their work ... Now behold, God is with us at our head, and His priests with the signal trumpets to sound the alarm against you. O sons of Israel, do not fight against the Lord, God of your fathers, for you will not succeed. (II Chron. 13:4–10, 12)

The campaign, however, does not go in Judah's favor. Jeroboam's troops surround and entrap Abijah's army until:

When Judah turned around and saw the fighting was before and behind them, they cried out to God, and the priests blew the trumpets ... God routed Jeroboam and all Israel before Abijah and Judah. Israel fled before Judah, and God delivered them into their hands.... 500,000 chosen men of Israel were slain.... Abijah pursued Jeroboam and captured some of his cities – Bethel.... (13:14–17, 19)

This dramatic depiction is striking on several accounts. At the simplest level, there are the frightening numbers of casualties – half a million dead from the north! Was Abijah not a little excessive in his ruthless determination?

---

and seems to indicate an everlasting promise, as salt is a preservative; see Rashbam ad loc. For more on this expression, see Y. Barkai, "Covenant of Salt," *Bar Ilan Daf Hashavua*, http://www.biu.ac.il/JH/Parasha/Korach/bar.html [Hebrew].

More centrally, Abijah's braggery seems out of place for a man whose administration fosters idolatry. Chronicles presents Abijah as mocking the illegitimate worship of Bethel,[4] yet when he eventually captures that city, he fails to destroy those very shrines, which continue to function well after this war.

Some of the dissonance between the depictions in Kings and Chronicles may be explained by the different perspectives of these two books. Chronicles supports the house of David and disdains the northern kingdom. It champions centralized worship in Jerusalem and the role of the priests rejecting any obfuscation of their status. To the degree that Abijah supports these national institutions, Chronicles endorses him. In contrast, the book of Kings focuses on idolatry, refusing to forgive any strains of it. The text assesses Abijah based solely on this criterion, branding him a failure and a sinner.

A RABBINIC VIEW

The Talmud rejects Chronicles' whitewash of Abijah:

> "Jeroboam could not muster strength again during the days of Abijah; God struck him down, and he died" (II Chron. 13:20) – R. Shmuel said: Do you think it was Jeroboam [who died]? No! It was Abijah.[5] And why was he struck down?
>
> R. Yoḥanan said: Because he shamed Jeroboam publicly. As it states: "[...]a great multitude, and having with you the golden calves that Jeroboam made as gods for you" (13:8).
>
> Resh Lakish said: [Abijah was punished] because he ridiculed Ahijah the Shilonite. As it states: "worthless men gathered about him, scoundrels" (13:7). Is he labeling Ahijah a scoundrel?!
>
> The rabbis said: [Abijah was punished] because idols came into his control, but he failed to destroy them. As it states:

---

4. See I Kings 12:29, cited below.
5. According to the chronology outlined in I Kings (15:9), Asa was crowned in Jeroboam's lifetime. The verse cited from Chronicles must therefore be referring to Abijah's death, not Jeroboam's. See Rabbi Yosef Kara on 15:7.

> "Abijah pursued Jeroboam and captured some of his cities – Bethel" (13:19), and it states: "He placed one [golden calf] in Bethel and the other he placed in Dan" (1 Kings 12:29). (Jerusalem Talmud, *Yevamot* 16:3)[6]

This Talmudic discussion demonstrates Ḥazal's keen reading of the Bible and their skill in linking diverse sources. Abijah reigns for only three years, dying shortly after his military engagement with the northern kingdom. The Talmud blames his sickness and subsequent death upon his sins, finding the clues to these offenses in his smug oration prior to the war. Three scholars probe Abijah's harsh words, penetrating his righteous veneer. R. Yohanan condemns the public shaming of Jeroboam, a legitimate Israelite king; after all, if Abijah was serious about his criticism, he might have found more discreet channels through which to convey his objections to Jeroboam, rather than publicizing them as war propaganda.[7] Resh Lakish contends that Abijah cannot legitimately depict Jeroboam's rise to kingship as a power grab, supported by an unlawful rabble, when this monarchy was ordained by a prophet. The other rabbis reject Abijah's claim of the moral high ground when he himself fails to remove the idolatry from Bethel. Such a king is in no position to admonish Jeroboam.

This critique of Abijah's jingoistic speech closes the gap somewhat between the perfect image of Abijah in Chronicles and the harsh judgment of the book of Kings. Chronicles refers us to more information in the "midrash of the prophet Ido" (13:22), which has disappeared in the course of history. One can only wonder what such a book might add to our understanding of this king and what Ido communicated to Abijah in his short reign.

---

6. See also *Gen. Rabba* 65:20.
7. *Gen. Rabba*, op cit., goes further, with R. Levi accusing Abijah of disregard for human dignity in his treatment of the corpses of the northern soldiers who fell in battle. This accusation of cruelty, of an inability to stop the war, relates to the enormous figure of half a million war dead, indicating an overzealous desire to inflict death and destruction on Jeroboam and Israel – who were, after all, fellow Jews.

ASA

Abijah's son and heir, King Asa, represents a welcome change for the kingdom of Judah, as he follows God enthusiastically.[8] The book of Kings describes his removal of idolatrous icons and the eradication of the institution of the *kadesh* (15:12). The driving force behind the culture of *avoda zara* appears to have been the king's grandmother – Maachah of Ammon – who evidently imported her religious practices from her native land. Asa removes her *mifletzet* – a statue of sorts, or an object of worship – and abolishes her standing as *gevira*.[9] Having removed the idolatry, Asa turns his attention to renovating and funding the Temple and to boosting the service of God among the people. Religiously, these are good times for Judah.[10]

THE WAR WITH BAASHA

King Baasha of Israel advanced against Judah, and he fortified Ramah to prevent anyone belonging to King Asa of Judah from

---

8. Even regarding the good kings of Judah, the text stresses that the *bamot*, regional sacrificial altars, remain (15:14). The impression, however, is that Asa did not personally participate in this ritual, even if the nation did.

9. Although we lack full details about the *gevira*, it would seem that she was generally the king's main wife. See also I Kings 11:19, referring to the *gevira* in Egypt, as well as II Kings 10:13 and Jeremiah 13:18 and 29:2, which refer to this position. Accordingly, the *gevira* seems to have enjoyed a high royal standing. This might explain why the name of the ascendant king's mother is frequently recorded in the book of Kings. As for Maachah, she appears to have had significant religious influence. Later queens Jezebel (II Kings 16–21) and Athaliah (II Kings 11) dominated religiously or administratively, respectively, although it is difficult to conclude whether they reflect the Israelite or Phoenician *gevira* tradition.

10. II Chronicles provides a more detailed biography of Asa than Kings, describing a spectacular military victory over the army of Zerah the Kushite of Ethiopia. Once again, this military campaign is replete with charismatic religious speeches (II Chron. 14:10) – a hallmark of Chronicles – followed by God's immediate response. (The use of the Hebrew verb n-g-f [plague] is common to the Abijah and Asa accounts, as are many other leading words and phrases.) Furthermore, Chronicles charts incremental stages of Asa's religious revival, culminating in a covenantal ceremony in the king's fifteenth year, in which the nation restates its allegiance to God after a protracted period in which there has been "no true God, no guiding priest, and no Torah" (15:3).

going out or coming in. So Asa took all the silver and gold that remained in the treasuries … and sent them to Ben-Hadad … of Aram, who resided in Damascus, with this message: "There is a pact between you and me …; I herewith send you a gift of silver and gold; go and break your pact with King Baasha of Israel, that he may withdraw from me." Ben-Hadad responded to King Asa's request; he sent his army commanders against the towns of Israel and smote … all the land of Naphtali. When Baasha heard about it, he stopped fortifying Ramah and remained in Tirzah. King Asa mustered all Judah with no exception, and they carried away the stones and timber with which Baasha had fortified Ramah …. (15:17–22)[11]

The tense standoff between Asa and Baasha is described in restrained, controlled language. We are left with many questions. What has instigated this conflict? What exactly is this "Ramah" that Baasha builds, and does it really threaten Judah? How should we assess Asa's bribe of Ben-Hadad, inviting him to attack Baasha? Is this policy correct?

Let us try to fill in the gaps. It seems that Judah under Asa enjoys a welcome sense of stability. The smooth Davidic royal succession contrasts with the political upheavals that have plagued the northern kingdom; Jeroboam's son Nadab reigned only two years before his assassination by Baasha, from the tribe of Issachar. One imagines that this political insecurity is not the sole factor in the north's decline. As a result of this deterioration, we witness mass migration southward toward Judah:

And he [Asa] gathered all of Judah and Benjamin, and those who had settled with them from Ephraim, Manasseh, and Simeon, for

---

11. Chronicles' dating of this war is highly problematic. The text records that the battle took place in the thirty-sixth year of King Asa, but this is impossible: Baasha reigned for only twenty-four years, from Asa's third year to his twenty-sixth (1 Kings 15:33, 16:8). Radak (15:34) and Ralbag (15:17) count the thirty-six years from the split of the kingdom.

many had defected from Israel when they saw that the Lord, his God, was with him. (II Chron. 15:9)

This population attrition in the north is the first factor in explaining Baasha's building of the Ramah – he seeks to stem the tide of emigration from north to south, "to prevent anyone belong to Asa King of Judah from going out or coming in" (1 Kings 15:17).

A second motivation is to reclaim territory. In the previous war between Abijah and Jeroboam, the Judean king captured land all the way northward to Bethel. Ramah is only nine kilometers north of Jerusalem. With this frontier-building act, Baasha is essentially moving the southern border back to its original position as he invades Judah.

Be the causes as they may, the construction of an impermeable barrier hemming in Judah and restricting access to the north is perceived by Asa as an act of aggression.[12] Our chapter indicates the construction of a wall and possibly other fortified structures, as we read of stones and timber. Other sources refer to a moat or trench dug to impede movement.[13] In short, Baasha cuts off the access roads, making passage between Judah and Israel impossible.

The Appeal to Aram, and Asa's Illness

Asa resolves the impasse by appealing to Aram (Syria), bribing the its king, Ben-Hadad, to attack Israel. Ben-Hadad complies, abrogating his peace agreement with Baasha and attacking and capturing the entire Galilee panhandle, the Hulah Valley from Ijon (near Metulla) and Dan to the Sea of Galilee. This hefty conquest is a devastating blow for Baasha. A massive segment of Israel passes into enemy hands, and Baasha, distracted by his problems with the Arameans in the north, abandons his provocation of the southern kingdom.

---

12. Obstruction of passage can certainly lead to armed conflict. A contemporary illustration of a military action of this sort is Egypt's blockade of the Straits of Tiran in 1967, which led to the Six-Day War.

13. Jeremiah 41:9 describes a moat or pit that "King Asa had constructed on account of King Baasha of Israel." From the combination of sources in Jeremiah or Kings, it seems that Baasha builds a wall and Asa digs a moat of sorts in self-defense.

Asa's action, notwithstanding Baasha's provocative wall building, is highly problematic. The act of turning against one's brother by
paying a foreign power to attack Israel seems reprehensible. How is this
move perceived by the Bible? The text here is strikingly silent. Does it
approve of Asa's action?

The commentators identify a clue in a seemingly innocuous detail
in the concluding line of the account in Kings:

> In his old age, Asa suffered from a foot ailment. (15:23)

They see this enigmatic tidbit as divine punishment:

> Because he sent to Ben-Hadad, as if he himself had no legs to go
> to war, ...God gave him this illness. (Ralbag)

In other words, if Asa must engage in aggression, he should at the very
least not employ a foreign country to attack Israel.[14]

A more serious critique emerges from an incidental reference in
the book of Jeremiah. Jeremiah describes the treacherous assassination
of Gedaliah, the Jewish governor appointed in the aftermath of the Temple's destruction and killed by Jewish political opponents. This terrible
act of violence precipitates a mass flight of the surviving Jewish population from the land of Israel, intensifying the devastation of the land
after the destruction. From the Talmud's perspective, this assassination

---

14. The Talmud (*Sota* 10a) proposes that this illness was God's punishment for a rather
strange sin – Asa's drafting Torah scholars and bridegrooms into his army. Let us
explain this comment by defining two halakhic categories of armed conflict. Jewish law exempts certain civilians from fighting in a standard war (*milhemet reshut*),
whereas in a war of national survival (a *milhemet mitzva*), the entire civilian population is drafted, including Torah scholars and "the groom from his room and the
bride from her wedding canopy" (*Sota* 8:7; Maimonides, *Mishneh Torah*, Laws of
Kings 7:4). The Talmud's specification of this infraction implies that Asa used all
the emergency measures at his disposal, mobilizing even civilians ordinarily exempt
in a standard war. In other words, Asa over-reacted, misjudging Baasha's buildup as
an existential threat. Asa was punished for his excessive zeal and lack of caution in
fighting his own nation.

is a national calamity, warranting the institution of an annual fast day (*Tzom Gedalia*). In recording the murder, Jeremiah writes:

> The cistern into which Ishmael threw all the corpses of the men he had killed in the affair of Gedaliah was **the one King Asa had constructed on account of King Baasha of Israel.** (Jer. 41:9)

Gedaliah's corpse and those of his associates are thrown into the moat that was dug in this standoff between Baasha and Asa. Jeremiah's pedantic intertextual reference links these two awful events. The prophet groups the assassination of Gedaliah together with the dreadful conflict of Asa and Baasha, establishing them in Jewish history as twin landmarks of heinous killing and devastating infighting.[15]

CONCLUSION

This chapter charts the religious decline and recovery of the kingdom of Judah. It also records the ongoing tension between Judah and Israel, which frequently flares into warfare. Ironically, Asa's religious upturn is marred by conflict with his neighbor in the north. With the advent of the next king of Judah – Jehoshaphat – relations between north and south will change, as the two kingdoms join in a formal alliance.

---

15. We have noted that the conflict between Baasha and Asa focuses on a place called Ramah. Ramah is better known from a verse in Jeremiah: "a voice is heard in Ramah; …Rachel is crying for her sons, who are no more" (Jer. 31:15). Most commentators assume that her wailing is associated with this site due to the exile of the Jews from Ramah in Jeremiah 40:1. In light of our chapter, however, Ramah infamously symbolizes *sinat hinam*, groundless hatred within the Jewish people. This subtext is especially poignant considering that in the war between Asa and Baasha, Rachel's sons are fighting one another – the sons of Benjamin, allied with Judah, against the sons of Joseph: Ephraim and Manasseh!

1 Kings 15–16

Northern Turbulence

I f the southern state of Judah has had its ups and downs, the picture north of the border is significantly worse.[1] Religiously, Jeroboam's reforms become the norm, and unlike in Judah, the leadership fails to restore a pure mode of worship. Internally, each royal dynasty is brought to its untimely end through acts bloody assassinations, as opportunists repeatedly seize the throne. The following timeline of the northern kings (with dotted lines indicating a revolt or assassination) clearly demonstrates this state of affairs.

Jeroboam – 22 years
Nadab – 2 years

Baasha – 24 years
Elah – 2 years

Zimri – 7 days

Omri – 12 years

---

1. From 1 Kings 15:25 until the end of the book, the focus shifts to Israel, the northern kingdom.

Jeroboam's heir, Nadab, is assassinated by Baasha, from the tribe of Issachar. This revolt takes places as the nation is engaged in military conflict with the Philistine city of Gibbethon. Baasha takes advantage of King Nadab's presence in the war camp to kill the newly appointed monarch – only two years into office – and usurp the throne. As if this were not enough, he murders all of Jeroboam's offspring, decimating the royal family.[2]

Baasha's rule lasts twenty-four years, but his son, Elah, fares no better than King Nadab. Our one dismal glimpse of Elah's palace shows the king in a drunken stupor. After only two years in power, he is killed in a coup by Zimri, the commander of half the chariotry. This act of treachery gives rise to the pejorative biblical idiom "Zimri, murderer of your master" (II Kings 9:31), designating a subordinate guilty of cowardly treason.[3]

Zimri's political ambition is unmatched by his popularity, and his reign lasts a mere seven days. The army marches against the capital, Tirzah, to unseat him. Understanding that his revolution has failed, Zimri burns down the palace around himself in an act of suicide.

Several years follow in which there are two contenders for the throne:[4] Tibni and Omri. Omri, the chief of staff, eventually gains national support and is crowned king, and Tibni is killed.[5] With two rival candidates for the throne, these years are dogged by national infighting and a leadership vacuum.

---

2. Compare the act of Abimelech in Judges 9:5 and Saul's promise to David in I Samuel 24:21. The common practice in the case of an insurrection by an outsider was to execute the entire royal line in order to eliminate all contenders for the throne. An example of where such a tactic failed is found in II Kings 11:1–16, where (Queen) Athaliah kills all the male offspring of the king, but baby Joash is snatched from the dead, only to later become king.

3. This epithet is pronounced against the army officer Jehu by the evil Jezebel.

4. Rashi computes this five-year period: Zimri rules in the twenty-seventh year of Asa; Omri rules in Asa's thirty-first year. Since Zimri reigns only seven days, that leaves a five-year interim period. Others calculate the years differently

5. Yehuda Kiel, *Da'at Mikra, I Kings*, commentary on 16:21 [Hebrew].

The cumulative picture of this period offers little but violent upheaval. Furthermore, the disastrous civil war instigated by Baasha ends with the Aramean king Ben-Hadad seizing the north (15:16–22). Thus, for fifty-two dismal years, the northern kingdom lacks any stability or success. These are difficult times.

DIVINELY ORDAINED?

The Bible clearly states that Baasha has been divinely mandated to destroy Jeroboam and his family:

> As soon as he [Baasha] became king, he struck down all the house of Jeroboam; he did not spare a single soul...**in accordance with the word that the Lord had spoken through His servant Ahijah the Shilonite** – because of the sins Jeroboam committed.... (15:29)

Yet we later read:

> The word of the Lord came through the prophet Jehu son of Hanani against Baasha and against his house, due to all the evil he had done..., in being like the house of Jeroboam, and because he had struck him down. (16:7)

If God approved of Baasha's destruction of the royal house of Jeroboam and of his deposing King Nadab, why is Baasha condemned for the selfsame acts? Rashi explains:

> Since he [Baasha] committed the same sins, he had no right to kill him [Nadab]; hence, he was punished for his murder. Similarly, we find, "I will visit the blood of Jezreel upon the house of Jehu" (Hos. 1:4) – since Jehu failed to follow a path different from that of Ahab, he was punished for his murder. (Rashi on I Kings 16:7)

The house of Jeroboam was found guilty of forbidden religious practices. Had Baasha eschewed those practices, then his act of deposing the house of Jeroboam would have been justifiable; he would have been acting in God's agency. However, Baasha lacked the moral right to eliminate Jeroboam and his family, since he followed the same sinful path.

Ralbag adds a different dimension to Rashi's perspective, arguing that Baasha's motives in killing Jeroboam's descendants were personal rather than judicial or religious:

> One must question why this was considered a sin; after all, had Ahijah the prophet not transmitted the word of God that this would befall the house of Jeroboam? ...We can suggest that he [Baasha] was punished since he had clearly acted not [as punishment] for Jeroboam's sins, as he himself followed those practices, nor did he do this to fulfill God's word…, but rather out of an evil heart, so that he would be king and no one could contest his monarchy. Furthermore, he was punished because he killed him at a time when he [Nadab] was fighting God's wars against the Philistines…. (Ralbag on 15:29)

Abarbanel notes that the structure of this story contains a striking symmetry, equating Jeroboam and Baasha and underscoring their shared culpability:

> After Baasha killed the house of Jeroboam for its sins, and he himself committed the same sins, it is only appropriate that he should be punished in the same manner…. What would happen to Baasha's son was that which happened to Jeroboam's son: Just as Nadab [son of Jeroboam] ruled for two years, so did Elah [son of Baasha]. And just as Nadab was assassinated, so was Elah, fulfilling the words of the prophet that Baasha would suffer the same fate as Jeroboam. Look how incredible the similarities are![6]

---

6. Abarbanel, p. 572 in the standard edition.

The symmetry is indeed remarkable:

	House of Jeroboam	House of Baasha
Length of reign	22	24
Length of son's reign	2	2
Prophet's words:		
King	I raised you **from among the people** and made you leader of My people, Israel	I raised you **from the dust** 1 and made you leader of My people, Israel
Sin	You have made for yourself other gods... **you have provoked Me to anger** (14:9)	You walked in the ways of Jeroboam... **to provoke Me to anger** by their sins (16:2)
Punishment	I will cut off from Jeroboam every last male in Israel – bondsman and freeman. I will **burn up** the house of Jeroboam as one burns dung, until it is all gone (14:10)	I am about to **burn up** Baasha and his house, and I will make your house like that of Jeroboam son of Nebat (16:3)
	Anyone belonging to Jeroboam who dies in the town shall be devoured by dogs, and all who dies in the open country shall be devoured by the birds of the sky (14:11)	Anyone belonging to Baasha who dies in the town shall be devoured by dogs, and all who dies in the open country shall be devoured by the birds of the sky (16:4)
Fulfillment	When he [Baasha] ruled... he killed off all the house of Jeroboam; he did not spare a single soul... as God spoke (15:29)	When he [Zimri] ruled... he killed off all the house of Baasha; he did not spare a single male (16:12)

The northern kings remain entangled in the sins of Jeroboam, and each successive ruler lacks the moral justification to depose his predecessor. Though God wishes to see Jeroboam removed from the national leadership, Baasha fails to act more faithfully toward God, and therefore he finds himself equally blameworthy.

THE DIVINE PLAN AND HUMAN DECISIONS

On the basis of this discussion, we will devote a few words to how the Bible illustrates and communicates God's justice in history. There are two dimensions to events in the Bible. First, there is the Godly dimension, governed by divine reward and punishment. Second, there is the worldly realm – a function of human decision-making.[7]

Frequently, a biblical passage will combine the two dimensions – the Godly and the human – but this overlap does not indicate that God is intervening, manipulating, or even actively guiding human decisions. A few examples should illustrate this point.

1. In chapter 2, Abiathar is banished from Jerusalem by Solomon:
   Solomon dismissed Abiathar from the office of priest of the Lord, **thus fulfilling what the Lord had spoken** at Shiloh regarding the house of Eli. (1 Kings 2:27)
   Solomon exiles Abiathar for his own political reasons; he receives no instruction by God. The Bible injects its own (divine) perspective that this occurrence fulfilled an ancient prophecy (see 1 Sam. 2:32–33).

2. In chapter 12, we read Rehoboam's harsh and insensitive response to the nation:
   The king did not listen to the people; **for the Lord had brought it about** to fulfill the promise that the Lord had made through Ahijah the Shilonite to Jeroboam son of Nebat. (12:15)

---

7. For more on these ideas, see Yehuda Kiel, *Da'at Mikra, 1 Samuel* (Jerusalem: Mossad Harav Kook, 1981), Introduction, 48–49 [Hebrew]; Yehuda Elitzur, *Israel and the Bible: Studies in Geography, History and Biblical Thought*, ed. Yoel Elitzur and Amos Frisch (Ramat Gan: Bar-Ilan University Press, 1999), 253–60 [Hebrew].

God does not blind Rehoboam morally or politically; He does not force his hand. Rehoboam makes his own (erroneous) administrative decision. But the Bible's "voice" interjects that this human, political decision is the fulfillment of God's word. There is no curtailment of free will; in fact, the opposite is true. When Rehoboam exercises his free choice, deciding on a tough response to the nation, the Bible informs us that this act aligns with a divine decree.

3. In the book of Judges, Samson expresses his intent to marry a Philistine woman:

> His father and mother did not realize that this was the Lord's doing; He was seeking a pretext against the Philistines. (14:4)

Samson genuinely fell in love with this woman. He was not coerced by God; he made his own decision. But in hindsight, the Bible looks at the event and sees the hand of God guiding history. The prophet tells the reader that God is exacting His vengeance against the Philistines, even as Samson makes an independent, this-worldly decision. Once again, the biblical text articulates a coalescence of the Godly and human dimensions.

These are but three instances of a phenomenon found throughout the Bible.[8] Applying this understanding to our chapter, it is quite clear that when Baasha and Zimri each seized the throne, they had no idea that their act was part of a divine plan. They were motivated by ambition; they wanted power. It is the prophetic narrator of the book of Kings who interjects, reminding the reader that these murders accord with God's plan – in Baasha's case, "in accordance with the word that the Lord had spoken through His servant Ahijah the Shilonite" (1 Kings 15:29). We should not think Baasha had religious or righteous motives when he "killed off all the house of Jeroboam; he did not spare a single soul" (15:29). His story affords us yet another window into God's historical plan within the orbit of human actions.

---

8. For further examples, see Joshua 11:19–20; 1 Samuel 2:25; and 11 Samuel 17:14.

1 Kings 16

Omri and Ahab: An Introduction

King Omri and his royal dynasty are the answer to the crisis of instability in the northern kingdom. Omri's reign is characterized by political security, military strength, and peace and cooperation between the northern and southern kingdoms. His development of a new capital city, Samaria, brings a spirit of renewal to the kingdom of Israel.

Omri's opening advantage is his rise to power as a popular leader; he is the people's choice (16:21–22).[1] Omri's widespread backing establishes his monarchy on a stable footing. He extends his power beyond his borders; both the Bible and other sources record Omri's conquest of neighboring Moab.[2]

---

1. In this instance, the term *ha'am* (lit., the people) might refer to the military, as in 16:15–16. See Yehuda Kiel, *Da'at Mikra, 1 Kings* [Hebrew].
2. See II Kings 1:1. In addition, the Mesha Stele (c. 850 BCE), unearthed at the site of ancient Dibon (Dhiban, Jordan) in 1868 and now housed in the Louvre, records Omri's control of Moab and King Mesha's revolt against Israel (see II Kings 3).

Ironically, this stability and prosperity is in inverse proportion to his monotheistic commitment. Omri and his son Ahab are described at the outset as kings who were more evil than all who preceded them.[3] As we shall see, these two aspects of Omri's reign – economic prosperity and spiritual decline – are far from disconnected.

SAMARIA

> In the thirty-first year of King Asa of Judah, Omri became king over Israel for twelve years; he reigned in Tirzah for six years. He bought the hill of Samaria from Shemer for two talents of silver; he built [a city on] the hill and named the city he built Samaria, after Shemer, the owner of the hill. (16:23–24)

In these lines, we read of Omri's purchase of a site on which to build a new capital city. What motivates him to shift the capital from Tirzah to Samaria?

Omri's predecessor, Zimri, burned the palace down, taking his own life (16:18). Omri therefore inherits a dilapidated royal center. He has two choices – he can renovate the royal city in Tirzah or begin again. He chooses the second option, living in Tirzah for the first six years of his reign while designing, supervising, and constructing a magnificent, well-fortified city in Samaria. The fact that, centuries later, Samaria withstood a three-year siege by the fierce Assyrian army[4] testifies to the city's impressive strength, storage facilities, and defense installations. By the time Omri moved to Samaria, six years after assuming the throne, the city was probably already built in the grandest, most modern fashion. This transfer of the capital establishes Omri as a planner and forward-thinker.

But the primary motivation for moving the capital is strategic. Tirzah was a central Canaanite town in Joshua's era.[5] Jeroboam adopted it as his capital (14:17),[6] but Tirzah was off the beaten track, facing

---

3. 1 Kings 16:25, 33.
4. See 11 Kings 17:5.
5. See Joshua 12:24.
6. While Jeroboam's kingdom began in Shechem (1 Kings 12:25), its capital moved to

eastward, toward the desert, and lacking direct access to international trade routes, specifically to the Mediterranean sea ports. Omri bases his foreign policy on his alliance with Phoenicia.[7] To this end, he places his capital close to the north-south road – the main internal Israelite byway – but, more important, on a central east-west artery, allowing access to the coast. Samaria became the capital until the fall of the northern kingdom, and was later known by its Greek name, Sebastia.

Shemer and the Land of Israel

The text mentions the purchase of the land and stresses its original ownership by Shemer. It is quite astounding that Omri, who crafts this location into a metropolis, fails to name the city after himself, preserving instead the identity of the original landowner.

> This purchase is a positive reflection upon the kings of Israel, in that they did not expropriate land belonging to citizens [even for royal purposes], but rather paid for it in full. (*Da'at Mikra, 1 Kings*)[8]

This point is especially poignant in light of a later episode in which Omri's son, Ahab, attempts to wrest land from his neighbor Naboth. Naboth spurns the king's proposal on principle:

> God forbid I should give you my ancestral inheritance. (21:3)

In a reflection of a fundamentally Jewish value system as regards the land of Israel, the entire land returns to its ancestral owners in the Jubilee year (*yovel*). The sovereign is not the master of the land. God is, and He has entrusted it to the national body politic, with each family proudly

---

Tirzah shortly thereafter (14:17).

7. There were economic and security reasons for this alliance. In these chapters, Ben-hadad of Syria is depicted as a major regional military force. Omri's alliance with Phoenicia likely aimed to resist Syrian pressure as well. See W.F. Albright, *The Biblical Period from Abraham to Ezra: An Historical Survey* (New York: Harper and Row, 1949), 61–63.

8. See Kiel, *Da'at Mikra, 1 Kings*.

taking responsibility for its estate. Omri therefore perpetuates the identity of Samaria's ancestral owner, recognizing that he himself is not the master of the land. For a king of Omri's power, this is no small statement.

Ḥazal appreciate his connection to the land of Israel, praising him for his building of the city of Samaria:

> R. Yoḥanan said: Why did Omri deserve to be king? Because he added a city in the land of Israel. (*Sanhedrin* 102b)

RELIGIOUS LOW POINT

Spiritually, however, the kingdom has reached its lowest point yet:

> Omri did evil in the eyes of the Lord; he was worse than all who preceded him. He followed all the ways of Jeroboam son of Nebat and the sins he committed and caused Israel to sin…. (16:25–26)

This passage is somewhat contradictory. If "Omri followed all the ways of Jeroboam," then why is he "worse than all who preceded him"? We can suggest that it is Omri who sets the negative trajectory of the kingdom by aligning it economically, culturally, and religiously with the wealthy trading region of Phoenicia.[9] The worst of this alliance is the marriage of his son Ahab to a Phoenician princess. With this union, Omri plants the seeds of religious waywardness, which bear their poison fruit during the reign of Ahab.[10]

AHAB

> Ahab son of Omri became king over Israel in the thirty-eighth year of King Asa of Judah, and Ahab son of Omri reigned over Israel in Samaria for twenty-two years. Ahab son of Omri did more evil in the eyes of the Lord than all who preceded him. Following the sins of Jeroboam son of Nebat was trivial for him; he took as a wife Jezebel, daughter of Ethbaal, king of the Phoenicians, and

---

9. Ralbag offers a different explanation.
10. See Micah 6:16, in which Omri is placed in the same sinful category as his son Ahab.

he went and served Baal and bowed to it. He set up an altar to Baal in the temple of Baal that he built in Samaria. Ahab made the *ashera*, and Ahab continued to anger the Lord, God of Israel, more than all the kings of Israel who preceded him. (16:29–33)

Ahab marries the daughter of the king of Sidon, Ethbaal. The Baal suffix reflects the spiritual allegiances of Phoenicia. Classic Israelite names also frequently express religious affiliation, as they bear the suffix Yah or Yahu (as in Adoniyah/Adonijah, Yedidyah/Jedidiah, Ḥizkiyahu/Hezekiah, Yoshiyahu/Josiah, etc.), referring to God's name YHVH. Jezebel's father's name highlights the pagan orientation of Phoenicia.[11]

The alliance with Phoenicia thrusts Baal worship into the very center of life in the northern kingdom. Jezebel, Ahab's wife, is an ardent and ruthless missionary of Baal. With her hundreds of idolatrous prophets,[12] she outlaws the worship of God and persecutes those who prophesy in His name (18:4, 13; 19:2).[13] Jezebel's lack of conscience[14] is unprecedented even against the corrupt political backdrop of the northern kingdom. Her dominance of her husband coupled with her fearless resolve contribute significantly to Israel's spiritual deterioration.[15]

---

11. Jezebel's name is unparalleled in ancient Near Eastern sources. Some have speculated that it is an abbreviation of *Avi-Zevul* – "My father is a ruler"; the word *zevul* (as in Zebulun and in Judges 9:27) found in Phoenician and Ugaritic sources indicates leadership. However, the transition from *zevul* to *zevel* is seen as a prophetic midrash of sorts, a parody of this wicked queen's name; *zevel* means manure! This motif is reinforced by the reference to dung in Jezebel's curse in II Kings 9:37. See Moshe Garsiel's article on names in the Ahab story and the intertextual wordplays they create: "Midrashic Name Derivations in the Elijah Cycle," in *Gevaryahu Jubilee Volume* (Jerusalem: Kiryat Sefer, 1989), pp. 149–55 (Hebrew).

12. It appears that there was more than a single ensemble of prophets; see I Kings 18:19, 22, where beyond the 400 prophets of Baal, 450 Ashera prophets are denoted as "eating at Jezebel's table."

13. Ahab himself threatens a prophet of God in 22:26–27.

14. See especially the story of Naboth's vineyard in chapter 21.

15. In the book of Kings, kings rather than their wives are generally singled out for punishment. Yet Jezebel receives her own condemnation from God (21:23). Her influence upon Ahab is noted in 21:25. See also the fulfillment of God's prophecy in II Kings 9:35.

The effects are overwhelming. Under Ahab, Baal becomes the official religion. The Israelites have dabbled in other gods, but always perceived a fundamental alignment with the God of Israel. Now, with the temple of Baal functioning as the official and exclusive center of worship in the capital, the leadership has discarded the God of Israel entirely! We can thus appreciate why Jeroboam's sins are deemed "trivial" in comparison to Ahab's.

How could Ahab, an Israelite king, fall so thoroughly into the hands of Baal, a foreign deity? In today's Western world, with its separation between religion and state (at least to some extent), we fail to understand the degree to which economic and political alliances went hand in hand with religious orientation in antiquity. Throughout the Bible, whenever Israel allies itself economically and militarily with a regional power, wider societal and cultural effects – including religious influences – are not far behind.[16] In a contemporary analogy, countries militarily and economically allied with the West are generally receptive to its cultural norms, adopting many aspects of its worldview and ideological priorities as well as its fashion, food, and other features of its lifestyle. Similarly, in seeking the economic and political strength of Phoenicia, the northern kingdom opens itself up to Phoenician culture in its entirety, including its gods. In the words of the famed scholar of the ancient Near East, W.F. Albright:

> In judging the frequent triumphs of Canaanite polytheism in Israel, we must always bear in mind that polytheism had a popular appeal in many ways like that of the dominant secularism of our own age. The wealth, science, and aesthetic culture of that age were lined up on the side of Canaanite religion.... Compared with Phoenicia, the lands of Judah and Israel were very poor, very rustic, and far behind the spirit of the day in fashions, arts of civilization, and material pleasures of life. All the sinister fascination of the elaborate proto-sciences of magic

---

16. Examples include the Assyrian influence on Ahaz (II Kings 16) and Manasseh (ibid. 21).

and divination was marshaled in defense of polytheism against the stern, almost savage simplicity of Mosaic theology. When Israelite women employed the same amulets as their Canaanite friends in order to ward off evil spirits, they unconsciously made it more difficult to save their children from the perils of the Canaanite way of life. The extraordinary thing is that the way of Moses succeeded in Israel in spite of the forces drawn up against it![17]

BAAL AND THE RAIN

The chapters we are about to study chronicle the epic struggle between two personalities – Ahab, king of Israel, and his nemesis, the great prophet Elijah. Ahab and Jezebel's Baal worship constitutes the focal point of the tension, but the medium that generates much of the drama is a drought. Elijah withholds rainfall to pressure Ahab and his nation to abandon their commitment to Baal. Why is rain chosen as the means of influencing Ahab? Is there a connection between Baal and rain?

Baal is the rain or storm god, responsible for fertility and agricultural success. The Talmud even refers to a field irrigated exclusively by rain as a *sedeh Baal*, a "Baal field."[18] The primary agricultural and economic drawback in Eretz Yisrael and Phoenicia – two lands essentially on the same geographical continuum – is lack of rain. With no great rivers to provide irrigation, the land of Israel relies solely on rainfall. which is unpredictable and sporadic.[19] Hence the enormous attraction to Baal. The Torah asserts that total commitment to God's laws is the only means of guaranteeing rain. Baal worship, however, ostensibly offered an alternative guarantee of rainfall, and thus economic stability and prosperity. The desperate Israelite farmer, whose crops and livelihood were threatened by drought, might have felt that a visit to the local priest of Baal was an excusable religious infraction if it were to ensure his family's survival.

---

17. Albright, *Biblical Period*, 61.
18. *Moed Katan* 2a–b; *Bava Batra* 28a.
19. See Deuteronomy 11:10–12.

We should not dismiss Baal as merely a figurine or molten image –
whole worlds of mythology bolstered its worship. Baal constituted the
male representative of the rain god. Its female counterpart, Ashera, took
two forms: a tree or a female image or figurine, frequently a pregnant or
nursing woman. The theory was that Baal (the rain) fertilized Ashera
(the tree).[20] This union of male and female led to cultic sexual rites in
the temples of Baal; the sexual union of male and female temple prostitutes (*kadesh* and *kedesha*)[21] would simulate and stimulate the god's
bringing the desired rainfall and its ensuing abundance. Thus, we can
appreciate the connection made by the Torah (for example, in Leviticus
18) between idolatry and illicit sexual practices.

This background may help us understand the allure of this deity,
which seemed to exhibit an almost magnetic attraction for the Jewish
people from the time of the Judges (Judges 2:11) through the Temple's
destruction (11 Kings 23:4).

HIEL OF BETHEL AND THE CITY OF JERICHO

As we continue to study the text that introduces Ahab and his kingdom,
we encounter a mysterious and seemingly disconnected verse:

> During his [Ahab's] reign, Hiel of Bethel built Jericho; he laid
> its foundations at the cost of Abiram, his firstborn, and set its
> gates in place at the cost of Segub, his youngest, in accordance
> with the words that the Lord had spoken through Joshua son of
> Nun. (1 Kings 16:34)

What does the building of Jericho have to do with the death of Hiel's
sons? Furthermore, what is the relevance to Ahab? We cannot claim
these stories are unrelated; the verse explicitly links them with the phrase
"During his reign." Why?

The story of Hiel is based upon an ancient curse recorded in the
book of Joshua. After the fall of Jericho, Joshua pronounces an oath
condemning anyone who rebuilds the city:

---

20. Baal and Ashera appear together in 1 Kings 18:19.
21. See Deuteronomy 23:18–19.

> Cursed of the Lord be the man who builds the city of Jericho: he shall lay its foundations at the cost of his firstborn, and set its gates at the cost of his youngest. (Josh. 6:26)

Hiel abrogates this oath; he builds Jericho and suffers the consequences. But why does this peculiar curse resurface at this specific juncture?[22]

Unraveling Jericho

One approach is to frame this episode within the context of the national conquest and, conversely, the threat of exile. Jericho is the first city that Israelites captured in Canaan. Joshua vows that the city will be abandoned to ruin as a living monument, an everlasting sign of God's victory at that site. Hiel's obstinate rebuilding of Jericho at huge personal loss represents the undoing of the miraculous entry into the land, removing God as the national benefactor and savior, and unraveling the divine mandate that bestowed the land on the nation. By implication, Hiel is, in some manner, inviting exile and the retraction of God's protection and providence. Accordingly, his actions are connected with the reign of the idolatrous king Ahab, whose regime of Baal threatens the very tenure of Israel in its land.

Crisis of Values

A simpler approach views this event from the perspective of national priorities, or the degree to which the nation is in touch with its identity.

The entry into Canaan is a formative event for the Israelite nation. Time after time, God instructs the people to enact ceremonies that remind them of the significance of the historical moment. Some events are designed to highlight the process that they themselves are experiencing (such as via the ceremony at Mount Ebal and the celebration of Passover). Others involve the construction of memorials for future

---

22. Some have viewed this anecdote as a footnote to the worship of Baal. For example: "It was a frequent practice – in an effort to placate their gods – to kill young children and bury them in the foundations of a house or public building at the time of construction.... [Thus,] 'In his days did Hiel of Beth-Elite [*sic*] build Jericho: he laid the foundation thereof in Abiram his firstborn....'" Howard E. Vos, *An Introduction to Bible Archaeology* (Chicago: Moody Press, 1953), 19.

generations, such as the stones raised from the Jordan riverbed and imprinted with the text of the Torah.

> In time to come, when your children ask their fathers: "What is the meaning of these stones?" tell your children: "Here the Israelites crossed the Jordan on dry land." (Josh. 4:21; see also 4:6)

In other words, these monuments are intended to educate, to instill a legacy, a sense of national heritage and historical importance. Similarly, the ruins of Jericho symbolize the miraculous victory of the founding of the country for all eternity.

What does it take for Hiel to build upon a national heritage site? Imagine if a property developer sought to build luxury housing on the Gettysburg battlefield or turn the palace of Versailles into an amusement park! If someone turns a national icon into a real-estate development, it reflects a vacuum of national values and education, a total lack of pride in, understanding of, and appreciation for a nation's history and priorities.

If Hiel can rebuild Jericho, then the damage caused by Ahab's reign is profound and far-reaching. The Israelites have abandoned their Jewish heritage.

ENTER ELIJAH!

It is at this juncture that we meet the powerful personality of the prophet Elijah, who enters the story unannounced and – in characteristic Elijah fashion – with a devastating pronouncement:

> As the Lord lives, the God of Israel whom I serve, these years will have no dew or rain except at my word! (1 Kings 17:1)

Again, this line seems to be a non-sequitur. What is the connection between the events here? The Talmud offers an ingenious solution, creating a cohesive new reading that links the disjointed verses:

> What is the sequence here? Elijah and Ahab went to comfort Hiel in his mourning. Ahab said to Elijah: "Is it possible that the curse of the student [Joshua] was fulfilled, and the curse of Moses our

teacher was not? After all, it states, '[if] you turn aside and worship other gods…. God's anger will burn against you, and He will shut up the heavens, and there will be no rain' (Deut. 11:16–17). All Israel is serving idols, and the rain has not stopped!"

Immediately, Elijah said, "As the Lord lives, the God of Israel whom I serve, these years will have no dew or rain except at my word!" (Rabbi Yosef Kara, based on *Sanhedrin* 113a)

According to this creative reconstruction, Elijah and Ahab meet when they come to comfort Hiel after the death of his sons. Presumably, the conversation at the *shiva* house turns to Joshua's curse and whether Hiel's sons died because of it. Ahab rejects the Torah's morbid pronouncements. After all, he says, Moses' curses are clearly ineffective! Deuteronomy declares that if the nation practices idolatry, rainfall will be withheld. I have promoted idolatry like no other king of Israel, says Ahab, yet the rain is falling – in fact, the country's economy is booming!

This "quote" of Ahab focuses our attention on the critical difficulty regarding his reign. Ahab abandons God, yet his kingdom flourishes. In fact, this king's prosperity and idolatry both find their source in Phoenicia; perhaps his adoption of Phoenician culture is the secret of his success! Ahab has not witnessed or experienced a contradiction between his religious orientation and the national fortune.

At this point, Elijah steps in and swears in God's name: "As the Lord lives…there will be no…rain except by my word." Elijah will uphold the honor and commitment of God; he will enforce the Torah's pledge, the divine stipulation. If Ahab continues with his idolatry, there can be no rain. And indeed, the upcoming chapters describe a terrible three-year drought.

Elijah's outburst raises serious questions. If he is outraged, why is God not angry? Is Elijah correct? Furthermore, is he making his radical pronouncement as an emissary of God? It is to the fiery figure of Elijah, and these questions, that we shall now turn our attention.

I Kings 17

Three Years of Drought and Three Miracles

Elijah the prophet has become a fascinating symbol in Jewish life. According to tradition, he visits each and every circumcision ceremony,[1] his presence is felt at the seder table, and he is commonly known as the herald of the Messiah.[2] His biblical persona, however, is rather different. Elijah is a zealot (19:10, 14)[3] – agitated, demanding, and passionate; he is the brusque, itinerant prophet who causes fire to descend from heaven to earth, and who ends his life by ascending heavenward in a fiery chariot (II Kings 2:11).

The captivating tale of his determined fight against Ahab's regime of Baal begins with Elijah's fierce and bold announcement of a

---

1. See Malachi 3:1; *Pirkei DeRabbi Eliezer* 29; *Zohar*, Genesis 93a.
2. Malachi 3:23. For more on Elijah in the *aggada* and in Jewish folklore, see *Encyclopedia Judaica* (Jerusalem: Keter, 1972), vol. 6, s.v. "Elijah" (cols. 635–40).
3. Elijah is further identified with another biblical zealot, Phinehas; see *Midrash HaGadol*, Numbers 25:12, as well as *Yalkut Shimoni* and other midrashim. I deal with this midrash at the close of our discussion of I Kings 19.

devastating drought, which lasts three years, until his showdown against Baal at Mount Carmel. The story spans three chapters of I Kings:

> Chapter 17 – Three years of drought
> Chapter 18 – Elijah's confrontation with Ahab, the contest on Mount Carmel, and the advent of rain
> Chapter 19 – Elijah's crisis at Mount Horeb, and the appointment of Elisha

Several other episodes in the book of Kings feature Elijah,[4] but the story told in chapters 17–19 is a single continuous narrative, an epic religious, national, and personal drama.

DID ELIJAH INITIATE THE DROUGHT?

> Elijah the Tishbite, an inhabitant of Gilead, said to Ahab: "As the Lord lives, the God of Israel whom I serve, these years will have no dew or rain except at my word." (17:1)

With these words, Elijah proclaims a three-year drought (as indicated in 18:1). When we read this verse, we are disoriented by the suddenness of it all. The Bible customarily provides biographical background regarding its main characters, and a prophet is frequently introduced with the drama of his inaugural prophecy.[5] In contrast, the description of Elijah as "the Tishbite" from Gilead hardly explains the identity of this powerful prophet.

A key question intrigues us. Is the mysterious Elijah proclaiming this famine independently or upon God's command? On the one hand, the phrase "As the Lord lives… whom I serve," implies divine subservience. On the other hand, the assertion that there will be no rain "except at **my** word" seems to portray Elijah as the instigator of the drought.

---

4. See I Kings 21 (the vineyard of Naboth) and II Kings 1 (the confrontation with the messengers of King Ahaziah of Israel); and 2 (Elijah's miraculous death).
5. As are Moses at the burning bush (Ex. 3), Gideon (Judges 6–7), Samuel (1 Sam. 1–3), Isaiah (Is. 6), Jeremiah (Jer. 1), and Ezekiel (Ezek. 1–3).

Elijah's Zeal

The commentaries are divided on this point. Some insist that Elijah initiates the drought independently:

> Elijah did this without a divine command and without permission, but rather by his own will and choice, to pursue his zealousness for God. (Abarbanel)

> Elijah decreed concerning the rainfall in his zealousness for God because of the worship of idolatry, as it is written in the Torah, "[if] you turn aside and worship other gods and bow down to them, God's anger will burn against you, and He will shut up the heavens, and there will be no rain" (Deut. 11:16–17). He was sure God would fulfill his pronouncement. About this type of action, it says: "You pronounced a decree, and [God] fulfilled it for you" (Job 22:28). (Radak)

The radical conclusion of these commentators is that Elijah initiates the cessation of rainfall in his outrage over Ahab's violation of God's law. It is as if the prophet decides that God Himself is failing to fulfill His own Torah. After all, God decreed that when the nation turned to "other gods," God would "shut up the heavens" and withhold rain. Elijah makes the pronouncement and, curiously, God listens!

Rabbi Elchanan Samet supports this view:

> Significantly, Elijah himself makes no mention of any divine source of his mission. He does not introduce his declaration with the words "So says God," nor does he formulate his oath in such a way that we may understand that it is God's words that he is speaking.... More important, we reach this very conclusion from Elijah's language. The very need to utter an oath, together with the personal formulation of the oath, demonstrates that this withholding of the rainfall is an independent initiative on the prophet's part. A regular prophetic mission – in which the prophet foretells, in God's name, the punishment that will come upon Israel – requires no oath. But when the prophet decrees

of his own will, and his listeners understand his words correctly, then his oath comes to strengthen their faith in the fulfillment of his decree.[6]

This perspective portrays Elijah as engaged in a personal quest to prove God's power beyond any reasonable doubt and to demonstrate and publicize the falsity of Baal worship. Elijah's religious passion in instigating this drought is radical – he is more zealous than God Himself! – yet he fully expects God to support him in this endeavor.

By God's Word

Other commentators view Elijah as God's agent:

> Elijah, **by God's command**, issued a most severe decree in withholding dew and rain throughout those years, until [he] would allow them to fall, **as a messenger of God.** (Ralbag)

> There is no doubt that his [Elijah's] words were from God. (Rabbi Joseph ibn Kaspi)

Prof. Uriel Simon adopts this view in his reading of this story:

> …the text goes on to state both explicitly and emphatically that Elijah went to Wadi Cherith (17:2) and from there to Zarephath (17:8), back to Samaria (18:1), in obedience to divine commands. Are we to infer from this conspicuous contrast that the omission of a divine command to appear before Ahab means that Elijah brought such a severe drought on Israel on his own initiative and that he was willing to risk so daring an oath on the same basis? The rejection of this hypothesis is more plausible and more in keeping with the personality of Elijah as deployed in the rest of the

---

6. Elchanan Samet, *The Elijah Narratives* (Jerusalem: Maaliyot Press, 2003), 30 [Hebrew]. Note that an abridged English translation of this Rabbi Samet's book appears on the Virtual Beit Midrash, http://vbm-torah.org/eliyahu.htm.

story, as well as the explicit statements in his two prayers – one to revive the child (17:20) and the other to bring down fire (18:36).[7]

We thus have two diametrically opposing views. Is God commanding Elijah, or is Elijah issuing a decree that God supports? Is Elijah the zealous prophet of God, or is he simply God's loyal and obedient servant?

As we study chapter 17, we shall work with both of these readings.

THREE YEARS – THREE STORIES

Chapter 17 is critically placed between Elijah's decree of the drought (17:1) and God's command that he bring rain (18:1). The chapter contains three miraculous incidents, which continue Elijah's story against the backdrop of the national drought and the ensuing famine:

17:2–7	Wadi Cherith – ravens bring food to Elijah
17:8–16	Zarephath – miraculous production of food
17:17–24	Zarephath – the death and revival of a boy

These three stories represent a progression in Elijah's miraculous power. In the first story, food is miraculously procured and delivered to him by ravens, but the food itself is natural and non-miraculous.[8] In the second story, flour and oil are produced unnaturally. In the third story, it is not food that Elijah produces, but life itself, as he miraculously revives the child.

Upon closer examination, we can discern additional modes of progression. Let us chart the literary structure of the narrative:

---

7. Uriel Simon, *Reading Prophetic Narratives* (Bloomington: University of Indiana Press, 1997), 160.

8. Some explain this story in a completely non-miraculous manner, arguing that these were not ravens (*orvim* in Hebrew), but people from a town called Orev (see Judges 7:25); see Rabbi Yosef Kara based on *Gen. Rabba* 33:5.

   There is further discussion regarding the origin of the food. According to the Talmud, it came either from Ahab's table or from that of Jehoshaphat, king of Judah (*Sanhedrin* 113a). Perhaps the first opinion implies that Elijah, just like Ahab, is somewhat responsible for the nation's ruin.

Introduction

> ...**these years** will have no dew or rain except **at my word.**
> (17:1)

1. Wadi Cherith: Elijah alone

   > And (*Vayehi*) **the word of God** came to him, saying: "**Go**
   > from here...." And at the **end of a year** (*yamim*), the wadi
   > dried up, for there was no rain in the land. (17:2–3, 7)

2. Zarephath: Elijah and the widow

   > And (*Vayehi*) **the word of God** came to him, saying: "Get up
   > and **go** ...." And she and he and her household ate for a **year**
   > (*yamim*)...according to the **word of God**.... (17:8–9, 15–16)

3. Zarephath: Elijah, the widow, and her son

   > And (*Vayehi*) after these things...and the **word of God** in
   > your mouth is true. (17:17, 24)

Conclusion

> And (*Vayehi*) after many **years** (*yamim*), the **word of God**
> came to Elijah in the third **year,** saying, "Go appear before
> Ahab, and I will send rain...." (18:1)

This story is clearly divided into three scenes. An essential element of
the story is the passage of time, as each **year** is carefully measured.[9] As
each year passes, the famine intensifies. In the first scene, as the famine
begins, there is water in the wadi, and food is available for the birds to
bring, but at the end of the year, the wadi is dry, and Elijah must move
on. In the second episode, he meets a woman foraging for two simple
pieces of wood with which to bake her final provisions – as she tells
him, "...we shall eat...and then die" (17:12). People are dying of hunger.
The third scene reveals the depth of disease that regularly accompanies
famine: The woman's child falls sick and dies. Though this incident is

---

9. Here the word *yamim* (lit., days) indicates a year. For other examples of this usage,
   see Genesis 24:55, Leviticus 25:29, and 1 Samuel 27:7.

not explicitly attributed to the famine, Elijah's language – "...**even** to this widow with whom I live will You bring calamity, slaying her son?" (17:20) – indicates that this boy's death reflects the plague gripping the nation. Thus, the three scenes depict the growing severity of the famine.

A further progression involves Elijah's location. In the first scene, he is living in a wadi, apparently outside Ahab's jurisdiction. Later (18:10), we read of Ahab's desperate efforts to locate Elijah, yet the prophet eludes him, demonstrating his superiority over the king. Elijah's second location, "Zarephath, which is by Sidon" (17:8), is also outside Ahab's borders and beyond his reach; Elijah is still in hiding. But this location takes him to the heart of Baal country, to the homeland of Ethbaal and Jezebel. Elijah's ability to produce food and create life within the jurisdiction of Baal accentuates its inability to likewise care for the population, which underscores the triumph of God's word over Baalism.

After charting the ascending scale of this chapter, we wish to understand its message. How does it contribute to the wider drama of Elijah?

THE RAVENS AND THE WIDOW

The choice of the raven as the conveyor of food to Elijah demands some probing. On the one hand, the raven's large size makes it ideal for transporting food. Furthermore, Noah also sends out a raven in search of a means of subsistence. Yet this parallel may point to a shared trait of Noah and Elijah – their extreme disengagement from society.

However, the raven is an "unclean" bird (Lev. 11:15) and widely viewed in folklore as cruel. Psalms 147:9 speaks of the "offspring of the raven that call out," and Job 38:41 adds that the raven fails to feed its young, leaving them hungry. Why does God choose this callous bird as His messenger? Malbim explains:

> He [God] orchestrates His sustenance through ravens, which are cruel by nature, so he [Elijah] should remember that he similarly has been cruel to the nation, killing them by famine.

Rashi adopts a similar approach regarding the drying of the water in the wadi:

> "The wadi dried up" (17:7) – So he [Elijah] would understand the need for rain … for it was severe in God's eyes that Israel was dying by famine.

These commentators view Elijah as actively withholding the rainfall; God utilizes a variety of media to indicate to him that the time has come to exercise compassion. Elijah, however, appears to be impervious God's prompting.

This line of thinking is valid regarding the widow in Zarephath as well. In the introductory scene, we are witness to a dreadful image, as the widow collects a few twigs in order to cook her last meager rations – a little flour and oil. Elijah arrives and requests water, then food. He adds insult to injury by insisting that she "make me a small cake **first**, and bring it to me, and for you and your son **afterward**" (17:13). How can Elijah be so insensitive? Does he not see the woman's suffering? Even if he knows God will perform a miracle (17:14), is this emotional indifference necessary?

> The main point is so he will see … the suffering of a widow and orphan, upon whom God Himself has mercy, and concerning whom He warns against causing them suffering (Ex. 21:22). For were it not for him [Elijah, who was to reside with them], the two of them would die. As she says to him: "That I may prepare it for myself and for my son, that we may eat it and then die." From them, he will see that a great many like them, among the masses of Israel, will die of hunger. And because he is good, he will pray for mercy for them, that there be rain and dew by his word. (Rabbi Moses Alshikh, *Mar'ot Hatzov'ot*)

Samet's Approach

These observations lead Samet to view the escalating intensity of chapter 17 as expressive of God's increasing impatience with Elijah. In his passion and zeal for God, the prophet has decreed a national famine, but in so doing he has afflicted the country with epidemic and death. God Himself cajoles Elijah to recant, to show compassion and rescind his decree.

Elijah's first encounter with the results of the drought takes place at Wadi Cherith…. This demonstrates to him the destructive effects of the cessation of rain *with regard to the land* – its streams and its plant and animal life. But the drying up of the wadi is also significant *for Elijah himself*, since he is dependent on its water. Nevertheless, **this [demonstration] does not cause him to retract his oath**….

The second encounter takes place at the gates of Zarephath. Here, Elijah views the meaning of the drought on the *human level* – and specifically what it means to the weakest sectors of society, a widow and an orphan. But here again, the suffering of the woman and her child because of drought and famine, *although affecting Elijah himself*, since his sustenance depends on them, **does not cause him to retract his oath.** To overcome the problem that has presented itself, he invokes a miracle that will allow him to continue living a whole year in the widow's home in Zarephath.

Elijah's third encounter with the results of the drought takes place at the end of the year of lodging with "the woman who was mistress of the house" (17:17), with the death of her son. Now Elijah is forced to contemplate the most tragic consequences of the famine: the death of a poor, orphaned child, illustrating the fate of many more like him. Once again, the event *affects Elijah's personal fate*: The child's mother blames him for the death and asks him to leave.[10]

According to this approach, the thrust of the story is how God seeks to dislodge Elijah from his intransigent refusal to capitulate. In the end (18:1), God orders Elijah to stop the famine.

Samet's reading, while rooted in traditional commentaries, is difficult both textually and logically.

Textually, God instructs Elijah explicitly throughout the chapter, and the prophet is fully responsive to His guidance. As noted, the repetition of the phrase "the word of God" (17:2, 8, 16, 24) emphasizes

---

10. Samet, *The Elijah Narratives*, 68–69.

Elijah's utter obedience.[11] It is difficult to perceive him as completely responsive to God yet impossibly resistant to His intent.

Logically, if God really opposes the extended drought, let Him end it sooner. Would the Almighty really wait three years rather than intervene directly in the prophet's plan?[12]

Rather, we might suggest that God gives Elijah His full backing, deliberately concealing his location from the evil Jezebel.[13] From the next chapter (18:4, 10), we know the government has been hunting and executing prophets of God, and that the powers that be have been searching desperately for Elijah. God spirits him away, procuring his food miraculously, shielding him, and waiting until the moment He decides to end the famine.

Simon's Approach

This approach is adopted by Simon, who reads the chapter in a manner diametrically opposed to that of Samet. As we have seen, Simon suggests that the initial oath is issued by God, and therefore God is driving the drama of chapter 17 in its entirety.

For Simon, the threefold story charts three stages in the initiation and development of Elijah as a prophet. Elijah begins the chapter as an unknown figure, possibly resembling the anonymous *ish Elokim* (man of God) of chapter 13. How can an untried, novice prophet muster the nerve to confront the king? Chapter 17 functions as a lengthy introduction to Elijah; we follow his divine apprenticeship as God trains him for his forthcoming mission.

---

11. In chapter 17, the single instance in which we sense a spirit of opposition toward God on Elijah's part is his assertive outburst in his first prayer, in verse 20. Interestingly, this prayer fails to revive the child. Only after Elijah's physical attempts to resuscitate the child, followed by his adoption of a humble and submissive mindset in his second prayer (verse 21), does God accede and revive the widow's son. It would seem that God responds when Elijah adopts a servile stance, not a defiant one.

12. Samet maintains that the prophet is given autonomy to instigate and sustain the drought despite God's opposition. At the same time, God chooses not to intervene, even shielding and sustaining the prophet. Samet terms this paradoxical approach "revolutionary." He states: "Eliyahu's decree arouses God's criticism of him, though it is God Himself who actually fulfills it" (*The Elijah Narratives*, 38).

13. See Ralbag and Abarbanel loc. cit.

In the first scene, Elijah does not escape to Wadi Cherith independently; God sends him there to hide. Throughout the entire chapter, in fact, it appears that the prophet functions in **response** to God. God uses Elijah's **word** as the instrument of His **word**,[14] and it is by God's **word** that he goes to the wadi. Elijah's disconnection from Ahab represents God's estrangement from the nation.

The second scene depicts Elijah in contact with others. God instructs him that "I have designated a widow to feed you" (17:9), but Elijah must locate the woman and convince her, by his powers of personality and persuasion, to put the prophet's needs before her own. (Simon assumes that she identifies him as a man of God; otherwise, why would she obey him? The proof is that she swears by the name of "the Lord, **your** God" [17:12], though he has not yet mentioned God!)

Here, Elijah confronts not a king, but rather a lowly widow, yet he subjects her to a test of faith. Her reward for passing that test is ongoing sustenance. In Wadi Cherith, God miraculously provides food for Elijah; but in Zarephath, He also provides for others – the widow and her son. Furthermore, Elijah is not merely receptive; in Zarephath he becomes active – commanding, convincing, and creating the miracle, "according to **the word of God** spoken through Elijah" (17:16).

The third scene represents a crisis. Things go wrong; despite the widow's hospitality toward the man of God, her son dies. She accuses Elijah, "What harm have I done you that you come here to recall my sin and kill my son?" Elijah does not contest the woman's harsh accusation. Instead, he takes her child and appeals to God. His prayer is accepted, and God restores life to the boy. Note the words that close this episode and bring the chapter to a climax. In contrast to her fierce accusation earlier, she affirms:

Now I know that you are a man of God and the **word of God** in your mouth is true. (17:24)

---

14. The words *devar Hashem* (word of God) appear six times in the chapter and act as a *leitwort* of sorts (as does *davar* [word], without reference to God). Moreover, the entire chapter revolves around proving that God's word is in Elijah's mouth.

For Simon, the theme of chapter 17 is the maturation of Elijah as a prophet during the famine.

> When he hides in Wadi Cherith, in accordance with an explicit command, he is subordinating his personal life to the demands of his mission, much like prophets before him and after him. In Zarephath, however, he is called upon to be increasingly active and independent. At first he bears a divine command and must get its recipient to repose her confidence in the messenger, put her trust in the sender, and obey His word. Later he is the target of the widow's bitter complaint and her advocate before his God. When the widow complies with his command and when the Lord responds to his prayer, Elijah knows – and so does the reader – ...that he is a genuine and faithful prophet....[15]

After this rigorous training, Elijah is ready to meet Ahab the king, and the challenges he will face on the national stage.

CONCLUSION

We have clearly demonstrated the threefold progression of this story; however, the meaning of this escalating structure is open to interpretation. Is this a story of Elijah's religious indignation, a tale of how God tries to make him renounce his principled stand? Alternatively, Elijah is God's representative and mouthpiece, and this is a story of how God mentors and trains the inexperienced prophet to gain the faith and confidence needed to confront even the most threatening kings.

---

15. Simon, *Prophetic Narratives*, 168.

Showdown at Mount Carmel

This chapter tells one of the Bible's most famous stories: the dramatic contest between the four hundred prophets of Baal and the lonely prophet Elijah to procure fire from heaven. Elijah's eventual triumph is a victory for God and Israel, a testimony to God's truth and the falsehood of Baal.

Our chapter opens as God instructs Elijah that the time has come to bring the rain.

> …the word of God came to Elijah in the third year, saying, "Go appear before Ahab, and I will send rain upon the earth." (18:1)

The drought is to end. But the rain cannot fall without Elijah's challenge to Ahab and to the nation. God is instigating the great contest of faith at Mount Carmel.

THE NATION

It seems as though the excruciating and devastating three-year famine has been orchestrated to lead specifically to this finale. But to whom is this spectacle directed?

> Now, send and gather **all Israel** to me at Mount Carmel. (18:19)

Even if this phrase represents something of an exaggeration (as it is unlikely that the entire nation will attend), it reflects the prime objective of the great assembly. At Mount Carmel, Elijah seeks to engage the nation as a whole, and it is to the assembled throngs that he directs his words and activities. Elijah seems uninterested in debating Ahab, the renegade king. Nor does Elijah address the prophets of Baal; in fact, he virtually ignores them. His energy and actions are geared exclusively toward the Jewish people.

But what does Elijah wish to say? His opening line expresses his clear motive:

> Elijah approached the people and said, "How long will you waver between two opinions? If the Lord is God, follow Him; but if Baal is God, follow him!" But the people said nothing. (18:21)

There are several important details in this verse. First, note the opening verb, *vayigash*, which is echoed later in the chapter (18:30, 36). Elijah deliberately approaches the nation. This approach seeks to stimulate a reciprocal movement – the nation's return to God.

Elijah's challenge pinpoints national religious clarity and commitment as his focal concern. The people were content to dabble in Baal worship while retaining an Israelite identity that viewed God as their deity. This wavering or dual loyalty is anathema to Judaism, which sees the rejection of other gods as an essential condition of belief in God. In Judaism, there is only a single commitment; any peripheral gods constitute idolatry.[1]

---

1. See 1 Samuel 7:3–4, in which Samuel exhorts the people to worship God exclusively. In *Exploring Exodus*, Nahum Sarna explains how difficult it was to be monotheistic

Elijah insists that the people cease their flip-flopping, this flirting with Baal. He uses the verb *p-s-ḥ*, which indicates jumping or leaping.[2] The people need to resolve their dual commitment and dedicate themselves absolutely and exclusively to God.

The verse concludes with the nation's response, or lack thereof: "But the people did not answer at all." Israel is mute, noncommittal; the people are confused and passive.[3] It is this inarticulacy, reflecting their religious ambivalence, that Elijah intends to shake.

OBADIAH

Delving more deeply into the chapter, we detect that it comprises three episodes:

verses
1–19	Elijah's reappearance to Obadiah; the meeting with Ahab
20–40	The contest at Mount Carmel
41–46	Elijah's waiting for the rain

The opening verse of the chapter reports that Elijah has been instructed to end the famine. We might anticipate an immediate encounter between him and Ahab. Instead, we meet one of the king's senior courtiers:

---

in a polytheistic world. Judaism was harshly intolerant of other gods, unlike the cultures surrounding ancient Israel. The Bible frequently equates idolatry with adultery, because even people who worshipped idols understood marital fidelity as an exclusive and inviolable commitment. This paradigm communicated the faithfulness God expected of His people. See Sarna, *Exploring Exodus* (New York: Schocken, 1986), 141–2.

2. God is described as leaping over the Jewish houses in Exodus 12:13, 27 – hence the name of the resulting holiday, Pesah. Alternatively, both Radak and Ralbag suggest a motion of limping or hobbling (the Hebrew word *pise'ah*), as in a person unable to retain their balance, shifting weight from one foot to the other, but lacking independent stability. This too would seem an apt metaphor for Israel as they limp, seeking to lean on various deities to support their instability. See also J. Walsh, *1 Kings* (Collegeville, Minnesota: The Liturgical Press, 1996), 248.

3. In a similar vein, see Rabbi Joseph B. Soloveitchik, "Redemption, Prayer, Talmud Torah," *Tradition* 17:2 (Spring 1978): 23–42.

> ...Obadiah feared God exceedingly. When Jezebel killed God's prophets, Obadiah took one hundred prophets and hid them in two caves, fifty in each, and supplied them with food and water. (18:3–4)

Elijah's encounter with Ahab numbers a mere four verses; in contrast, the description of the God-fearing Obadiah and his dialogue with Elijah takes up fourteen verses![4] Why this preoccupation with Obadiah? Why must Elijah meet Obadiah as a prelude to his tense encounter with Ahab?

Some claim that this passage is a literary device, notching up the tension in the lead-up to the drama at Mount Carmel. Others suggest that it is a matter of protocol: Ahab is to be summoned to Elijah (by Obadiah), rather than the prophet's subordinating himself to the king.[5] We will suggest a different approach.

TWO MASTERS

Who is Obadiah? His very name indicates his religious orientation; he serves God – *oved Yah*. Moreover, he subverts Jezebel's roundup of the prophets of God, supporting and sustaining one hundred of them in a cave. Obadiah recognizes Elijah and greets him with great veneration:

> ...he bowed down to the ground and said, "Is it really you, my master (*adoni*) Elijah?" (18:7)

While Ahab addresses Elijah as a "betrayer of Israel" (18:17), Obadiah has a different assessment of the prophet. Immediately, Elijah responds:

> Go tell your master (*adonekha*), "Elijah is here." (18:8)

---

4. In terms of the storyline, if verse 2 were followed by verse 17, the reader would not sense anything missing.

5. Elchanan Samet, *The Elijah Narratives* (Jerusalem: Maaliyot Press, 2003), 104 [Hebrew]. See also Dr. Yael Ziegler, "*Haftarat Ki Tissa*," in Aharon Eldar, ed., *Maftirin BaNavi* (Jerusalem: Jewish Agency for Israel, 2010), 134–37. There she portrays the compassionate Obadiah as a contrast to Elijah, who demonstrates insensitivity to the national suffering he creates by declaring a famine. I have adopted a different approach.

Obadiah uses the word *adon* to address Elijah, yet Elijah uses it to denote Obadiah's more obvious superior, King Ahab. This word recurs throughout the next few verses (10, 11, 13, 14), sometimes in reference to Elijah and other times in reference to Ahab. Essentially, Obadiah is caught between conflicting commitments and allegiances; who is his ultimate master?

Elijah seeks to send Obadiah to summon Ahab, but Obadiah is concerned that if Elijah disappears, Ahab will kill him. To reassure the frightened Obadiah, Elijah swears in God's name that he will indeed meet Ahab that day.[6] As Obadiah goes to deliver the message, he is transformed into Elijah's messenger – God's messenger.

---

6. Elijah uses the same language to reassure the widow of Zarephath (1 Kings 17:14). There is, in fact, a complex parallelism between chapters 17 and 18. We may identify an extensive array of literary connections:

   (A) Wadi Cherith and Obadiah:
   - a. 17:3 – "Wadi Cherith" ("Kerit" in Hebrew) / 18:4 – "When Jezebel killed (*behakhrit*) God's prophets"
   - b. 17:4 – "I have commanded the ravens to provide for you (*lekhalkelkha*)" / 18:4 – "He provided them (*vekhilkelam*) with bread and water"
   - c. 17:6 – "...the ravens brought him bread..., and he drank from the stream" / 18:4 – "bread and water"

   (B) Elijah with the widow of Zarephath and with Obadiah:
   - a. 17:10/18:5, 7 – Elijah approaches a person foraging for wood or straw outside the city
   - b. 17:12/18:9–10 – Refusal to comply with Elijah's request; language of "as the Lord, your God, lives"
   - c. 17:14/18:15 – Elijah's reassurance in the name of God: "So says the Lord, God of Israel," or "As the Lord of Hosts lives"
   - d. 17:12/18:9, 13 – The specter of death ("...and we shall eat it and then die" / "...you deliver me into in Ahab's hand to slay me," "he [Ahab] shall slay me")
   - e. 17:19 – "To remember my sin (*avoni*)" / 18:9 – "How have I sinned (*chatati*)?"

   (C) Elijah's revival of the dead boy and Elijah's actions at Mount Carmel:
   - a. His appeal to God, accusing Him of acting inappropriately, causing destruction and death: 17:20 – "O Lord, my God, why have You brought tragedy also upon this widow I am staying with, causing her son to die?" / 18:37 – "And let this nation know that You are the Lord, God, and have turned their hearts back"
   - b. Threefold action: 17:21 – Stretching himself over the boy / 18:34 – pouring water three times

Obadiah personifies the dilemma of the nation. Israel feels torn between two masters, God and Baal. Keep in mind that both promise the desperately needed rainfall. Obadiah is Ahab's closest minister, yet he also fears God "exceedingly." Obadiah himself is "wavering between two opinions"; Elijah forces him to choose. This is the precursor to Israel's choice.

MOUNT CARMEL

Elijah summons Jezebel's prophets of Baal to a showdown at Mount Carmel. Two coordinates identify this setting: the Kishon stream (18:40) and the direct access to Jezreel, site of Ahab's winter palace (18:46). Both of these match the Carmel mountain range, near today's Haifa.[7] Why does Elijah choose this location?

There are two possible explanations.[8] First, Elijah wants to challenge Baal on its own turf. The Carmel is perennially green. Even during a protracted drought, when vast tracts of countryside turns to parched hues of yellow and brown, the Carmel mountain range retains

---

c. Prayer and God's miraculous response (it is even plausible that the life-giving rainfall parallels the restoration of life to the child)

d. Knowledge of God: 17:24 – "Now I know that you are a man of God and the word of God in your mouth is true"/ 18:36 – "Let it be known that You are God in Israel and I am your servant..." 18:39 – "...they [the people] fell on their faces and cried, 'The Lord – He is God!'"

What is the meaning of these parallels? Just as Elijah must use the full power of his personality to convince the widow that he bears the word of God and she should therefore forgo her self-interest to obey and provide for him, he must prevail upon Obadiah to endanger himself in order to present him to the king. Once again, we are dealing with Elijah's charismatic influence, which compels people to follow his (and God's) dictates despite their personal preferences. This supports Simon's view of chapter 17 as Elijah's apprenticeship in preparation for the great confrontation of chapter 18. For more on this parallel, see Uriel Simon, *Reading Prophetic Narratives* (Bloomington: University of Indiana Press, 1997), 209–17; and Samet, *The Elijah Narratives*, 114–15.

7. Other places are known as Carmel as well – for example, in the southern region of Judah (see Josh. 15:55 and I Sam. 25:2).

8. Both theories may be found in an article by Dr. Yisrael Rosenson. See Y. Rosenson, "Elijah at Carmel: From Geography to Literary Interpretation," *Tallelei Orot*, 10 (5762): 197-204 [Hebrew].

its freshness. For the Baal worshippers, then, this is a region in which Baal – the rain god – exercises particular control. A victory over Baal in this location is indisputable.

Second, the Carmel lies between two cultures. From its peak, one can look northward to the coastline and the trading areas under Phoenician administration and influence. Looking southwest, one sees the hills of Samaria, the ancestral portion of Ephraim – the Israelite heartland.[9] If Israel is "wavering between two opinions," two cultural systems, two religious orientations, the Carmel is positioned at the fulcrum between them. The venue of this test reflects, once again, the choice that the people must make: Israel or Phoenicia?

ACTIVATING THE PEOPLE

Elijah acts as a master choreographer, planning the events of the day of the contest in order to bring the people to a point of faith. As mentioned, his original call to exclusive commitment to God is met with stony silence. At that point, Elijah unveils his challenge of bringing down fire from heaven to consume the sacrifice, with the goal of demonstrating God's ultimate power beyond any doubt. The Baal worshippers begin in an advantageous position: There are more of them, and Elijah lets them choose the animal they will sacrifice.

The day is divided into time periods:

1. morning until noon (18:26)
2. noon (18:27)
3. afternoon, "until the bringing of the *minḥa*" (18:29)[10]
4. at the "bringing of the *minḥa*" (18:36)

Elijah masterminds the day in order to manipulate its events to maximal advantage.

---

9. Eretz Yisrael's borders expand and contract. At times we lose the coastal plain or the Jezreel Valley to foreign conquest, but the hill country including the portion of Ephraim is consistently part of Israelite territory, from the nation's entry into the land until the fall of Samaria.
10. Yehuda Kiel, *Da'at Mikra*, *1 Kings* [Hebrew], suggests that this refers to the hour of the afternoon sacrifice in the Temple at Jerusalem.

For the first half of the day, Elijah remains passive, simply waiting, allowing the prophets of Baal to occupy the audience's attention. The prophets dance all morning, and the text describes this movement with the verb *p-s-ḥ* (18:26), the same language used to describe Israel's religious oscillation (18:21), indicating that the nation's "wavering between two opinions" is tantamount to Baal worship.

By noon, the Baal worship has yielded no heavenly fire, and the Israelites are bored. Now Elijah has everyone's attention. He taunts the priests of Baal, using cynicism and comedy; his stand-up routine is something new and entertaining. This tactic throws the Baal prophets into a desperate frenzy, as they raise their voices and slash themselves with sharp blades until they bleed (18:28).[11]

The text highlights the absence of any response to the antics of these prophets. In the morning, we are told that "there was no voice and no response" (18:26). By late afternoon, the lack of response is stronger: "…no voice, no response, **no one listening**" (18:29).

THE UNITY OF THE NATION

Elijah has exhausted the opposition and exposed its inability to produce fire from heaven. But he is not interested merely in proving God's power; he seeks to heal the nation, spurring it to respond. Late in the day, he beckons the people with the same verb, *vayigash*, that was previously met with silence: "Approach me!" he says. This time, without hesitation, "the entire nation approached him" (18:30).

Elijah uses symbols to represent the heritage and unity of Israel:

1. He repairs the altar with twelve stones, "…for the twelve tribes of the sons of Jacob, to whom the word of God had come, saying, 'Israel will be your name'" (18:31).
2. He instructs the people to pour twelve jugs of water (four jugs, three times) (18:33–34).
3. He prays to "the God of Abraham Isaac, and Israel" (18:36).

---

11. A modern example of such practices may be the Shiite *Ashura* ceremony, in which participants cut and beat themselves until their blood flows freely.

Continuing the education of his audience, Elijah repairs the altar rather than building a new one; thus he conveys that there is room for *teshuva*, repentance and rehabilitation. The number twelve is particularly interesting, given that we are discussing a kingdom split into two, where the northern kingdom does not represent the nation in its entirety. Nonetheless, Elijah establishes that the nation is one, all descended from a single Jacob. And ever since Jacob, God has not changed His relationship to His people.

RESPONSE

We have drawn attention to the theme of silence and vocalization, which constitutes a key feature of this story. The *leitwort* of the chapter is the verb *a-n-h*,[12] "answer" or "respond." The trial of whether God will "respond" with fire is the pivotal stimulus in determining whether Israel will find its own voice in calling out to God. Elijah skillfully guides the nation to become more vocal and active, more engaged as the day progresses:

At the start	…the people said nothing. (18:21)
After Elijah's initial proposal	Then all the people said, "What you say is good." (18:24)
Late in the afternoon	Elijah said to all the people, "Approach me!" and the entire nation approached him. (18:30)

Elijah repairs the altar alone, but then he activates his audience:

> Then he said to them, "Fill four jars with water, and pour [it] on the offering and on the wood"; "do it again," he said, and they did it again; "do it a third time," he said, and they did it a third time. (18:34)

Now we see the people actively engaged.

---

12. The verb *a-n-h* appears seven times in these lines. See 18:24–29, 37. The verb *k-r-a* (call) recurs here as well.

Elijah's prayer expresses his explicit goal:

> Answer me, O Lord, answer me! And let **this nation** know that
> You are the Lord, God. ..." (18:37)

Indeed, after fire descends from the heavens to consume Elijah's sacrifice:

> When the people saw this, they fell on their faces and cried, "The
> Lord – He is God! The Lord – He is God!" (18:39)

Elijah has achieved his objective: The people have made their commitment to God. In that twilight hour – the *ne'ila* hour at the end of the day – Israel proclaims its undivided religious allegiance. This conviction is reinforced by what follows: The people capture the Baal prophets, and Elijah executes them (18:40).

AHAB'S RESPONSE

This great day culminates in Elijah's turning to Ahab with a dramatic pronouncement:

> Go up, eat and drink, for there is the sound of much rain
> [approaching]. (18:41)

We have not heard from Ahab throughout the day's proceedings. However, the execution of the prophets of Baal cannot have taken place without royal approval. Moreover, the instruction "Go up" suggests that Ahab, along with the impassioned throngs led by Elijah, have descended to the Kishon stream to execute the priests of Baal.

The events of the day have signaled a striking religious turnaround for Ahab. This transformation is especially remarkable considering his bitter clash with Elijah only a few hours earlier:

> Ahab said to him: "Is that you, O betrayer of Israel?" He retorted,
> "It is not I who have betrayed Israel, but you and your father's
> house, by forsaking the commandments of God and going after
> Baalim." (18:17–18)

Now Ahab is a changed man. He follows Elijah's instructions precisely; the prophet tells him, "Go up, eat and drink," and "Ahab went up to eat and drink" (18:42). The eating and drinking reflect Ahab's joy at the impending rain and his approval regarding the slaughter of the prophets of Baal, whose guilt is self-evident.[13]

Elijah responds to Ahab's religious reversal by exhibiting the respect due to a religiously loyal Jewish king. In a grand gesture of servitude, the prophet runs before Ahab's chariot all the way back to his palace in Jezreel (18:46).[14] Prof. Uriel Simon writes:

> It is clear that Elijah's running before Ahab's chariot is intended to honor the king. He lets him know with unparalleled clarity that nothing he has done was meant to subvert the monarch's rule and undermine his authority. On the contrary; at the sight of the prophet with girded loins, running in a heavy rainstorm… a distance of some twenty-five kilometers – we can sense the enthusiasm with which he is restoring to the king that which appertains to the king and the joy with which he [Elijah] is finally returning to his own people.[15]

One unexpected observation we may make pertains to Ahab's passivity and compliance with Elijah. After Obadiah's fraught concerns about the king's violent fury, we might have anticipated an encounter with a seething, malevolent tyrant. Instead, Ahab is open to influence and quick to

---

13. Different suggestions have been made regarding the significance of Elijah's instruction to Ahab to "eat and drink." Radak proposes that Ahab has been fasting due to the drought; breaking his fast reflects the breaking of the tension, as the drought is over. Simon claims that Ahab's eating indicates his approval of the killing of Jezebel's prophets (*Prophetic Narratives*, 197). This reading is based upon biblical depictions of people sitting down to eat and drink after pronouncing the demise of an enemy, thereby expressing their satisfaction. See Genesis 37:25 (Joseph's brothers, after casting him into the pit) and Esther 3:15 (Haman and Ahasuerus).
14. See Rashi on 1 Kings 18:46. The Bible presents a standard practice of kings heralded by runners – see 1 Samuel 8:12. Recall that two heirs to the throne – Absalom and Adonijah – each had "fifty people running" before their carriages (11 Sam. 15:1; 1 Kings 1:5).
15. Simon, *Prophetic Narratives*, 197.

cooperate with Elijah. It is possible that Ahab has met his match with the powerful Elijah. Possibly the miraculous events of the day have overwhelmed the king. Alternatively, Ahab assesses that Elijah holds the key to the rainfall; hence his agreement to Elijah's plan. But Ahab's swift acquiescence to Elijah's test at Mount Carmel, his silence throughout the dramatic contest, as well as the absence of any resistance or official royal pronouncement as the four hundred prophets are slaughtered all raise questions about Ahab's personality and religious obduracy. At the close of this chapter, we discover an Ahab who is impressionable and manipulable. Has he now set a new course of devotion to God, or will other forces and events lead to further fluctuations in Ahab's religious allegiances?

Elijah Prays for Rain

Thе great spectacle at Mount Carmel ends with an enigmatic postscript:

> Elijah said to Ahab, "**Go up**, eat and drink, for there is the sound of much rain [approaching]." And Ahab **went up** to eat and drink; Elijah, meanwhile, **went up** to the top of the Carmel, stretched himself out the ground, and put his face between his knees. He said to his servant, "**Go up**, please, and look toward the sea"; he **went up** and looked and reported, "There is nothing"; seven times, Elijah said, "Go back." And the seventh time, he reported, "Behold! A small cloud, like a man's hand, is **rising** from the west"; and he [Elijah] said: "**Arise**! Tell Ahab, 'Hitch up your chariot, and go **down** before the rain stops you.'" Meanwhile, the sky grew black with clouds, there was wind, and a downpour fell; Ahab mounted his chariot and drove off to Jezreel.
>
> And the hand of the Lord had come upon Elijah; he tied up his skirts and ran before Ahab all the way to Jezreel. (18:41–46)[1]

---

1. The bolded words indicate the sevenfold repetition of the verb *a-l*, indicating ascent,

In this scene, Elijah is deeply ensconced in prayer, in what appears to be a protracted, tense wait for the rain. Repeatedly, he anticipates a signal, some indication that the rain will indeed come. His assistant moves back and forth, frantically scanning the horizon for the relief of a raincloud, only to report in disappointment and frustration, "There is nothing."

This tension is surprising. After all, in verse 41, Elijah seems certain of imminent rainfall, informing Ahab that the rain is approaching, and encouraging him to celebrate the termination of the national drought. Furthermore, the miraculous fire that signaled God's acceptance of Elijah's sacrifice appears to be a direct indication that He intends to bring rain. Finally, we know precisely God's intent; chapter 18 opened with an explicit pronouncement regarding the arrival of the rain:

> …the word of God came to Elijah in the third year, saying: "Go appear before Ahab; then I will send rain upon the earth." (18:1)

Is Elijah fearful that God might not bring the rain in fulfillment of His word?

Another source of puzzlement is the time span of this scene. The story begins as both Ahab and Elijah stand at the Kishon stream, where the prophets of Baal were executed. There, Elijah instructs Ahab, "**Go up**, eat and drink, for there is the sound of much rain [approaching]," and in clear compliance with Elijah, "Ahab **went up** to eat and drink." Elijah does not accompany Ahab. He makes his own way **up** – in a parallel action indicated by the same verb, *a-l-h* – ascending to the top of Mount Carmel with the aim of praying and waiting.

The process of prayer that follows Elijah's ascent seems to take quite a while. Yet, after seven cycles of prayer, once the initial cloud is viewed, Elijah has enough time to dispatch his servant with an urgent message for Ahab, who is apparently still at the Carmel! Elijah manages

---

as well as its opposite, *y-r-d*. The vertical axis plays a central role in all the Elijah stories. See II Kings 1, where the drama revolves around who will go up and who will come down. In II Kings 2, there is also an up-and-down motif, especially as Elijah is raised heavenward in a storm.

to descend the mountainside in time to run as a herald before the chariot of the king.

Did Ahab simply take his time? Or did Elijah's prayer, described in slow motion, actually transpire with great speed?[2]

Furthermore, what does this episode add to the wider story? In verse 46, we find ourselves at essentially the same point in the storyline as we were in verse 41. In both verses, we find Elijah encourages Ahab to hurry to Jezreel because the rain is on its way. How does to the intervening passage enhance the drama of this chapter?

COMMENTATORS

Radak explains the need for Elijah's prayer :

> Elijah was sure God would bring the rain as He had promised, "I will send rain upon the earth" (18:1), ... but he prostrated himself [in prayer] before God to expedite the rain, **so it would fall when Ahab was still there!** (Radak on 18:41–42)

Ralbag too sees an educational motive in Elijah's actions:

> Elijah wished the rain would fall immediately, so they would understand that their sins had caused the drought. That is why the rain came the moment they engaged in their return to God. (Ralbag on 18:42)

Accordingly, Elijah wishes either to impress Ahab or to drive home his message to the nation. Radak resolves the time problem elegantly, with Ahab deliberately waiting for Elijah:

> He [Ahab] did go up to his carriage in order to travel to Jezreel to eat and drink. But when he realized that Elijah had gone to

---

2. One simple resolution is offered by Radak (in his second interpretation): When Elijah told Ahab, "Go up, eat and drink," he meant on Mount Carmel, not at his palace in Jezreel. While Ahab was feasting, Elijah was praying. We shall follow an alternate direction.

the top of the Carmel to pray, he waited for him, not departing until he saw the outcome. (Radak on 18:42)

These answers to our questions are very sensible and practical, but we will suggest an additional dimension to this story.

THE THREE KEYS

Let us begin with the word *vayighar*, which describes Elijah's prayer posture here.[3] This rare verb appears twice in 11 Kings, in the episode of the Shunammite woman and Elisha's revival of her son:[4]

> ...he [Elisha] **stretched himself out** upon him; the boy's body grew warm. He [Elisha] turned away and walked back and forth in the room and then went up and **stretched himself out** upon him once more; the boy sneezed **seven times** and...opened his eyes. (11 Kings 4:34–35)

Why is this verb used only in these two stories?

At an initial level, one may suggest that Elijah is granting renewed life to the earth with the advent of the rainfall. The drought placed a stranglehold on the country. Now Elijah resuscitates the land with the same technique that induced God to restore life to the widow's child.

---

3. Radak describes two distinct stages of prayer, each with its own posture. First, Elijah stretches himself out on the ground, and thereafter, he prays seated with his head between his knees.

4. In the antecedent of this story, when Elisha's master, Elijah, revives the son of the widow in Zarephath (1 Kings 17:15–22), Elijah's actions are described in a similar manner: "He stretched himself out on the boy three times" (17:21). There, however, the verb used is *vayitmoded* rather than *vayighar*. In that context, there is a threefold repetition rather than a sevenfold one.

   Nevertheless, other textual cues link Elijah's revival of the child and our story. The verb a-l-h appears prominently in both incidents; Elijah ascends to the attic to revive the boy just as he ascends the mountain to bring rain. Both instances also involve prayer; unlike in chapter 17, we are not privy to the content of Elijah's *tefilla* in chapter 18, but his posture of "head between his knees" appears to be one of intense prayer.

God's Three Keys

I believe a Talmudic midrash offers a deeper understanding:

> Elijah prayed that God give him the key to the resurrection of
> the dead, but he was told from Heaven: Three keys were never
> entrusted to an agent [remaining exclusively in God's possession]:
> the key to childbirth, the key to rain, and the key to the resurrec-
> tion of the dead. You already have the key to rain, and you [also]
> want the key of the resurrection of the dead?! (*Sanhedrin* 113a)

This fascinating *aggada* proposes that there are three "keys" held by God
alone: those of childbirth, rain, and resurrection. The common denomi-
nator of these three keys is that each involves life and death. Birth and the
resurrection of the dead are quite obviously matters of giving or creating
new life. Rain shares this central feature in that it determines personal
and national survival; who will live and who will die.[5]

This Talmudic passage addresses a question that lurks in the background throughout the Elijah stories, as he seems to make pronouncements and perform miracles independently: Is Elijah acting by God's
agency, or is he instigating acts with which God somehow follows along?
The Talmud answers that God "lends His keys" to Elijah; the prophet is
granted unusual power, as he holds a tool that is customarily in God's
jurisdiction. Yet God makes it clear to Elijah that the power He has
vested in him has its limits. God is firmly in the driver's seat.

Therefore, Elijah must pray before reviving the widow's son,
imploring God to restore the boy's life. He does not hold the key to
resurrection; that power belongs to God. Similarly, our image of Elijah
climbing to the mountaintop in order to stretch out on the ground in
prayer transmits the message that he has no independent control of the
rainfall. Whether Elijah decreed the drought independently or loyally
pronounced God's word, the key to rain is firmly in God's hands. Elijah
must pray for the rain to come.

---

5. See *Berakhot* 5:2: "The strength [of God in bringing] the rain is recited in [the bless-
    ing of] the resurrection of the dead."

The number seven, explicit in this story, is rooted in the Creation narrative.[6] Our cycles of seven – Shabbat and the Sabbatical year – reflect God's mastery of nature, His total control of the natural world. Lest there be any doubt as to God's central role in the granting of rain, this image – Elijah's desperate prayer – demonstrates that rain is under God's absolute jurisdiction.

---

6. In other narratives, the number seven seems to express God's control. In Jericho, for example, after Israel makes seven circuits on the seventh day, with seven priests sounding seven ram's horns, the city falls, and the spoils of war belong to God – because, ultimately, it is God who fought the battle.

1 Kings 19

Prophet in Distress

E lijah has just experienced his greatest success, bringing the people to a rousing proclamation of monotheistic commitment, roundly defeating the prophets of Baal. He should be on top of the world! Yet our chapter opens with a melancholy, disheartened Elijah wandering desperately into the desert and begging God to end his life:

> He prayed that he might die: "Enough!" he cried; "now, O Lord, take my life, for I am no better than my fathers." (1 Kings 19:4)

What is agitating Elijah? Why is he suddenly so depressed?

THE CHALLENGE AND THE FAILURE

We recall the scene in which the jubilant Elijah escorts Ahab to the royal palace in Jezreel:

> Once he [Ahab] allied himself with Elijah, he was accorded the honor befitting a king, for at that moment he had repented. He [Elijah] sought to draw him closer to the service of God. (Malbim on 18:46)

Ahab returns to the palace excited, reporting the impressive events of the day – the contest and the fire from heaven – to his wife and advisers. But Jezebel, resolute and unimpressed, sends a message to Elijah that he is now subject to a royal death warrant:

> When Ahab told Jezebel all that Elijah had done and all of how he had put all[1] the prophets [of Baal] to the sword, Jezebel sent a messenger to Elijah, saying, "Thus and more may the gods do,[2] if by this time tomorrow[3] I have not made you like one of them [the slain prophets]." (19:1–2)

Jezebel, a religiously impassioned woman, sets the noxious spiritual tone of the kingdom. She has banned the worship of God and executed the prophets loyal to Him (18:4). Conversely, the four hundred prophets of Baal "eat at Jezebel's table" (18:19) – Jezebel's rather than Ahab's. When Elijah confronts Ahab, he is in essence picking a fight with Jezebel, and when he kills her prophets, she retaliates by resolving to kill him. Interestingly, Jezebel enables Elijah to escape, announcing his death "tomorrow." She need not actually kill him; she is happy to see him disappear for another three years!

PERSONAL OR NATIONAL?

Elijah flees Israel to the kingdom of Judah. Initially, we sense that he is driven by concern for his personal welfare; logic tells us that he could

---

1. Yair Zakovitch points out that the threefold repetition of the word *kol* (all) indicates the huge impact made upon Ahab by the events at Mount Carmel. See Zakovitch, "A Still, Small Voice: Form and Content in 1 Kings 19," *Tarbiz* 51 (1982): 329–46 [Hebrew].

2. In Hebrew, the plural is quite deliberate, as denoted by the verbs *ya'asun* (may they do) and *yosifun* (may they add).

3. It is strange that Jezebel delays Elijah's execution to "tomorrow" rather than eliminating him immediately. *Da'at Mikra* assumes that the prevailing religious fervor precluded his assassination that very day. Jezebel assesses that she will be unable to persuade Ahab to kill him immediately. Rabbi Elchanan Samet suggests that even as queen, Jezebel was bound by law (as with Naboth in chapter 21) and needed some time to devise a legal case for executing Elijah. See Yehuda Kiel, *Da'at Mikra, 1 Kings* [Hebrew]; Samet, *The Elijah Narratives* (Jerusalem: Maaliyot Press, 2003), 259 [Hebrew].

have lived safely in Judah. But then, curiously, he ventures into the desert to die.[4] He has given up. The turnaround from Jezebel's death warrant to Elijah's self-imposed death wish is articulated by the sevenfold repetition of the word *nefesh* (life):[5]

19:2	"Your life (nafshekha) will be like the life (nefesh) of one of them"
19:3	Elijah flees "for his life" (*el* nafsho)
19:4	"He prayed to die (*Vayishal et* nafsho *lamut*): 'Enough!' he cried; '...take my life (*kaḥ* nafshi)...'"
19:10, 14	"they seek to take my life" (nafshi *lekaḥta*)

In this regard, it is worth noting the symmetrical inversion of the verb *l-k-h*. Because Jezebel seeks "to take my life" (*nafshi* lekaḥta), Elijah pleads with God: "take my life (kaḥ *nafshi*)." Ironically, Elijah's death wish brings Jezebel's threat dangerously close to fulfillment. Within the precise time frame of her promise to kill him – "tomorrow" (19:2) – Elijah finds himself at the end of "a day's journey into the wilderness" and prays to die (19:4).[6] He is mysteriously abandoning the struggle, surrendering, as he allows Jezebel to win.

We are at a loss to explain Elijah's sudden despair. After all, he exhibited fearless confidence when confronting Ahab. He flouted Jezebel's ban on the worship of God and her execution of His prophets. Why does this death threat prompt Elijah's collapse?

---

4. The borders of Eretz Yisrael extend "from Dan to Beersheba" (Judges 20:1; I Sam. 3:20; II Sam. 3:20, 17:11, 24:2; I Kings 5:5). Due to the sparse rainfall, agricultural sustenance is incredibly difficult south of Beersheba. Only unusual desert societies, such as the ancient Nabateans, survived in those conditions. Elijah's flight to this region recalls the story of Hagar and Ishmael, which takes place in the "desert of Beersheba," where Hagar leaves the faint Ishmael "under one of the bushes" to die (Gen. 21).

5. In the Bible, the word *nefesh* indicates the physical – "life," or "body" – rather than the spiritual connotation of the literal translation, "soul." When we are told to afflict our *nefesh* on Yom Kippur (Lev. 23:27), that means fasting – denying the body, not the soul. On festivals, we are permitted to do work for *okhel nefesh* (Ex. 12:16) – food for the body, not the soul. Similarly, in Psalms, *nefesh* refers to one's life, not one's spiritual destiny.

6. See Zakovitch, "A Still, Small Voice."

The answer lies in understanding that Elijah's desire to die is a function of his ideology and strategy. The wider context is critical here. Elijah, in God's name, has orchestrated a three-year drought that has brought the nation to its knees. It has been an excruciating process, with the prophet living in exile for three years. Yet he has succeeded in turning the king around and drawing the nation to proclaim allegiance to God. But now, in a single day, the entire project – this huge educational endeavor – lies shattered, in ruins.[7] In the words of Prof. Uriel Simon, Elijah "decides that all his achievements were spurious. The depth of his fall and despair is in proportion to the height of his expectation and self-confidence."[8] Elijah evidently expected things to turn out differently. He has misread Ahab, anticipating a more determined response. In contrast, he quickly discovers that just as he has influenced Ahab, Jezebel has swung events in the opposite direction. Ahab and the entire kingdom are religiously paralyzed by her overwhelming influence. Without removing Jezebel, there is no hope. The transformation of national priorities is clearly going to be a more arduous, complex, and protracted process than Elijah thought.

This is articulated in Elijah's words on Mount Horeb:

> I have acted zealously for the Lord, God of Hosts, for the Israelites have forsaken Your covenant, destroyed Your altars, and killed Your prophets by the sword; and I alone am left, and they seek to take my life. (19:10)

Elijah equates the entire nation with the evil queen! From his perspective, they are Jezebel's accomplices. Therefore, his success amounts to nothing.

---

7. Moses also seeks his own death in Numbers 11:15. There too, he is gripped by intense despair, as notwithstanding the nation's encampment for an entire year at Mount Sinai, the people are obsessed with meat en route to the Promised Land. Moses' frustration and disappointment lead him to abandon national leadership and to seek to end his life. For more on the Moses-Elijah connection, see later in "1 Kings 19: Prophet in Distress."

8. Uriel Simon, *Reading Prophetic Narratives* (Bloomington: University of Indiana Press, 1997), 202.

Elijah lies down to die but is woken and revived by an angel. This *malakh* sent to revive him is the inverse of the *malakh* Jezebel dispatches to end his life (19:2).[9] The angel feeds him and informs him that "the way is great before you" (19:7). As Simon writes, "The provision of his needs in the wilderness attests to the Lord's concern for his servant and makes him aware that his mission is not over yet."[10]

> He walked forty days and forty nights to the mountain of God at Horeb. (19:8)

It would seem that the angel leads Elijah to this momentous venue.[11] But why must he visit this mountain in particular? And what does God communicate to him at this mysterious encounter? How does God plan to convince Elijah to continue?

THE CONVERSATION AT MOUNT SINAI

> And He said, "Go out and stand on the mountain before the Lord";

---

9. See this and other observations in Zakovitch, "A Still, Small Voice."
10. Simon, *Prophetic Narratives*, 203. The angel feeding Elijah is reminiscent of the widow in Zarephath, for both feed him *uga* (cake). But two other unusual features of this episode attract our attention. First, the angel repeatedly touches Elijah (v. 5 and 7), an unusual act for an angel. Second, the cake that he is fed is an *ugat retzaphim*, a cake baked upon coals. What is the significance of these particular details? I believe that these take us to Isaiah chapter 6 – the dedication of Isaiah – in which Isaiah "lives among a people of unclean lips" and yet an angel "flew over to me with a live coal (*ritzpah*)…and touched it to my lips" (Is. 6:6). Isaiah then declares that he is prepared to assume God's mission to the nation: "Here I am; send me" (Is. 6:8). This interesting parallel forms a subversive subtext to the Elijah story. Isaiah, unfazed by the nation's wrongdoings, willingly undertakes his prophetic role. The coal touched to his lips empowers Isaiah, the novice prophet. This comparison underscores Elijah's self-absorbed abandonment of his prophetic mission. The prophet of fire is fed a fire-baked cake, and yet, unlike Isaiah, he refuses to respond, "Here I am; send me." Instead, he abandons his prophetic calling.
11. Mount Horeb is Mount Sinai. See, for example, Exodus 3:1; Deuteronomy 4:10, 5:2, 28:69. The use of Horeb in particular might be phonetic, as it resonates with the recurrence of the word *herev* (sword) in 1 Kings 19:1, 10, 14, 17 (twice).

> And behold, the Lord passed by,
> And a great and strong wind rent the mountain and broke the
>   rocks…,
> But the Lord was not in the wind;
> And after the wind, an earthquake; but the Lord was not in the
>   earthquake.
> And after the earthquake, a fire; but the Lord was not in the fire;
> And after the fire, a still, small voice.[12] (19:11–12)

How does Elijah respond to God's cryptic message?

> When Elijah heard it, he wrapped his face in his mantle and went
> out and stood at the entrance to the cave; … and He said, "What
> are you doing here, Elijah?" (19:13)

When prompted by God to articulate his mode of thinking, of being –
his mission and essence[13] – Elijah repeats his harsh words verbatim:

> I have acted zealously for the Lord, God of Hosts, for the Isra-
> elites have forsaken Your covenant, destroyed Your altars, and
> killed Your prophets by the sword; and I alone am left, and they
> seek to take my life. (19:14)

This highly enigmatic dialogue raises many questions. What is Elijah
trying to say to God? And what is God communicating to him? What
is the symbolism behind the wind, the earthquake, and the fire? And

---

12. This is a difficult phrase. We have used the familiar King James translation, but it fails
    to capture the language and mystery of the three Hebrew words: *kol* – a voice or
    sound; *demama* – silence; *daka* – thin, withered, or granular. Of course, the phrase
    is an oxymoron; if there is a voice or sound, it cannot be silent. The phrase has been
    understood variously as "a voice emerging out of the silence" (Rashi), a low-toned
    voice (Radak), or a mix of sound and silence (Ralbag).
13. Radak on 19:10 likens this question to God's famous inquiry of Adam "Where are
    you?" or to Cain after the murder of Abel: "Where is Abel, your brother?" It is a
    mode of "engaging in conversation to elicit a response" – in other words, prompting
    someone to talk to God, as God desires that man confront God and his own self.

what is the still, small voice? Furthermore, when prompted by God, why does Elijah repeat himself?

EXPLAINING ELIJAH

Here is Malbim's reading of this episode:

> "What are you doing here, Elijah?" – As if to say: The role of the prophet is to be among the people, to rebuke and to prophesy, not to go into seclusion in the wilderness and mountains.
>
> "And he [Elijah] responded" – Here I am! I cannot be a prophet who teaches and guides this nation, for my zealotry regarding their evil acts has killed me. I executed the prophets of Baal, and now they seek to kill me! I cannot continue with my mission.
>
> …He [God] showed him that God is to be found not in the wind, earthquake, and fire, but only in the voice of silence, and from this His messengers should learn the lesson: not to make a loud noise or burn like fire, as did Elijah in his zeal for God, in his cessation of the rain and his execution of the prophets of Baal. Rather, God sends His messengers to approach the people with a quiet voice, to persuade the nation with bonds of love and gentle words.[14]

In other words, Elijah expresses his frustration at the collapse of his master plan. God encourages a more moderate approach of "love and gentle words." Does Elijah accept God's message? Clearly not. Elijah stands at the entrance of the cave. Again God asks him:

> "What are you doing here, Elijah?" – Why do you not return to your prophetic mission, guiding the nation without zeal and turbulence?

---

14. Of course, there are other approaches. Radak suggests that the revelation at Mount Sinai is Elijah's reward for his successes upon Mount Carmel. However this explanation has its difficulties, such as why God relieves Elijah of his mission – is there no more work to do? And if Elijah has succeeded so absolutely, why does he desire death?

> And he repeated that he could not abandon the way of zeal for God, for he was zealous for God's name.
>
> ... And because he expressed his desire not to return to prophecy, due to his zeal, He commanded him to anoint Elisha. (Malbim)

Elijah speaks the language of fiery passion. He knows what is true, and when the world around him fails to correspond to the truth that burns within, he cannot accept the travesty. He cannot accept a government of Israel that is hostile to God. He cannot stand that God will sit by and watch as the nation adopts Baal as its deity. According to Malbim, we might say that Elijah holds God to a standard even higher than that which God demands of Himself![15] God wishes to function in the world

---

15. This point is made in the following midrash:

> Three prophets: One defended the honor of the father and the son, one defended the honor of the father but not the son, and one defended the honor of the son but not the father.
>
> Jeremiah defended the honor of the father and the son, as it says, "We sinned and transgressed; You did not have mercy" (Lam. 3:42).... Therefore, his prophecy was doubled....
>
> Elijah defended the honor of the father but not the son, as it says, "I have acted zealously for the Lord, God of Hosts" (1 Kings 19:14). What does it say [regarding this]? "Go, return... anoint Elisha son of Shaphat... in your stead as prophet over Israel" (19:15–16) – "in your stead," as if to say: "I cannot tolerate your prophecy."
>
> Jonah defended the honor of the son but not the father. What does it say? "And the word of the Lord came to Jonah second time..." (Jonah 3:1) – [He spoke to him] a second time and no more. (*Mekhilta DeRabbi Yishmael, Massekhet DePasha* 1)

See Jonathan Sacks, "Leadership and Crisis," in Jeffrey S. Gurock and Yaakov Elman, eds., *Hazon Nahum: Studies in Jewish Law, Thought, and History Presented to Norman Lamm on the Occasion of His Seventieth Birthday* (New York: Yeshiva University Press, 1997), 8–10, where Rabbi Sacks argues that this scene advocates a model of leadership that fails to acknowledge and express solidarity with the nation.

In a fascinating midrash cited below, *Pirkei DeRabbi Eliezer* 29 explains that God forces Elijah to attend every Jewish circumcision ceremony and thereby witness Israel's commitment to the covenant. This way, God denounces Elijah's misplaced zeal and his invalid accusation of Israel:

> He [Elijah] said: "I have acted zealously for the Lord, God of Hosts..." (1 Kings 19:14). God replied "You are always zealous! By your life! Every time Israel

via the "still, small voice"; Elijah wants fire, thunder, and earthquake. He cannot accommodate a world in which Jezebel can rule with a free hand, and he does not understand why God will not bring the world to order. Even when God instructs him to act differently, Elijah informs Him that he cannot; he is made of different stuff. Elijah cannot identify with the "still, small voice"!

We frequently hear Elijah demand uncompromising compliance from the people around him. Even God is not immune to Elijah's biting criticism:

When the child dies:

> "O Lord, my God! **Even to this widow with whom I live** will You bring calamity, slaying her son?" (17:20)

At Mount Carmel:

> "Answer me, O Lord, answer me! And let this nation may know that You are the Lord, God, and **have turned their hearts back.**" (18:37)

Elijah cannot tolerate a world that does not accord with truth. He burns with fire. And so, in this momentous scene, the great prophet effectively resigns. God accepts his resignation, and informs him that He is to appoint Elisha in his stead.

ELIJAH AND MOSES

When reading these chapters, one is struck by similarities between the biblical figures of Moses and Elijah.[16] In our chapter alone, there are numerous contact points: the angel in the desert (as at the burn-

---

perform[s] the covenant of *mila* (circumcision), you will be made to see it with your own eyes!" From here, the rabbis instituted the placement of a seat of honor for [Elijah,] "the angel of the covenant" (Mal. 3:1) [at the ceremony].

16. See a very lengthy list in *Yalkut Shimoni*, Kings 209 and a comprehensive article, A. Hakham, "Moses and Elijah," *Bar Ilan Daf Hashavua*, http://www.biu.ac.il/JH/Parasha/eng/kitisa/hak.html.

ing bush),[17] the miraculous forty days without eating or drinking, and, of course, Elijah's rendezvous with God at Mount Sinai. Furthermore, the chapter ends with the appointment of Elijah's disciple, Elisha, who will succeed him, much as Joshua, Moses' student, became his successor. (Even the name Elisha – "God will save" – matches the meaning of Joshua!) The chapter is filled with hidden references to Moses.[18]

But the parallel created by the focal scene of this chapter is the most evocative: Moses also visited God in the cave, or "nook," on Mount Sinai. It was at that site, in that selfsame mysterious cave, that the momentous debate raged between Moses and God, as Moses demanded Israel's forgiveness despite the grave idolatry of the golden calf (Ex. 33:17–23). At that great epiphany, God's presence, or essence, passed by Moses to utter the cardinal attributes of divine mercy:

> And God passed over his face and proclaimed: The Lord, the Lord, a God compassionate and gracious, slow to anger, abounding in kindness and truth, extending kindness to the thousandth generation, forgiving iniquity, transgression and sin. (Ex. 34:6–7)

What is the historic significance of the cave at Mount Sinai? At that spot, Moses heroically defended his people when they had been found guilty of idolatry. At that cave, God revealed Himself as a merciful God, expressing His desire and capacity to for generosity and forbearance. God wants Elijah to learn from the great prophet Moses, the defender of Israel, who invoked the covenant to save the nation.[19] Elijah doesn't get the hint!

---

17. See Exodus 3:2.
18. In previous chapters, Elijah also exhibits characteristics similar to those of Moses: The building of the altar on Mount Carmel with its twelve stones reminds us of the twelve stones alongside the altar built by Moses at Mount Sinai. At the inauguration of the Tabernacle, Moses, like Elijah, brings fire from heaven to consume the *korbanot*. In both cases, the people react by "falling on their faces." In 1 Kings 18, Elijah kills the prophets of Baal, much as Moses executes the perpetrators of the golden calf. Elijah flees the country after killing the prophets of Baal, just as Moses flees Egypt after killing an Egyptian. Later (11 Kings 2), Elijah splits the Jordan River in imitation of the parting of the Red Sea. Finally, neither Moses nor Elijah has a known burial place.
19. Moses speaks of the oath to Abraham, Isaac, and Jacob, using the language and

How wide, then, is the gulf that separates Moses and Elijah! Moses pleads for the nation; Elijah blames the nation. On the one hand, Moses knows how to present God's demands to the people – he rebukes them for their part in the golden calf and kills the perpetrators. But on the other hand, it is Moses who boldly stands before God to demand national forgiveness. In contrast, Elijah stands in the name of God and accuses the nation of abrogating the covenant. The cave at Sinai should have resounded with the mandate to defend and shield the nation despite its sin. Instead, Elijah chooses to bemoan, malign, and accuse Israel of breaching the covenant.

THREE TASKS

As a result, God relieves Elijah of his mission and instructs him to anoint three people to leadership positions:

1. Hazael as king of Aram – a king who eventually devastates the northern kingdom (II Kings 13:7, 22–23)
2. Jehu as king of the north – a king who eventually kills and replaces the royal house of Omri and Ahab
3. Elisha as Elijah's successor

These three actions represent a three-pronged response to Elijah's outrage. In the long term, God answers Elijah's appeal. He will destroy the house of Omri. To that end, the first task – the appointment of Hazael as king over Aram – puts a foreign leader in place who will devastate the northern kingdom. This is a national punishment emanating from an *external* source. Second, Jehu will rise to the throne in the northern kingdom by assassinating Ahab's son Jehoram. Jehu brings about an *internal* political reordering and the end of the royal dynasty of Omri. Third, the appointment of Elisha replaces Elijah, enabling continued spiritual guidance after the latter's personal breakdown.[20]

---

imagery – "stars of the heavens" (Ex. 32:13) – of the Covenant between the Parts (Gen. 15).

20. Interestingly, Elijah complies only with the final instruction. He appoints Elisha without delay, but he never anoints Haza'el or Jehu. Malbim suggests that Ahab's

THE APPOINTMENT OF ELISHA

God introduces Elisha as Elijah's successor, and we are curious as to his suitability for this role. The scene in which Elijah meets Elisha is a wonderful example of the contrast between these two men.[21] We meet Elisha as he is plowing with twenty-four oxen (19:19). It is apparent that his family owns the farm, so we are dealing with wealthy landowners. Elisha clearly works on the farm and pulls his weight.

Without introduction or explanation, Elijah flings his cloak over Elisha. Immediately, Elisha seems transformed, abandoning his work and running after him.[22] But then Elisha stops and says:

> "Let me kiss my father and mother goodbye, and then I will fol-
> low you".... He turned back from him and took a yoke of oxen
> and slaughtered [them] ... and gave it to the people, and they
> ate; then he arose and followed Elijah and became his assistant.
> (19:20–22)

Elisha speaks about running back to "kiss" his parents goodbye, but he gets distracted and ends up saying goodbye to the entire farm, slaughtering the oxen and providing a feast for the whole community! One wonders what Elijah makes of this behavior. I presume that he is rather frustrated, puzzled by Elisha's penchant for social niceties while the mission of God awaits. Elijah is the perennial loner, the outsider, the prophet who lives apart from society and fails to make peace with it. Elisha demonstrates social sensitivity, an ability to comprehend that even a divine calling must be balanced with a human approach. In this sense, he is an

---

repentance (see 1 Kings 21) delayed the punishment of his royal dynasty. Both Radak and Ralbag claim that Elijah had intended to perform the first two tasks, but he met Elisha on the way and understood that rendezvous as a sign that Elisha was to carry out those missions instead.

21. For more on the contrast between these two prophets, see Rabbi Adin Steinsaltz, "Elisha: The Pragmatic Prophet," in his *Biblical Images* (Jerusalem: Maggid, 2010), 139–44. On the scene of the appointment of Elisha, see Rabbi Elchanan Samet, *The Elijah Narratives*, 327-47 [Hebrew].

22. Elijah has a manipulative effect on people. See, for example, 1 Kings 17:15 and 11 Kings 1:6.

apt replacement for Elijah, complementing the latter's uncompromising, principled stance with a more congenial attitude.

In conclusion, we see how the great Elijah, despite his immense successes, is unwilling to speak the language of God's *kol demama daka*, His "still, small voice." Elijah, who appreciates God's overwhelming force – the earth-shattering wind and the consuming fire – cannot tolerate a gentle, human leadership style. He is so impassioned for God, so indignant regarding Baal, that he cannot adjust to any setback, to society's slow progress. Elijah resigns as prophet, and God appoints his successor.

RABBINIC CONNECTIONS: PHINEHAS AND ELIJAH

We have already compared and contrasted Elijah with Moses. However, we would do well to explore the connection drawn by rabbinic sources between Elijah and Phinehas, who both bear the biblical title of "zealot" (Num. 25:11–12 and I Kings 19:10, 14).[23] With Phinehas, we meet a fearless, impassioned leader who can shed light on Elijah and his mission.

Phinehas takes the national stage as the men of Israel consort with the women of Midian in a frenzied mix of sexuality and idolatry (see Num. 25:1–9). His decisive, aggressive action halts God's plague and saves Israel. He kills an Israelite prince and his Midianite consort, and this zealotry is praised emphatically by God.

Let us now revert to the other "zealot," to Elijah. Malachi envisions an eschatological "day of the Lord" on which the evil will be punished and the righteous will survive. Interestingly, Elijah features in this futuristic vision:

> Behold, I am sending you Elijah the prophet before the arrival of the day of the Lord, that great and awesome day. (Mal. 3:23)

What is Elijah's role in preparing Israel for that day, a day that is depicted in harsh terms, "burning like an oven…all the wicked will burn like straw" (3:19)? One of the sins mentioned in Malachi, labeled as a "violation of the covenant of our forefathers" (2:11), is described as follows:

---

23. Indeed, I Kings 19 is the *haftara* for *parashat Pinhas*.

> Judah has broken faith; abhorrent things have been done in Israel
> and Jerusalem; for Judah has profaned that which is holy to the
> Lord – **he has married the daughter of alien gods.** (Mal. 2:11)

Judah's abrogation of the covenant, his betrayal, is his marriage to non-
Jewish women who worship idols. What is Elijah to do about this? How
will he prepare the Jewish nation for God's awesome day?

> He shall reconcile fathers with their sons and sons with their
> fathers…. (3:24)

In other words, the children born to mixed marriages, and raised in the
tradition of their pagan mothers, shall be restored to their fathers, who
will teach them to follow God![24]

What are the rabbis teaching us by equating Elijah with Phinehas? Phinehas took vengeance on a Jewish prince who consorted with
a foreign princess. By his violent act, he put a stop to the rampant idolatry in the Israelite camp. By analogy, the Phinehas model suggests that
Elijah sought to detach Ahab from Jezebel.[25] He was hoping to separate
this Jewish king who had "married the daughter of alien gods" from his
idolatrous wife. That is Phinehas-Elijah's legacy. Elijah led Ahab all the
way to Jezreel in the hope that he would take the next logical step and
distance (or possibly kill) Jezebel – but that didn't happen. Elijah's failure to sever Jezebel's hold on her husband meant that the infrastructure
of Baal was still in place, the government had not changed, and now the
spectacle of Mount Carmel appeared insubstantial and fleeting. Here
lies the root of Elijah's frustration and despair.

---

24. Maimonides, in *Mishneh Torah*, Laws of Kings 12:2, discusses how, in Messianic
    times, Elijah will establish the correct lineage of children born to mixed marriages.
25. I heard this explanation from Rabbi Yaakov Medan.

1 Kings 20

Tests of Faith

Elijah, as we have seen, perceives the spectacle at Mount Carmel as a failure. But beyond his initial reaction, we have not assessed Ahab's impressions. Is he inspired by God's fire descending from heaven, or is he, like Jezebel, impervious to what he has witnessed? Does the revelation at Mount Carmel have any long-term effect?

RELIGIOUS RESURGENCE

In 1 Kings 20, Ahab's court experiences a religious resurgence in which God features prominently and in which Baal and its supporters are strangely absent. The impressive band of four hundred prophets of Baal is missing from Ahab's court. Instead a lone prophet of God functions as a central adviser. Ahab acts upon the encouraging words of that prophet not once but twice in this chapter. Moreover, in a scene at the end of the chapter, we see how another such prophet must disguise himself so Ahab won't recognize him – indicating that the king is well acquainted with the prophets of God.

In this story, God encourages and nurtures Ahab's faith, offering him military victory: "And you shall know that I am God" (20:13, 28). God is reaching out to Ahab.

The absence of prophets of Baal and Ashera is striking.[1] When Jezebel was a central religious influence, prophets of God were persecuted; now they walk freely and advise the king. It appears that after the showdown at Mount Carmel, something fundamental has shifted in Ahab's world. In many ways, Elijah has succeeded!

Of course, we should not get carried away. Ahab is not perfect; his faith and his relationship with God's prophet fluctuate[2] and are frequently a function of self-interest. Yet, to his credit, he is actively engaged with the Israelite religion. It is Jezebel, not Ahab, who is ideologically attached to Baal.

ARAM

Aram constitutes the greatest threat to Israel's national security. Already during Baasha's reign, Aram invaded the north, seizing the Huleh Valley, north of the Sea of Galilee. Now tensions flare again as we read of Ahab's three battles against Ben-Hadad, king of Aram. In the first two campaigns, detailed in our chapter, Ahab is victorious. In the third battle (chapter 22), he will lose the war – and his life.[3]

Our chapter opens with the northern kingdom in grave danger. Ben-Hadad has besieged the capital city of Samaria with an enormous coalition of thirty-two other kings. The initial negotiations take the

---

1. Baal does not return to the royal court. In 1 Kings 22, we find four hundred prophets – a number associated with Baal – but they prophesy exclusively in God's name (22:12). Admittedly, these are false prophets. Nevertheless, there is a critical difference between false prophets and a regime based upon idolatry.
2. Despite the positive religious orientation at its start, chapter 20 ends with a clash between the prophet and the king, leaving a sour taste regarding their cooperation. Chapter 21 also charts a turnaround, recounting considerable friction between prophet and king; however, when condemned by Elijah for his unethical actions, Ahab responds with an act of repentance. Then there is a further downturn in chapter 22, as his prophet Zedekiah strikes the prophet, and the king imprisons him.
3. The aggression between Israel and Aram steadily escalates after Ahab's era, with Aram gaining the upper hand until the reign of Jeroboam son of Joash (II Kings 14:23). Aram's domination of Israel is expressed in II Kings 6:24–28 and 13:7, 23.

form of war messages sent back and forth between the siege camp and the besieged city.[4]

Here is the first exchange between Ben-Hadad and Ahab:

> And he sent messengers to Ahab...: "Thus said Ben-Hadad: Your silver and gold are mine; your beautiful wives and children are mine." The king of Israel replied...: "As you say, my lord, king: I and all I have are yours."

Ben-Hadad demands that the city surrender, and Ahab capitulates in the face of Aram's superior force. However, the messengers return with another directive:

> Thus said Ben-Hadad: "When I sent you the order to give me your silver and gold and your wives and children, I meant that tomorrow at this time I will send my servants, and they will search your house... and seize everything you prize and take it away." (20:2–6)

Ahab has acceded to Ben-Hadad's first demand. How will he respond to this second rapacious and intrusive instruction? Ahab's reaction is slow and deliberate. He first summons his advisers, giving them his feeling that this is no ordinary demand but essentially a provocation, a pretext for attack: "this man is bent on evil/destruction" (20:7).[5] They advise him not to comply, and Ahab informs Ben-Hadad:

> Tell my lord, the king: All that you demanded of your servant at first, I shall do, but this thing I cannot do. (20:9)

The commentators are puzzled. In his first message, Ben-Hadad proclaims that Ahab's money and family are his, and Ahab agrees! Now

---

4. The root *sh-l-ḥ* (send) is something of a keyword, featuring in a more intense form – *shilaḥ* (release) – at the end of the chapter. See 20:2, 5–7, 9, 17, 34, 42.
5. In Hebrew, the word is *raa*, usually translated as "evil." But in many contexts, it means annihilation or destruction. See Genesis 19:19; Exodus 32:12, 14; Jonah 3:10.

Ben-Hadad declares that he is coming to seize those items. What critical shift has taken place in the second demand? Why does Ahab comply so readily with the first message and reject the second? Ralbag explains:

> "I and all I have are yours" – I am under your governance, to serve you and pay tribute. (Ralbag)

In other words, the original demand is that Ahab capitulate to the military superiority of Aram, aligning himself with that nation as a vassal by paying taxes to the Aramean kingdom, but essentially governing his internal affairs independently. But Ben-Hadad's second message indicates that he intends to enter the city and seize Ahab's family and valuables. That is an act of humiliation, a violation of the international standard between vassal and sovereign.

Alternatively, as suggested by Rabbi Yosef Kara, the second message is a demand that Samaria submit to the enemy, allowing it to overrun and destroy the northern kingdom. In short, Ben-Hadad is uninterested in Ahab's political loyalty; rather, he seeks to crush him. It is precisely because of this existential threat that Ahab calls a cabinet meeting. His advisers also understand that this is no ordinary diplomatic demand. Essentially, Ben-Hadad's directive is an ultimatum, a declaration of war, and they advise him to reject the arrangement.[6]

---

6. In a rather mystifying reading of this exchange, Ḥazal state that Ahab would have accepted the seizing of his family by Ben-Hadad. However, his red line – "everything you prize" – was a Torah scroll! Ben-Hadad demanded that Ahab hand over his personal *sefer Torah*, his "prized possession." "R. Yohanan said: Why did Ahab deserve to reign for twenty-two years? Because he honored the Torah, which was given with twenty-two letters" (*Sanhedrin* 102b). According to this reading, Ben-Hadad seeks not to humiliate Ahab personally, but rather to remove Israel's national symbol. It is this attack on Israel's spiritual roots that Ahab rejects. Rashi comments: "Even though they [the Israelites] served idols, they respected the Torah."

    In this fascinating midrash, as Ahab faces the very survival of his kingdom, he discovers that what matters most to him is his Jewish identity. In a classic gesture that has been exhibited by many wayward Jews who in critical moments of danger or external pressure and anti-Jewish humiliation discover their Jewish roots, Ahab demonstrates that at his core is a Jewish sensitivity, a commitment to God. He may not observe the law, but he knows it is the essence of Israel's survival.

Ahab's taking counsel is interesting. He is open to influence and reason. In contrast, Ben-Hadad's pose smacks of arrogance as he boasts at the prospect of victory.[7] Interestingly, Ahab addresses Ben-Hadad as "my lord, king," indicating that he accepts the vassal agreement. Yet he is unwilling to surrender his kingdom! Ahab retains his national pride in the war of words, concluding the conversation with a wonderful, witty idiom:

> The king of Israel answered, "Tell him: 'One who puts on his armor should not boast like one who takes it off.'" (20:11)

This is the military version of the expression "Don't count your chickens before they hatch." Ahab warns Ben-Hadad not to boast of victory before the war has even begun.

THE PROPHET

Now Ben-Hadad activates the siege. In a precursor to later events, we are informed that he and his compatriots have started drinking (20:12). They are clearly not anticipating any action that day. After all, a siege can drag out for months, if not years; there is no need at this point to be on alert. The brief mention of Ben-Hadad's drinking with his fellow kings starkly contrasts the carefree, happy siege camp and the tense atmosphere inside Samaria. This disparity will be the key to Ahab's victory. By the time we reach verse 16, Ben-Hadad will be far from sober (though it is only noon!).

One probable textual source of this midrash is the righteous king Josiah's discovery of a Torah scroll after the dreadful period of idolatry led by the evil king Manasseh (see II Kings 22:8–12). The Talmud links Ahab and Josiah in that they were both killed in battle (*Megilla* 3a).

7. "May the gods deal with me, be it ever so severely, if enough dust remains in Samaria to give each of my men a handful" (I Kings 20:10), says Ben-Hadad, expressing his victory in terms of dust. It would appear that this metaphor was part of the vernacular in Aram, as in "For the king of Aram had destroyed the rest and made them like the dust at threshing time" (II Kings 13:7) and "Please let me, your servant, be given as much earth as a pair of mules can carry, for your servant will never again make burnt offerings and sacrifices to any other god but the Lord" (5:17).

At this juncture, the prophet enters the scene:

Thus says the Lord: Do you see this great multitude? I will deliver it into your hands today, and you shall know that I am the Lord. (20:13)

Ahab trusts the prophet, adopting God's advice as an operative plan and sending out a small attack force.[8] Attacking a huge army with a small unit of soldiers – in broad daylight, at noon – is hardly a recommended tactic, but that is precisely the point.[9] By following God's instruction against all odds, the improbable becomes possible. Seeing a meager 232 people emerging from Ahab's camp, and assuming that these are the first group of deserters abandoning the city and the bleak prospects of a prolonged siege, a drunken Ben-Hadad delivers an incoherent message to his sentries.[10] The tiny force is an advantage, and the army from Samaria wins the day.[11]

The victory has been orchestrated by God, and it is evident to all that God is the critical factor in this success. Even if, in retrospect, we can see the genius in sending a small force at midday, no one had intelligence information as to the enemy's inebriation, a key element in the

---

8. This military unit, identified in 1 Kings 20:15 as *naarei sarei hamedinot* – the "young men of the princes of the provinces" – is unknown elsewhere in the Bible. However, the word *naar* (young man) is familiar from military contexts; for example, see 1 Samuel 30:17, 11 Samuel 2:14, and Nehemiah 4:1.

9. The number of soldiers who follow the attack force in this verse – seven thousand – is interesting, because the last appearance of this figure was in regards to the "seven thousand – every knee that has not bowed to Baal" (1 Kings 19:18). This is an example of a literary technique throughout 1 Kings, in which elements of a previous chapter are echoed in the next. However, in this instance, the recurrence may have deeper significance. Might it allude to the fact that the people have been exonerated for their sins of idolatry? See Rashi.

10. Ben-Hadad's strange line – "If they have come out to surrender, take them alive; and if they have come out for battle, take them alive anyway" (20:18) – indicates that either way, the people should be taken alive. The classic commentators suggest that the incoherence and lilt are those of a drunken man.

11. For an interesting reconstruction of the battle conditions here, see Moshe Garsiel, *The Beginning of the Kingship in Israel: Studies in the Book of Samuel* (Raanana: Open University, 2008), vol. 3, 175–80 [Hebrew].

panic and confusion that ensued. God's hand is evident in this unpredictable reversal of fortunes.

The prophet, now allied with Ahab, cautions against overconfidence, informing the king that Aram will return next year (20:22). Once again, we are impressed by the close relationship between prophet and government.

THE SECOND WAR

The second battle, a year later, is framed in a religious context from the perspective of both Aram and Israel. The Arameans are convinced that their previous defeat was a victory for the God of Israel. And yet, by their assessment, in different geographic conditions, their Assyrian gods would be stronger:

> The ministers of the king of Aram said to him, "Their God is a God of the mountains; that is why they got the better of us; but if we fight them in the plain, we will surely get the better of them." (20:23)[12]

Ben-Hadad's mobilization extends beyond the religious sphere. Aram reorganizes its military forces to avoid repeating the disciplinary and organizational failures of the previous campaign (see 20:24–25). This is a battle Ben-Hadad intends to win. The Bible reports that Aram "covered the land," whereas Israel is described as "two flocks of goats" (20:27).

Against this backdrop, the prophet offers God's assistance yet again. Now that Aram has framed the campaign as a battle of the gods, God's reputation is at the center of the drama.[13] Again, the prophet nurtures and mentors Ahab, as God actively stimulates his faith:

---

12. A geographical perception of God was common in many cultures. As noted, Baal was a local god. Similarly, some explain that Jonah flees Israel on the assumption that God is not be manifest outside the land. As the rabbis state: "Anyone who lives outside the land of Israel is as if he has no God" (*Ketubbot* 110b).

13. In several instances in the Bible, God expresses His intent to actively to defend His reputation. See Exodus 32:12; Numbers 14:4–16; Deuteronomy 32:27; Joshua 7:9; and Ezekiel 36:22, 32.

The man of God approached and spoke to the king of Israel, "Thus said the Lord: This is what the Lord says: Because the Arameans have said: 'The Lord is a God of the mountains, but He is not a God of the lowlands,' I will deliver this vast army into your hands, **and you shall know that I am the Lord.**" (20:28)

BEN-HADAD'S SURRENDER AND AHAB'S CAPITULATION

The war is fought in the plain of Aphek, east of the Sea of Galilee.[14] The Israelites gain the upper hand, decimating the enemy. The remaining 27,000 troops take shelter in the city, but the city wall collapses on them. It seems as if God is fighting for Israel. Now it is Ben-Hadad's turn to find himself under siege, trapped, as he "takes refuge in the town, in an inner room" (20:30):

> His officials said to him, "Look, we have heard that the kings of the house of Israel are merciful; let us go to the king of Israel with sackcloth around our waists and ropes around our heads – perhaps he will spare your life." Wearing sackcloth around their waists and ropes around their heads, they went to the king of Israel and said, "Your servant Ben-Hadad says, 'Please let me live'".… (20:31–32)

This masquerade is designed to make Ben-Hadad look vulnerable, arousing Ahab's sympathy and evoking the mercy for which kings of Israel are famed.

> The sackcloth … was the manner of prisoners of war, and the ropes around their heads, as if they were on the verge of being hanged. They aimed to say: O Master, King, we are your prisoners of war, and we understand that we should be executed, if not for your manifest mercy. (Abarbanel)

---

14. Garsiel suggests that it was fought on the banks of the Sea of Galilee around Ein Gev. Yehuda Kiel, however, opines that the battle took place in the Golan Heights. See O. Bustenai and M. Garsiel, eds., *Encyclopedia of the World of the Bible, I Kings* (Tel Aviv: Davidson-Atai, 1994) [Hebrew]; Kiel, *Da'at Mikra, 1 Kings* [Hebrew]. Others have placed the war near today's Afula, in the Jezreel Valley.

Ahab falls for the trick; his reaction is startlingly positive:

> …the king answered, "Is he still alive? He is my brother!"

Whereas Ben-Hadad's men initially addressed Ahab from a subordinate position, speaking of Ben-Hadad as "your servant," now Ahab addresses him as "my brother"!

This sudden "brothering"[15] of Ben-Hadad prompts a rapid shift in tone by Ben-Hadad's astute negotiators:

> The men took this as a good sign and were quick to pick up his word[16] – "Yes, **your brother** Ben-Hadad!" they said. (20:33)

And when the two kings meet, they negotiate a cease-fire with economic advantages for Israel:

> "Go and get him," the king said; when Ben-Hadad came out, Ahab had him come up into [his] chariot. He [Ben-Hadad] said: "I will return the cities my father took from your father, and you may set up your own market areas in Damascus, as my father did in Samaria." [Ahab said,] "On the basis of this treaty, I will set you free"; so he made a treaty with him and set him free. (20:33–34)

EXPLAINING AHAB

The Bible is highly critical of Ahab's failure to kill Ben-Hadad. What is motivating Ahab? Upon an initial reading, we may well propose that Ahab simply spots a good business opportunity. He is aware that a generation earlier, during the reign of Baasha, Aram captured vast tracts

---

15. This fraternal motif may be a play on Ahab's name, which in Hebrew contains the word *ah*, "brother." See Garsiel's article on names in the Ahab story and the intertextual wordplays they create: "Midrashic Name Derivations in the Elijah Cycle," in *Studies in Bible and Jewish Thought: H.M.Y. Gevaryahu Jubilee Volume*, ed. B.Z. Luria (Jerusalem: Kiryat Sefer, 1989), 149–55 [Hebrew]. Ḥazal also interpret Ahab's name in Hebrew, Ahav, homiletically, declaring him "a brother (*ah*) to Heaven but a father (*av*) to idolatry" (*Sanhedrin* 102b).

16. The Hebrew here is cryptic and grammatically complex.

of the Galilee (see 15:20). Rather than executing Ben-Hadad, here is a chance to leverage the situation and recoup lost territories. In addition, Israel is being offered unrestricted export access to Damascus, a rare opportunity to penetrate a foreign market. The revenues from such a move could be enormous. Ahab maximizes his military advantage, accruing huge benefits for the nation at large and its treasury.

Some have deemed Ahab's motives political-military rather than economic. Archaeological evidence points in this direction. The Kurkh Monolith, an Assyrian document describing the wars of the Assyrian king Shalmanesser III, details a military alliance between the king of Aram and Ahab (who is described as unusually powerful).[17] Historians have speculated that, aware of the looming Assyrian threat, Ahab sought a military alliance with Ben-Hadad against Assyria, as his forces alone were insufficient.[18]

These theories regarding Ahab's motives are certainly plausible, but when we study the text, we are jarred by the wistful lilt of his speech, his abject sentimentalism: "Is he still alive? He is my brother!" This response is alarming. Why does Ahab perceive this man as a brother? Here is a rival king who has attacked him twice, who humiliated him in Samaria, and about whom he has said, "See! This man is bent on destruction" (20:7)!

Nehama Leibowitz makes an enlightening suggestion. In discussing a similar situation, in which King Saul spares Agag, king of Amalek, she addresses the case of Ahab:

> The text [in the book of Samuel, regarding Amalek] records nothing else but the hankering after the spoils of war. Why, then, did Saul spare Agag, it may be asked?
>
> It may be answered that he was loath to slay a king. **Class solidarity overlooks all other considerations.** (Note too that Ahab, one of the kings of Israel ... did not show mercy to just any

---

17. The Kurkh Monolith was found by J.E. Taylor in 1861; it is currently on display in the British Museum.
18. See Prof. Avraham Grossman, "1 Kings 20 and 22: The War between Ahab and Aram," http://www.daat.co.il/daat/tanach/rishonim/grosman6.htm [Hebrew].

of his enemies, but only to a royal adversary, the king condemned to utter destruction, calling him "brother" even when they both sent their armies against each other to annihilate and exterminate each other. In like manner, the kings of Europe banded together to rescue their French royal counterpart from the French Revolution. They were inspired not by international brotherhood, but by class solidarity.)[19]

In other words, we are talking about a VIP club, a royal fraternity. Ahab spares Ben-Hadad simply because he shares his rank. Even between warring kings, it would appear that a royal, as a royal, deserves special treatment! Ahab has not made a calculated administrative decision after discerning that the economic benefits exceed the effectiveness of war; this is unadulterated favoritism! In this light, Ahab's act of "mercy" becomes morally reprehensible.

But there is a deeper religious problem here, which is articulated by the fourth appearance of a prophet, at the end of the chapter.

THE JURIDICAL PARABLE

The final scenes of this chapter depict a strange series of events in which the prophet instructs someone to injure him and then disguises himself and approaches the king. Bearing the message that God is far from happy with Ahab's pardon of Ben-Hadad, the prophet issues a severe condemnation:

> Thus says the Lord: Because you have set this man free, whom I had doomed (*ish ḥermi*), your life shall be forfeit for his life, and your people for his people. (20:42)

Why is the prophet's disguise necessary? Why can he not simply stop the king's carriage and speak God's word? Why must he resort to a theatrical trap? Prof. Uriel Simon has noted this type of masquerade

---

19. Nehama Leibowitz, "King Saul's Offence," in Leibowitz, *Studies in Vayikra* (*Leviticus*) (Jerusalem: World Zionist Organization, 1980), 316.

in several stories in the Bible, identifying them as a sub-genre he terms the "juridical parable."[20] In such a presentation, the storyteller presents

> …a fictional tale with a realistic plot dealing with an act of law-breaking, told to someone who has committed a transgression or is intimately involved in the matter, with the aim of getting him to unwittingly pass judgment on himself.[21]

The offender will be caught in the trap only if he does not detect that the parable addresses him. To this end, the speaker disguises the parable as a legal case and creates some discrepancy between it and the offender's situation. In our story, the masking/bandaging of the wounded prophet has a dual effect: It hides his true identity, so Ahab does not realize he is being challenged by a prophet, and it also allows the latter to adopt the guise of a wounded soldier fresh from battle, thus reinforcing the parable.

But here we encounter some difficulty. The juridical parable must accord somewhat with the real-life situation, but must also obscure and disguise it, or else the parable will not elicit the desired response. We seek a correlation, on the one hand, along with a distortion, or an in-built discrepancy. Yet in our case, the discrepancy is too great. In the prophetic parable, the man is explicitly told, "Guard this man! If he is missing, it will be your life for his" (20:39). But we fail to locate an explicit instruction to Ahab that Ben-Hadad was to be killed or even incarcerated![22] Why, then, is Ahab condemned for letting him go?

In answering this question, we must appreciate the status of the king in ancient warfare. As in chess (which reflects such warfare), victory cannot be declared unless one has eliminated the king. Despite the loss

---

20. Examples include 11 Samuel 11:1–4, 11 Samuel 14, and Isaiah 5:1–7.
21. Uriel Simon, *Reading Prophetic Narratives* (Bloomington: University of Indiana Press), 112. See also Simon's "The Poor Man's Ewe-Lamb: An Example of a Juridical Parable," *Biblica* 48 (1967), 207–42.
22. Because of this jarring discrepancy, the Jerusalem Talmud (*Sanhedrin* 11:5) – and in its footsteps, Rashi – insists that Ahab indeed had been told explicitly not to favor or release Ben-hadad.

of 130,000 soldiers, Ben-Hadad could still save face; he would return to his nation and organize a victory parade.[23] As long as the enemy king is free, Ahab's "victory" is debatable. The only decisive determinant of victory is the death of the enemy leader. Ben-Hadad understands this only too well. When he subsequently fights Ahab yet again, he instructs his archers to target the king:

> Do not fight anyone, small or great, except the king of Israel. (22:31)

So is Israel, in fact, victorious under Ahab, or do his actions essentially squander the triumph, allowing it to evaporate? An answer may be found in chapter 22, where we read that a mere three years later, Ben-Hadad flouts all his promises. With this king at large, God's victory is short-lived.

JERICHO AND THE SPOILS OF WAR

The battle of Jericho (Josh. 6–8) presents a useful parallel with which to illustrate the severity of the clemency extended to Ben-Hadad. The prophet of our chapter labels Ben-Hadad *ish ḥermi*, a man sentenced to die (as *Targum Yonatan* renders it). The word *ḥerem* is crucial in the case of Jericho, which is, of course, another battle God fights for Israel. In that episode, a man named Achan appropriates various items from the spoils (*ḥerem*) of war and is sentenced to death for his crime. There are some interesting parallels between that narrative and ours:

1. Kings: "And these encamped opposite these for seven days…" (20:29)
   Joshua: "They marched around the city once…they did this six days. On the seventh day…" (6:14–15)

---

23. A few contemporary examples of this phenomenon: Anwar Sadat annually celebrated Egypt's "victory" in the Yom Kippur War. After the Second Lebanon War, despite his bombed-out headquarters, Hassan Nassrallah staged a victory parade in the streets of Beirut. And when NATO fought in Libya in 2011, the combat ended only when the national leader – Col. Muammar el-Qaddafi – was executed.

2. Kings: "The prophet approached: So says God:...I will deliver this massive force into your hand..." (20:28)
   Joshua: "Joshua said:...God has delivered you the city" (6:17)
3. Kings: "the wall fell on 27,000 survivors" (20:30)
   Joshua: "the wall collapsed" (6:20)

The victory at Jericho is characterized by a ban on the spoils: "The city is banned (*ḥerem*), and all its contents are God's..." (6:17). Why are the spoils of this battle sacrosanct? In ancient warfare, the spoils belong to the victor, the triumphant party. In Jericho, it is not man who fells the city, but God. The victory is His, and hence, the booty belong not to man, but to God. By taking from these spoils, Achan "betrays" Israel[24] and its Benefactor. He takes the symbol of God's victory for himself, as if to say, "We fought this war; it is ours – not God's."

Returning to our chapter, Rashi translates the phrase *ish ḥermi* as "the man of My battle," intimating that it is not within Ahab's jurisdiction to release this man. Ben-Hadad is God's prisoner, not Ahab's. As we have seen, Ahab capitalizes upon this military victory to gain politically, territorially, and economically. He seeks to reap personal profit from God's triumph. Ahab's misappropriation of the victory is a violation of God's role in the war.

Note that in the juridical parable presented to Ahab, the man is blamed not for failing to execute the prisoner, but rather for being so preoccupied that the prisoner gets away! Ahab too allows his prisoner to slip away. But unlike in the parable, the prisoner does not simply escape – that would be bad enough! Rather, Ahab plea-bargains; he makes a deal! In this outrageous act, he fails to acknowledge that this is God's victory and that he has no right to leverage it for his own advantage.

IN CONCLUSION

Behind the state politics and military negotiations of chapter 20, God's presence is palpable. Throughout the chapter, God ensures Israel's victories, and the prophet accompanies Ahab's decisions, guiding his tac-

---

24. In another interesting parallel, Achan is labeled a "betrayer" (Josh. 6:18, 7:25), and so is Ahab (1 Kings 18:18).

tics and boosting national confidence. In the final battle, however, Ahab sidelines God's role and uses the military defeat to his advantage instead of as a springboard to faith. Thus, from God's perspective, he has squandered the victory and undermined his status as king.

1 Kings 21

A Perfect Murder

At first blush, this chapter could not be more straightforward. It is the story of a simple man who gets in the way of powerful, ruthless people. Naboth has something the king and queen want, and he is a nuisance. They have him "disposed of," murdering Naboth in a political setup and seizing the prize piece of real estate that they so desperately seek. Elijah the prophet is sent to condemn King Ahab's abuse of power.

Upon a closer reading however, this tale provides a fascinating landscape in which to examine the intriguing pathology of sin and the revolutionary power structure of Israelite society.

THE INHERITANCE OF HIS FATHERS

> And it came to pass after these things that Naboth the Jezreelite had a vineyard, which was in Jezreel, next to the palace of Ahab, king of Samaria. Ahab spoke to Naboth, saying, "Give me your vineyard, that I may have it for a vegetable garden, because it is near my home, and I will give you a better vineyard instead; or if you prefer, I will give you its worth in money." Naboth said to Ahab, "God forbid I should give the inheritance of my fathers to you." And Ahab came home sullen and displeased.... (1 Kings 21:1–4)

In these opening lines, the protagonists are depicted as products of their geography: "Naboth the Jezreelite had a vineyard, which was in Jezreel" – he is a Jezreelite; it is the cornerstone of his identity. He is contrasted with "Ahab, king of Samaria," a city far from Jezreel, who is nonetheless the king. At the outset, this description transmits two contrasting perceptions. First, Naboth is way out of his depth; after all, he, a commoner, is defying the king! Second, conversely, this king resides in Samaria; he is a foreign implant in Jezreel. His jurisdiction is elsewhere, and it is Naboth who is the permanent local fixture.

Naboth refuses the king on principle: "God forbid I should give the inheritance of my fathers to you." In other words, I cannot sell you my vineyard even if I wish, because God has mandated me to preserve this tract of land in my family. This response reflects no lack of respect for Ahab or disregard for the high office of the king. Naboth simply sees the issue as a matter of faith.

But is Naboth correct? Is a Jew forbidden to sell land? In *parashat Behar*, the selling of land in Eretz Yisrael is permitted only under dire financial duress. Moreover, if unfortunate circumstances lead to the sale of the ancestral estate, the family of the land's original tribal owner is to "redeem" that land, restoring it to the family (see Lev. 25:25). This practice is familiar to us from the book of Ruth, in which Boaz redeems the property of Elimelech. In the Torah, this mitzva is preceded by the following verses:

> The land shall not be sold in perpetuity, for the land is Mine, and you are sojourners and residents with Me. And throughout the land of your possession, you shall give redemption to the land. (Lev. 25:23–24)

Moreover, we read in the book of Numbers:

> An inheritance shall not be transferred from one tribe to another, for each person of the children of Israel shall cleave to the **inheritance of the tribe of his fathers**, that the children of Israel may inherit, each individual the **inheritance of his fathers**. (36:7–8)

This is the origin of the phrase spoken by Naboth, "the inheritance of my fathers." The land is not ours to sell. God has entrusted it to us, returning it to the ancestral family unit each Jubilee (*yovel*) year if we have sold it in the intervening years. A Jew sells his inheritance only as a last resort!

ROYAL POWER AND PEOPLE POWER

But has the king no right to requisition land from his citizens? Indeed, when the prophet Samuel introduces what a monarchy entails, what the Talmud calls the "Law of the King," he appears to legislate that a king may seize any vineyard he desires:

> This shall be the custom of the king who will rule over you: he will take your sons and commandeer them for his chariot and as his horsemen, and they shall run before his chariot.... And he shall take your daughters as perfumers and cooks and bakers. And **he shall take the best of your fields and your vineyards** and your olive yards, and give them to his servants. (1 Sam. 8:11, 13–14)

However, the legal status of this passage is under dispute in the Talmud:

> R. Judah said in the name of Samuel: All that is mentioned in the "Law of the King" is permitted to the king. Rav said: This was told to them only to threaten them. (*Sanhedrin* 20b)

According to R. Judah, it is within Ahab's rights to expropriate Naboth's vineyard. But Rav disagrees. In his view, the regal powers listed in the book of Samuel are mere propaganda intended to discourage the nation from becoming a monarchy. According to Rav, the appropriation of property is beyond the king's legal jurisdiction.

Interestingly, Maimonides, who seems to rule like R. Judah, takes the legal middle ground:

> He [the king] may take fields and olive groves and vineyards for his subjects **when they go to war... if they have nothing to eat**, and he **must recompense** [the owner of the land]. (*Mishneh Torah*, Laws of Kings 4:6)

Maimonides asserts that the king has the right to requisition a field or vineyard, but only under very specific conditions. It must be a war situation, a case of urgent military food need, and he must compensate the land's owner for his financial loss.

Within our chapter, however, this legal debate seems immaterial. The storyline makes it clear that Ahab is powerless to commandeer this vineyard. His hands are tied, and everyone concerned understands that seizing Naboth's field is beyond the rights of the king. Even Jezebel needs to devise an intricate scheme of courtroom intrigue and fabricated evidence in order to indict Naboth. If it were legally straightforward for the king to requisition land, Ahab would have done so; Jezebel certainly would not have hesitated. We thus appreciate that in the Jewish state, the king's power was severely constrained. When it came to land rights, the citizen surpassed the sovereign.

We cannot overstate the significance of this law, as it showcases the autonomy of the citizen in ancient Israel.[1] Israel was a revolutionary culture that empowered its rank and file, preventing its being trampled or bullied by the ruling class. This democratic land culture is the very opposite of other ancient societies and is a tribute to Torah values.

THE TRANSFORMATION OF NABOTH'S REFUSAL

We have understood Naboth's refusal as based upon his deep ancestral connection to the land of Israel. In Ahab's mind, however, Naboth's principled and polite stand undergoes a radical transformation. Our chapter records his refusal four times, and a comparison between them is most instructive:[2]

---

1. See Rabbi Jonathan Sacks, *Covenant & Conversation* 5770: "*BeHar-BeHukkotai*, The Chronological Imagination," http://www.chiefrabbi.org/2010/05/08/covenant-conversation-5770-behar-bechukotei-the-chronological-imagination/#. UD8-_6CD4sY; Joshua A. Berman, *Created Equal* (New York: Oxford University Press, 2008); and J.A. Berman, "The Biblical Origins of Equality," *Azure* 37 (Summer 2009): 76–99.
2. The literary structures and comparisons used in these chapters are detailed in Yair Zakovitch, "The Tale of Naboth's Vineyard: 1 Kings 21," in Meir Weiss, ed., *The Bible from Within* (Jerusalem: Magnes Press, 1984), 379–405.

1. **Naboth** says: "God forbid I should give the inheritance of my fathers to you" (21:3).
2. **Ahab hears**: "I shall not give you the inheritance of my fathers" (21:4).
3. **Ahab tells Jezebel**: "[Naboth said,] I shall not give you my vineyard" (21:6).
4. **Jezebel hears**: "[Naboth] refused to give you [the vineyard] for money" (21:15).

The first record of the refusal (1), as voiced by Naboth, is phrased in religious terminology, "God forbid," and his reason is that his property is an ancestral inheritance. But Ahab returns home frustrated and irritated, and as he mulls over Naboth's reply, it takes on a personal tone (2). Note how the "God forbid" is dropped, and the "you" moves into the foreground of the sentence. Ahab recalls Naboth's response as devoid of lofty principles. At best, it sounds like family nostalgia and at worst, like a personal snub of the king.

By the time Ahab retells the story to his wife, Jezebel (3), Naboth's refusal has evolved into an act of defiance lacking rhyme or reason: "I shall not give you my vineyard." The vineyard has been divested of its ancestral associations, and the sole interpretation of Naboth's obstinacy is as an attempt to insult and disgrace the king, to flex his muscles toward the monarch.

In the final stage of this metamorphosis, Jezebel reads Naboth's refusal as emanating purely from greed (4). It as if she says: Naboth the ingrate refused to give you the field despite your generous offer!

This is a classic case of how we deal with cognitive dissonance, refashioning events to justify our emotions and frustrations. Rather than objectively accepting Naboth's refusal as a principled affirmation of Jewish heritage, backed by Torah law, Ahab grotesquely twists Naboth's ethical stand into an egotistical gesture of greed.

BETWEEN JEZEBEL AND AHAB

His wife, Jezebel, came to him and asked him, "Why are you so dispirited that you won't eat bread?" So he told her.... His wife,

Jezebel, said to him, "Now is the time to show yourself king over Israel; rise and eat bread and be cheerful; I will give you the vineyard of Naboth the Jezreelite." (21:5–7)

Ahab had "lay down on his bed and turned his face away, and would not eat" (21:4). He does not begin to entertain the thought of obtaining the field by illicit means. Jezebel, however, comes from a different royal culture, in which the limits placed on the king are absurd. She views the Israelite norms with disdain. At first she advises, "Now is the time to show yourself king over Israel," meaning that Ahab should simply execute Naboth. When she realizes that Ahab finds that option inconceivable, she tells her husband that she will take care of things.

Is Ahab to blame here or Jezebel? In chapter 18, we saw the appalling religious state of the nation when Jezebel's influence held sway. Chapter 20, while not describing a perfect monarch, portrays a receptive religious environment. Not coincidentally, Jezebel is noticeably absent in that context. Now, in chapter 21, Jezebel returns, and with her a degenerate and corrupt administrative culture.

One problem here is Ahab's inability to face Jezebel. Witness the way he tells her about his offer to Naboth:

To Naboth – 21:2	To Jezebel – 21:6
Give me your vineyard,	Give me your vineyard
that I may have it for a vegetable garden,	for money;
because it is near my home	if you prefer, I will give
and I will give you a better vineyard instead;	you another vineyard in
if you prefer, I will give you its worth in money	exchange

The difference is striking. In conversation with Naboth, Ahab is generous and accommodating, even diffident, and certainly humble. When he talks to Jezebel, he omits the way he justified his need for the field to Naboth; Jezebel would think he was ingratiating himself. Moreover, he reverses the order of his offer to make it sound more like a straightforward, hard-nosed business deal. He knows his wife values money,[3] so he speaks her language. But we know his offer was far more generous, and his tone kinder and more self-effacing. Ahab is clearly intimidated by his wife.

The Jerusalem Talmud picks up on this. The textual cue it cites is found at the end of the chapter, but its thrust is a sub-current throughout:

> "Indeed, **there was never anyone like Ahab,** who committed himself to doing what was evil in the eyes of the Lord" (21:25) – R. Levi taught this verse for six months in disparagement of Ahab. At night, Ahab came to R. Levi and asked him, "How have I sinned against you, and what crimes have I committed against you? Why do you read only the beginning of the verse, and not its end, '**at the instigation of his wife, Jezebel**'?" From that day forth, for the next six months, R. Levi expounded the verse in praise of Ahab. (*Sanhedrin* 10:2, 28b)

In its summation of Ahab as a sinner, the book of Kings specifies Jezebel's influence. Is Ahab the prime offender here, or is he merely instigated by his wife? How much blame lies at Ahab's door? Does Jezebel's incitement minimize his guilt?

THE MURDER SCENE

As we have mentioned Jezebel's culpability, we should examine the chilling deception that she so immaculately plans. A fast day is declared in Jezreel. An event of this sort generally indicates that some tragedy has befallen the community, such as drought, war, or disease; a fast is a call to repentance. Naboth is chosen to be the spiritual leader of the day, the man who will preach to the congregation and lead it in prayer.[4] This role proves him a highly respected member of the community. Just as he is solemnly immersed in earnest prayer, the unsuspecting Naboth is to be accused, tried, and executed.

---

3. See 1 Kings 21:15, where – as noted below – Jezebel mentions the money alone, not the exchange of vineyards.
4. See *Taanit* 2:1.

The calling of the fast bears not a small measure of cynicism. Jezebel is suddenly agitated for the relationship between man and God! ...But in truth, she is creating the conditions for the gravest crime towards God – the murder of Naboth.[5]

This elaborate trap is set by Jezebel in detailed royal letters addressed to the "elders and the nobles in his city" (21:8). These are civic leaders, respected men who all know Naboth, live in his town, and farm their fields alongside his. Yet they are so afraid of Jezebel that no one dares to challenge the conspiracy; the city leadership complies with the fabricated trial.

Nothing is left of the legal establishment; it is merely a rubber stamp for the crimes of this unbridled queen...a queen who appears from the outside as if she submits to the law. Everything looks absolutely legal.[6]

The "legal authorities" of Jezreel seem to know they must report to Jezebel as soon as Naboth has been executed: "They sent to Jezebel, saying, 'Naboth has been stoned and is dead'" (21:14). She has turned the city elders into her collaborators. This corrupt legal manipulation is standard practice for Jezebel. Everything bears the veneer of officialdom, but it is, in fact, a sham.

CLAIM OF IGNORANCE

Given Jezebel's sinister ambush of Naboth, can Ahab truly be implicated in the crime? After all, he is unaware of the charges leveled at Naboth and the manner in which he meets his death. He is uninvolved, disconnected. Jezebel makes all the arrangements and orchestrates the entire scheme. How can Ahab be viewed as an accomplice, let alone the prime suspect?

---

5. Zakovitch, "Naboth's Vineyard," 391.
6. Ibid.

Here the genius of the structure and style of this chapter comes to the fore. The narrative can be divided into five discrete scenes:[7]

	Characters	Setting
Scene 1	Ahab and Naboth	Naboth's vineyard
Scene 2	Ahab and Jezebel	the palace
Scene 3	Jezebel, elders, witnesses Naboth	Jezreel
Scene 4	Ahab and Jezebel	the palace
Scene 5	Ahab and Elijah	Naboth's vineyard

This simple chiastic structure is a wonderful prism through which to gain perspective on the story. One powerful example of the symmetry between scenes 1 and 5 is the way that Elijah is essentially the surrogate for the deceased Naboth! But for our purposes, we may discern that Ahab is present, even dominant, in every scene – except one: the middle scene, the drama of Naboth's fabricated trial and execution.

This absence, this silence, speaks volumes. On the surface, this is the perfect murder. Ahab genuinely knows nothing. He is absent from the crime scene, and there is no way to implicate him in Naboth's death. There are no carelessly discarded memos, no evidence, no trace of involvement. Yet his fingerprints are all over this act – though he is unaware of a single detail!

First, let us highlight the symmetry of the words with which Jezebel parts from Ahab and those with which she returns to him:

> **Rise** and eat bread and be cheerful; I will give you **the vineyard of Naboth the Jezreelite.** (21:7)

> "**Rise** and **possess the vineyard of Naboth the Jezreelite**, who refused to give it to you for money; for Naboth is no longer

---

7. Ibid., 381.

alive – he is dead." When Ahab heard Naboth was dead, Ahab **rose** and went down to Naboth the Jezreelite's vineyard to take **possession** of it. (21:15–16)

What does Ahab think has happened to Naboth? Does he ask? Does he care? Does he inquire as to whether Naboth's relatives have inherited the vineyard? What exactly does Ahab think when Jezebel says, "I will give you the vineyard of Naboth," and then declares shortly afterward that Naboth is dead, clearing the way for the king to take control of the vineyard he so desperately covets?[8]

Moreover, let us examine how Naboth is set up:

She wrote letters in **Ahab's name** and sealed them with **his seal** and sent the letters…to testify against him: you [Naboth] have reviled God and **king**. (21:8–10)[9]

The letters are signed in the king's name and sealed with his royal seal, and Naboth is accused of cursing the king! Ahab can feign ignorance; indeed, he doesn't know a thing. But the entire episode reeks of royalty. Had he taken a lie detector test, Ahab would have passed with flying colors, but this makes the act all the more monstrous.

Thus, though the prime mover in this story is Jezebel, God accuses Ahab of the murder! As Elijah famously confronts Ahab:

So says the Lord: Have you murdered and also taken possession?[10]

---

8. Jezebel's intimate involvement reverberates in Ahab's receipt of the news as well. See the subtle parallel (clearer in Hebrew) between "'Naboth has been stoned and is dead.' When Jezebel heard" (21:14–15) and "Naboth is no longer alive – he is dead. When Ahab heard" (21:15–16).

9. For parallels with the Purim story, see Dr. Yonatan Grossman, "Does the King Know of Haman's Decree?" The Virtual Beit Midrash, http://vbm-torah.org/archive/ester/10ester.htm.

10. The use of the verb *y-r-sh* is generally reserved for taking control of the land of Israel in fulfillment of the divine mandate of conquering it. The ironic usage in 21:15–18 (as well as in Judges 18) evokes a heroic act, a mitzva, and mocks Ahab's assertion of his power as cowardly bravado.

Prof. Yair Zakovitch comments:

> The scathing rhyme…"Have you murdered and also taken pos-
> session?" – that is, have you added shameful insult to criminal
> injury – is the whole intent of the story in a nutshell. The tale is a
> lesson in the responsibility of rule. The king may not avail himself
> of the claim of ignorance, especially in view of such clear indica-
> tions that he was not unaware of all that was afoot.[11]

IN CONCLUSION

Our chapter is linked to the previous one with the phrase "And it came
to pass after these things" (21:1). There are many connections between
the two stories. One of them is Ahab's returning to his palace "displeased
and furious" (20:43), a scene that recurs in our chapter (21:4). But there
is also one significant contrast between the two chapters. We should be
struck by the polarity between Ahab's generosity toward Ben-Hadad –
"we have heard that the kings of the house of Israel are merciful…perhaps
he will spare your life" (20:31) – and his heartlessness toward Naboth.
This stark dissonance underscores the helplessness and vulnerability of
the simple Jewish farmer as opposed to the diplomatic immunity of a
powerful foreign king. It demonstrates how a merciful king can become
deaf to morality when it serves his purposes.

We have examined the complex psychological background to this
murder, the internal justifications, the external incitement by Jezebel,
and the façade of detachment and innocence on Ahab's part. However,
there is one further dimension. Maimonides suggests that Ahab is a
prime example of the last of the Ten Commandments, "Thou shalt not
covet." He depicts Ahab as a classic victim of a vicious pathology of sin,
a pernicious domino effect of desire. Once a person allows himself to
crave objects belonging to another, that illicit emotion can become a
manic, dominating force, with devastating results:

> Desire leads a person to covet, and coveting leads to theft. For
> if the owner [of the object that one desires] is not willing to sell,

---

11. Zakovitch, "Naboth's Vineyard," 398.

even though one offers a hefty sum and pleads with him, then he will come to steal, as it is written, "They have coveted fields and stolen" (Mic. 2:2). And if the owner confronts him so as to save his property or prevent him from stealing, then he will come to shed blood. Go and study the story of Ahab and Naboth. (*Mishneh Torah*, Laws of Theft and Lost Property 1:11)

1 Kings 21

Accusation, Denial, and Repentance

THE CONFRONTATION

God sends the prophet Elijah to challenge and admonish Ahab at a specific time and place. In chapter 18, Elijah confronted him as he was riding through the parched, famine-beleaguered countryside to "find some grass to keep horses and mules alive" (18:5). Elijah's meeting point was deliberately chosen to catch Ahab in a moment of desperation at the drought-induced collapse of his country, humiliated by his indignity. Similarly, in our scene, Elijah is to address Ahab outside the palace walls, a setting that will incriminate him. God instructs Elijah:

> Go down and confront King Ahab of Israel, who resides in Samaria; he is now in Naboth's vineyard – he has gone down there to take possession of it. (21:18)

The objective is for Elijah to catch Ahab red-handed in Naboth's vineyard, surveying his new acquisition. Ahab strolls through the vineyard in a clear demonstration of his culpability, unable to deny that he has gained the field through illicit means. Here is the dialogue between Elijah and Ahab:

> Say to him, "So says the Lord: Have you murdered and also taken possession?"

> Say to him, "Thus says the Lord: In the very place where the dogs lapped up Naboth's blood, the dogs will lap up your blood, too."

> Ahab said to Elijah, "So you have found me, my enemy?"

> He said, "I have found [you]." (21:19–20)

Is Elijah's first statement a rhetorical question, or does he expect an answer?

> You committed murder! How do you now [have the right to] take his possessions?! (Malbim)

> "Have you murdered and also taken possession?" – This question aims at opening the conversation to hear an answer, even though the details are known. Like…"Where is Abel, your brother?" (Radak)

As a statement, this pithy line articulates Ahab's crime in concise and unequivocal terms. If its intent is to offer Ahab an opportunity to express his regrets, he clearly fails to admit his guilt.

The next sentence announces Ahab's punishment, condemning him to a dishonorable burial:

> In the manner in which Naboth died, in that he died an unnatural death, so Ahab will die. And in the manner in which the dogs licked Naboth's blood, so will the dogs lick your blood. (Ralbag)

Ahab will be treated precisely as he treated Naboth. Chapter 22 describes the actual punishment:

> The king died and was brought to Samaria, and they buried him there. They washed the chariot at a pool in Samaria where the

prostitutes bathed, and the dogs licked up his blood, as the word of the Lord had declared. (22:37–38)[1]

Denial

Ahab attempts to deflect the guilt. He depicts Elijah as his adversary – "So you have found me, my enemy?" By casting Elijah as such, Ahab dismisses the prophet's damning critique a personal attack rather than a divine moral pronouncement.[2] If this is a personal quarrel, then Ahab can absolve himself of the prophet's damning ethical standards.

In the next chapter, Ahab relates similarly to another prophet, Micaiah son of Imlah, taking his criticism as a personal affront:

> There is one man through whom we can inquire of God, but I hate him, because he never prophesies anything good **for me**, but only misfortune – Micaiah son of Imlah. (22:8)

For Ahab, it is all personal. The prophets are biased, hostile to the king. Ahab shirks his guilt with this mode of thinking. Refusing to allow the words of the prophet to penetrate, he remains unshaken.

Punishment

But Elijah is not finished. He continues by delivering God's decree regarding the downfall of Ahab's royal line:

> …because you have committed to doing what is evil (*ra*) in the sight of the Lord, I will bring disaster (*raa*) upon you and make a clean sweep of you; I will cut off from Ahab every male and every bondsman and freeman in Israel. I will make your house like the house of **Jeroboam son of Nebat** and the house of **Baasha** son

---

1. Similarly, the prophecy of the destruction of Ahab's line (21:21–24) is fulfilled in II Kings 9 during Jehu's rebellion. There, the divinely mandated assassination of the king (Ahab's son) takes place at Naboth's field (9:21, 25–26). Jezebel also meets her end in that chapter (9:10, 30–37).
2. This exchange is strongly reminiscent of the mutual accusations between Ahab and Elijah in I Kings 18:17–18.

of Ahijah, because of the anger with which you have angered and because you have led Israel to sin. (21:20–22)

This speech echoes warnings delivered to Ahab's predecessors – Jeroboam son of Nebat and Baasha. Both kings received similar prophetic pronouncements of their demise in response to their sinful regimes. The similarity in phraseology is easy to identify:

"I will bring disaster upon you" – compare 14:10 (and II Kings 21:12)

"A clean sweep of you (*uviarti aḥarekha*)" – compare 14:10, 16:3

"I will cut off from Ahab every male and every bondsman and freeman in Israel" – compare 14:10 and 16:11

"You have led Israel to sin" – compare 14:16; 16:2, 13

"All of Ahab's line who die in the town shall be devoured by dogs, and all who die in the open country shall be devoured by the birds of the sky" (21:24) – compare 14:11, 16:4

And now, Ahab follows Jeroboam and Baasha as, yet again, a prophet informs a king of Israel that his royal line is at its end.

TESHUVA

At this point, we witness one of the most bewildering aspects of this story – Ahab's sudden repentance and God's enthusiastic acceptance:

When Ahab heard those words, he rent his clothes, put sackcloth upon his flesh, and fasted, and lay in sackcloth and walked about subdued. And the word of the Lord came to Elijah the Tishbite: "Have you seen how Ahab has humbled himself before Me?" (21:27–29)

The reader anxiously awaits the downfall of Ahab and Jezebel and the termination of their evil rule. In this light, Ahab's sudden *teshuva* and God's enthusiastic acceptance of it are disconcerting. Can a person change so fast? Might Ahab's sackcloth and fasting be no more than sophisticated theatrics? If the king has indeed had a change of heart, what has prompted it? How has his initial denial of sin given way to contrition? Furthermore, why does God respond so immediately and magnanimously to Ahab's remorse?

Rabbi Elchanan Samet argues that Ahab's turnaround is rooted in verses 21–24, which equate him with Jeroboam and Baasha. When Ahab hears himself grouped in the infamous company of his fleeting and unheroic predecessors, his monarchy presented as yet another increment in the unfortunate fate of royal houses of Israel, he is deeply disturbed:

> It is specifically this comparison that hurts Ahab, since it implies that the house of Ahab will be nothing but a brief episode, devoid of influence, in the stormy history of the kingdom of Israel – like the houses of Jeroboam and Baasha. All of the enormous efforts at which Omri and Ahab had excelled – the creation of the new capital city, Samaria, … forging of courageous political ties with the former enemy kingdom of Judah (chapter 22) and with the kingdom of Sidon… the reinforcement of Israel's army and the leading of it to victory against the principal enemy of that generation, the kingdom of Aram (chapter 20) – all of this counts for nothing, and the royal house that has achieved it all will be cut off![3]

Samet's explanation rests on the order of the verses. Ahab does not repent when he faces Elijah in the field; it is only the latter's rebuke – not even the warning of the king's own demise – that induces *teshuva*.

One might propose a psychological explanation for this sequence. A personal attack is met by instinctive self-justification.

---

3. Elchanan Samet, *The Elijah Narratives* (Jerusalem: Maaliyot, 2003), 390–91 [Hebrew].

Later, as the defense mechanism of the accused is relaxed, the criticism begins to sink in. It might well be that Ahab initially defended himself when confronted by Elijah, only to rethink afterward and accept his guilt and responsibility.

Ahab's sackcloth, mourning, and fasting draw our attention to an intriguing symmetry:

Verse 4	Verse 27
... displeased and furious	... he rent his clothes, put sackcloth upon his flesh
he **lay down** on his bed	and **fasted**
and turned his face away[4]	and **lay** in sackcloth
and **would not eat**	and walked about subdued[5]

In verse 4, Ahab was depressed about Naboth's unwillingness to sell him his vineyard. He lay in bed, depressed and inactive. Now Ahab finds himself in a similar posture and state of mind. He is back at the beginning! Yet there is a significant difference in orientation: In the first scene, Ahab lay in bed in a passive state of depression; in the second, Ahab dons sackcloth, actively expressing remorse. In verse 4, Ahab has lost his appetite due to his envy and frustration; in verse 27, he *chooses* to fast. Prof. Yair Zakovitch captures the irony:

> All that has transpired between these two descriptions of the king's grief is a result of Jezebel's attempt to relieve her unfortunate husband's misery, to get him out of bed and feed him. And yet, as a comparison of the two descriptions shows, she has not succeeded; not only does Ahab's condition revert to what it was, it worsens: Jezebel's efforts are in the end a disservice.[6]

---

4. For a similar situation of desperation in which a king turns his face, see the case of Hezekiah and his prayer in II Kings 20:43.
5. Rashi and Ralbag suggest that Ahab walked barefoot, as one in a state of excommunication.
6. Yair Zakovitch, "The Tale of Naboth's Vineyard: 1 Kings 21," in Meir Weiss, ed., *The Bible from Within* (Jerusalem: Magnes Press, 1984), 403.

Questions of Sincerity

Our understanding of Ahab's *teshuva* is complicated by conflicting cues in the text. On the one hand, God informs Elijah that the king's remorse is heartfelt – "Have you seen how Ahab has humbled himself before Me?" (21:29) – and responds by deferring his punishment. Furthermore, Ahab's afflictions, acts unbecoming of a king, would seem to indicate significant internal upheaval.

On the other hand, looking ahead to chapter 22, we find Ahab yet again associating with false prophets, and striking and imprisoning a prophet of God – behavior inconsistent with the shamefaced demeanor depicted here. Moreover, one wonders whether the king's self-imposed suffering can undo the religious damage he has inflicted upon the nation. If shrines to Baal and Ashera exist around the country, why should Ahab's personal grief be significant? Let him repair the damage!

No wonder we find conflicting strains in the rabbinic sources regarding Ahab's *teshuva*. Perhaps he is a paradigm of sincerity:

> He sent for Jehoshaphat, king of Judah, and he would administer forty lashes to him three times a day, and with fasting and prayer he would arise and go to bed before God, and he occupied himself with Torah all of his days and never again returned to his evil deeds. (*Pirkei DeRabbi Eliezer* 43)

Or perhaps this is a shallow, cosmetic change in lifestyle:

> To what extent did he fast? If he was used to eating every three hours, he now ate only after six hours. If he usually ate every six hours, he now would eat only after nine hours. (*Pesikta DeRav Kahana, Shuva* 24:11)

Thus, Ahab's sincerity and the nature of his repentance remain a mystery, an open question. But what of Ahab's punishment? God indicates that it has been postponed:

> ...because he has humbled himself before Me, I will not bring the disaster in his lifetime; I will bring the disaster...in his son's time. (21:29)

As noted above, there are two dimensions of Ahab's punishment. His personal fate (predicted in 21:19) is not commuted; his blood is indeed lapped up by the dogs (22:37–38). He cannot absolve himself of responsibility for Naboth's murder. In this dimension, "there was never anyone like Ahab, who committed himself to doing that which was evil in the eyes of the Lord" (21:25). Only the fate of the house of Omri (21:21–24), Ahab's royal lineage and his broader leadership of the nation, is delayed in the wake of his remorse.[7]

PREMATURE CONCLUSION?

Chapter 21 ends with a conclusion of sorts, a summative assessment of Ahab:

> Indeed, there was never anyone like Ahab, who committed himself to doing that which was evil in the eyes of the Lord, at the instigation of his wife, Jezebel. He acted most abominably, straying after the fetishes (*gilulim*) just like the Amorites, whom the Lord had dispossessed before the Israelites. (21:25–26)

Why do we hear this summary at this juncture? A dramatic and detailed chapter 22 still lies ahead, narrating Ahab's royal court, his final battle, and his heroic death. Ahab is not dead yet!

Maimonides writes that the murder of Naboth represents the worst of Ahab's wickedness:

> Although there are sins more serious than bloodshed, they do not lead to the **destruction of civilization** as bloodshed does. Even idolatry, or – needless to say – prohibited sexual relations or desecration of Shabbat, are not like bloodshed [in this respect]. For these belong to the category of transgressions between man and God, while bloodshed belongs to the category of sins between man and his fellow. And anyone who commits such a sin is completely wicked, and all the commandments he may have

---

7. As a result, the kingdom is taken away in the lifetime of Ahab's son, and Jezebel's gruesome death is also delayed, as her punishment is included in that of the kingdom.

performed throughout his life are not equal in weight to this sin, nor will they save him from judgment.... We learn this from the example of Ahab, who was an idolater, as it is said of him, "But there was never anyone like Ahab, who committed himself to doing that which was evil in the eyes of the Lord.... He acted most abominably, straying after the fetishes..." (1 Kings 21:25–26); but when his sins and merits were set out before God, no sin made him deserving of being wiped out, nor did any other matter stand against him, like the blood of Naboth. (*Mishneh Torah*, Laws of the Murderer and Protection of Life 4:9)

One might argue that the most severe of Ahab's crimes was idolatry, a sin on a national scale, whereas the murder of Naboth was a personal offense, which did not influence the nation's ethical norms. Maimonides insists, however, that murder is at the top of the pyramid, as it causes "the destruction of civilization," the disintegration of society, undermining its cohesion and trust.

Is there a connection between Ahab's idolatry and his greedy and shameless pursuit of Naboth? Samet suggests that a link may be found in Ahab's attraction to pagan norms:

The foreign, pagan culture that entered Israel together with Jezebel introduced new concepts into Israelite society and into the Israelite royalty with regard to the status of the king and the norms of the monarchy. **Religious corruption** is the source of the moral and social corruption that ultimately characterizes Ahab's household. But it is specifically the **social corruption** – epitomized by the story of Naboth – that seals its fate.[8]

The idolatrous momentum was not detached from the belligerent royal culture, the heartless elimination of enemies and mere irritants, as instigated by Jezebel. The book of Kings deliberately summarizes Ahab and his corruption as he perpetrates this spineless act of murder, for it constitutes his lowest point.

---

8. Samet, *The Elijah Narratives*, 379.

JEZEBEL

> "The dogs shall devour Jezebel in the rampart of Jezreel." ... Indeed
> there was never anyone like Ahab... at the instigation of his wife,
> Jezebel. (21:23, 25)

God reserves His prime condemnation for the Jewish king Ahab, yet Jezebel receives a prominent share of the blame. From the story of Naboth,
and from the previous chapters describing the "450 prophets of Baal
and 400 prophets of Ashera who eat at Jezebel's table" (18:19), we know
Jezebel to be a driven woman who introduces foreign deities and alien
norms into the Israelite body politic. She corrupts her husband, Ahab,
and the nation at large. She constitutes the paradigm of infamy; she is
possibly the most evil woman in the Bible.

Jezebel's fate is more gruesome than that of her husband; her
body itself will be eaten by dogs. As we saw above, the book of Kings has
warned several kings and their dynasties that they will be "devoured by
the dogs," but this is generally a metaphor; it never actually transpires.
In Jezebel's case, however, it happens quite literally and is described
rather graphically:

> Then Jehu went to Jezreel. When Jezebel heard about it, she
> painted her eyes, arranged her hair, and looked out a window.
> As Jehu entered the gate, she asked, "Have you come in peace,
> Zimri, you murderer of your master?" He looked up at the win-
> dow and called out, "Who is on my side? Who?" Two or three
> eunuchs looked down at him. "Throw her down!" Jehu said. So
> they threw her down, and some of her blood spattered the wall
> and the horses as they trampled her underfoot. Jehu went in and
> ate and drank. "Take care of that cursed woman," he said, "and
> bury her, for she was a king's daughter." But when they went out
> to bury her, they found nothing except her skull, her feet, and
> her hands. They went back and told Jehu, who said, "This is the
> word of the Lord that He spoke through his servant Elijah the
> Tishbite: On the plot of ground at Jezreel dogs will devour Jeze-
> bel's flesh. Jezebel's body will be like refuse on the ground in the

plot at Jezreel, so no one will be able to say, 'This is Jezebel.'" (II Kings 9:30–37)

This scene showcases Jezebel as cold, controlled, aloof, and fearless. Anticipating her executioners, she doesn't run. She calmly sits and puts on her makeup and does her hair. And when they enter the palace, she confronts them, taunts them, accusing them of cowardice and betrayal! This scene gives us an inkling of Jezebel's powerful personality and helps us understand her devastating influence on the Israelite kingdom.

1 Kings 22

Ahab's Final Battle

I n chapter 20, Ahab signed a treaty with Aram detailing territory that would be returned to Jewish sovereignty. It appears that these agreements have not been honored. Thus, after three peaceful years, Ahab prepares for battle, confident in his military superiority and seeking to take Aram to task for abrogating its commitments.

Interestingly, Ahab's ally in this war is none other than Jehoshaphat, king of Judah. Jehoshaphat is exuberant about the alliance:

> I will do what you do; my troops shall be your troops, my horses shall be your horses. (22:4)

Unlike Ahab, Jehoshaphat is a devoted follower of God. Despite this stark disparity in religious commitment, he shares close family ties with Ahab, marrying his son to Ahab's daughter (11 Kings 8:18). In addition, Jehoshaphat engages in joint projects with the north, both military ventures (22:1–4)[1] and sea expeditions (22:50).[2] His language reflects his

---

1. See also 11 Kings 3.
2. See also 11 Chronicles 20:35–36.

enthusiasm at the unity of the nation after a long period of acrimonious division.

IS THERE NOT A PROPHET OF THE LORD?

The first half of the chapter depicts a scene at "a threshing floor at the entrance to the gate of Samaria" (22:10), where the two kings seem to have been viewing their troops in training. Amid this military mobilization, the kings are accompanied by "prophets, four hundred men." Possibly, the threshing floor was chosen as it was large enough to hold such a crowd.

In the classic Jewish tradition,[3] Jehoshaphat suggests that the king consult with God prior to embarking upon military conflict. At this point, all four hundred prophets speak repeatedly in unison:

> Go up, and the Lord will deliver [them] into the hands of the king. (22:6, 13, 15)

These prophets are Ahab's men. Jehoshaphat, however, is from Judah and views the large bands of prophets somewhat suspiciously. He questions their loyalty, [4]specifically requesting a "prophet of the Lord" (22:7). In response, Ahab summons Micaiah son of Imlah (22:9).

Uniqueness of Prophecy

Jehoshaphat's request allows us to examine some fundamental elements of Israelite prophecy. The Talmud asks how Jehoshaphat knew the four hundred prophets were not loyal to God. After all, they spoke in the name of God (22:12–13)! The Talmud relates the conversation between Jehoshaphat and Ahab:

---

3. See Judges 20:27, I Samuel 23:10–12, and II Samuel 5:19.
4. The number four hundred is familiar from I Kings 18 as the number of prophets of Baal. In our chapter, however, the prophets are unaffiliated with Baal; moreover, they speak like prophets of God, using the Tetragrammaton (21:12–13). Though this scene is staged (see 21:13), there appears to be a desire to engage prophets loyal to God rather than to Baal. This is further evidence of Ahab's ups and downs in his relationship with monotheism. In this scene, he has adopted the trappings of Baal but uses the name of God.

Jehoshaphat said, "Is there no prophet of the Lord...?"

He [Ahab] replied, "There are all of these [four hundred]!"

He [Jehoshaphat] responded, "I have the following tradition from my grandfather's house: The same communication is revealed to many prophets, but no two prophets prophesy with the identical phraseology." (*Sanhedrin* 89a)

In other words, Jehoshaphat maintains that two authentic prophets never express an idea in precisely the same manner. This is why you never see large clusters of genuine prophets, functioning in choreographed unison. When you see a group of "prophets" talking and acting the same, you can be certain their prophecy is false.

Why should this be so? If God has a message to deliver, why can it not be transmitted identically by multiple prophets? We can begin to answer this question if we understand the mechanism of prophecy, as described by Maimonides:

What is made known to a prophet during prophecy is done by way of parable, and he will immediately realize what the parable means. For instance, when Jacob the Patriarch saw the ladder with angels ascending and descending it, it was a parable representing monarchy and its subjection. Similarly, the animals Ezekiel saw, the "boiling pot" and "almond branch" Jeremiah saw, and all the other objects seen by the other prophets were also parables. Among the prophets, some...related what they saw in their prophecy and their interpretation of it. Others related just their interpretation. Occasionally they related only the parables [of the prophecy], as Ezekiel and Zechariah sometimes did. All the prophets prophesied by way of parables and riddles. (*Mishneh Torah*, Laws of the Foundations of the Torah 7:3)

In Maimonides' formulation, prophecy is transmitted by means of images, "parables," or visions. Part of the skill or gift of a prophet is the ability to decipher and interpret the visions or non-verbal communication. A prophet takes the parable or imagery and translates it into words.

Accordingly, the text transmitted by the prophet, the wording used to communicate God's message, is composed by the prophet himself. The prophet receives God's images and ideas, but he determines the phraseology. Therefore, no two prophets can prophesy with precisely the same text. It is impossible for two prophets (let alone four hundred) to emerge with the identical articulation of the non-verbal communication they have received.

Another point should be made on the basis of Maimonides' theory. He writes that there is one exception to his rule, and that is the prophecy of Moses. Only Moses was able to receive prophecy with the clarity of a verbal message, to hear a precise textual formulation from God. Thus, the *Chumash*, the five books of the Torah, is unlike any other prophetic work; the text itself is God's word.[5] In the books of *Nevi'im*, in contrast, the text was authored by the *navi*, and each prophetic work therefore has a unique literary style. Since the prophet Ezekiel wrote his book, and Isaiah his, and Zephaniah his, each used his own distinctive language and style to communicate God's content. Each book contains the literary hallmark of its human author.

Interestingly, Ḥazal identify one particular era in which "four prophets [Isaiah, Hosea, Amos, and Micah] prophesied concurrently" (*Pesaḥim* 87a).[6] Could a single prophet not deliver a message effectively? Apparently, God had something enormously important to communicate, and He wanted it said four **different** ways.

We have digressed somewhat, but I feel we have learned something valuable about prophecy. The message of God is refracted through the prism of the human mind and soul. No two prophets prophesy the same way, because no two individuals are the same. The philosophical implications of this idea are far-reaching. God's message reaches us in a fusion of the divine and the human.

---

5. Maimonides, *Mishneh Torah*, Laws of the Foundations of the Torah 7:6. See also, for example, Nahmanides' introduction to his Torah commentary.
6. Also *Bava Batra* 14b.

The corollary of this concept is that one characteristic of the Jewish prophet is his standing alone. Unlike Baal, God's prophet does not prophesy in a group. The prophet is initiated into his prophecy in a private encounter, and subsequently it is the solitary figure who boldly communicates God's word, however unpopular its message may be. And this aloneness sometimes translates into loneliness as well, a sense of isolation that is shared by several of the most formidable prophets: Moses,[7] Elijah,[8] Isaiah,[9] and Jeremiah.[10]

Prophetic Theater

Another hallmark of Israelite prophecy that is showcased in this chapter is the use of symbolic acts. The leader of the four hundred prophets, Zedekiah son of Kenaana, gesticulates with iron horns to symbolize Israel's victory over Aram. He explains their meaning:

> With these shall you gore the Arameans until you make an end of them. (22:11)

With this, Zedekiah participates in a rich tradition of prophetic drama: Jeremiah walks around Jerusalem with a yoke on his shoulders to demonstrate subservience to Babylonia (Jer. 27); Isaiah is told to walk barefoot and undressed to simulate a prisoner of war (Is. 20). Hosea is commanded to marry a harlot (Hos. 1); Ezekiel breaks the wall of his house (Ezek. 8), lies on his side for 390 days (ibid. 4), and makes a show of merging separate pieces of wood into a single branch (ibid. 37:16–17). Prophets of Israel were frequently commanded to dramatize God's message. Similarly, Ahab's false prophets boost their credibility by acting in this time-honored prophetic style.[11]

---

7. Numbers 11:14; Deuteronomy 1:9, 13.
8. I Kings 19:10, 14.
9. Isaiah 50:1–11.
10. Jeremiah 1:18.
11. According to Nahmanides on Genesis 48:22, the prophets' symbolic acts were not just theatrical; rather, they activated certain events. See also II Kings 13:14–19.

But why specifically iron horns? It seems that they reflect Moses' blessing to Ephraim:

> Like a firstling bull in his majesty, he has horns like the horns of the wild ox; with them he gores the peoples, the ends of the earth one and all. (Deut. 33:17)

Ephraim is an appellation for the northern kingdom (as in Is. 7 and Hos. 5). It thus makes sense that the horn, a symbol of military victory,[12] should be used to illustrate an Israelite military triumph.[13]

CYNICISM AND COURAGE

Micaiah son of Imlah has been summoned to appear before Ahab, and the king's courtiers give him the script, the mantra he should chant: "Let your words be like the rest of them; speak a favorable word" (1 Kings 22:13). If we had any doubt as to the legitimacy of the four hundred prophets, we now understand that the entire spectacle is nothing more than a fraud, a choreographed farce. Furthermore, we know Ahab is also aware of the ruse; when Micaiah meets the king, repeating the lines he has been dictated verbatim, the king responds:

> How many times must I adjure you to tell me nothing but the truth in God's name?! (22:16)

In other words, Ahab knows this "prophecy" by the four hundred prophets is nothing more than a synchronized, rehearsed show.

Micaiah confidently and audaciously taunts the king into admitting the inauthenticity of his own prophets. Indeed, this fearless prophet so enrages the leadership that Zedekiah strikes him, and the king imprisons him with meager rations, "until I come home safe" (22:27). Nonethe-

---

12. Psalms 75:5–6.
13. This approach is noted by Yehuda Kiel, *Da'at Mikra, I Kings* [Hebrew].

less, Micaiah holds his ground, declaring, "We will see who has to flee from room to room" (22:25), a direct reference to Ahab's failure in 20:30.[14]

AHAB

Israel tragically loses the battle, just as Micaiah predicted, and Ahab is fatally injured. The book of Kings stresses that his death an act of divine providence, informing us that Ahab was disguised, and yet "a man pulled back a bow randomly and hit the king of Israel between the folds of his armor" (22:34). The king is killed by a "random" shot, yet the arrow pierces the single weak point in Ahab's armor.

Ahab remains on the battlefield, presumably bleeding to death. Why does he stay at the front? Ahab seeks to encourage his troops, fully aware that once the national figurehead is dead, it is unlikely that the rank and file will continue fighting. For this reason, he instructs his men to keep him propped up in his chariot, though it will cost him his life.[15] The Talmud commends this selfless and heroic act.[16]

IN CONCLUSION

We now bid farewell to Ahab, a central figure for the past five chapters. Both the book of Kings and the Mishnah designate him as one of Israel's most evil kings:

> Three kings and four commoners have no portion in the World to Come: Three kings – Jeroboam, Ahab, and Manasseh. (*Sanhedrin* 10:2)

---

14. See Rabbi Mordechai Sabato's useful article, "Fate and Choice in the Story of the Death of Ahab," in Amnon Bazak, ed., *Al Derekh Ha'avot* (Alon Shevut: Tevunot, 5761), 397–419 [Hebrew].
15. Ahab is killed in fulfillment of prophecies in chapters 20 and 21. The manner in which he meets his end here reflects both these decrees: The national defeat and his death fulfill the prediction in chapter 20, while the dogs that lap up his blood fulfill the prediction in chapter 21.
16. *Moed Katan* 28b.

These kings lose their place in the World to Come due to their actions, each leading Israel to a deeper level of idolatry.

However, other rabbinic statements are more generous. R. Naḥman suggests that "Ahab was equally balanced" (*Sanhedrin* 102b), and in this vein the Talmud formulates a pun based upon his name, depicting him as "a brother (*aḥ*) to Heaven but a father (*av*) to idolatry" (ibid.). In other words, his devastating flaws are counterbalanced by his virtues. Ahab's biography bears out this ambivalence. To his discredit, he leads the northern kingdom to unprecedented degrees of idolatry out of a desire to ally himself with Phoenicia and appease his intimidating wife. He turns a blind eye as God's prophets are killed, and he feigns ignorance as murder is committed in his name. He ignores God's instructions when they are inconvenient for him. Yet, to his credit, he responds to God's prophets and abandons Baal after the great assembly at Mount Carmel, and God accepts his repentance.

What motivates Ahab? Sometimes, he seems easily influenced and manipulated. He can be swayed toward Baal by Jezebel, then inspired by Elijah to kill its prophets and become more committed to God.

However, beyond Ahab's impressionability, we might suggest another factor. Ahab finds God only when in dire straits, in existential danger. Whether at the end of three years of drought, or under siege at Samaria, or facing Elijah's threat to his royal legacy, Ahab always turns to God in the proverbial foxhole, when he has no other recourse. Whenever he feels at an advantage, he makes other decisions, frequently allying himself with other powerful forces. In this regard, Ahab's guiding principle is self-interest, whether personal or national. Incapable of making firm commitments, he fluctuates without regard for God's law or the prophet's warning.

In the final analysis, we remember Ahab for the dreadful regime of Baal that he introduced to Samaria and the northern kingdom. Ahab followed Baal when it served the national interest, and God when it suited him. Ahab thus personifies Elijah's famous accusation of the nation, "wavering between two opinions."

Jehoshaphat, King of Judah

King Jehoshaphat of Judah is a strong leader with impressive achievements, and his agenda of national reconciliation creates challenging dilemmas. His reign was a high point for the kingdom of Judah. By engaging in a close reading, we can extract significant information from clues and indicators embedded in the text, through which we will emerge with a picture of this great ruler.

> He walked in all the way of Asa his father; he did not turn aside from it, doing right in the eyes of the Lord.... The remnant of the *kadesh* (Temple prostitutes) who remained in the days of Asa his father, he expelled from the land. (1 Kings 22:43, 47)

Jehoshaphat's achievements build upon the firm base established by his father. As we learned in chapter 15, Asa reigned forty-one years, and his prime accomplishment was his anti-idolatry policy, eradicating pagan sites of worship and their cultural influence. In addition, Asa boosted the prestige of the Temple and ended the protracted civil war with the northern kingdom.

Jehoshaphat continues on this path. During his twenty-five-year reign (22:42), he did that which was "right in the eyes of the Lord" – in other words, he did not succumb to idolatry. The book of Kings informs us that he engages in a comprehensive campaign to rid the country of the *kadesh*, continuing the war against idolatry waged by his father.

"Jehoshaphat also made peace with the king of Israel" (22:44). Interestingly, Jehoshaphat extends his hand in peace toward the northern kingdom. Despite the idolatry in the north, this expression of unity passes without comment or evaluation at this stage.

Jehoshaphat presides over a period of enormous prosperity and political hegemony over the region:

> Now there was no king in Edom; a deputy was king. Jehoshaphat made ships of Tarshish to sail to Ophir for gold, but they did not sail, for the ships were wrecked at Ezion-Geber. (22:48–49)

Jehoshafat builds Ezion-Geber (today's Eilat).[1] This shows that he has the means to build and maintain a seaport far from the nation's capital and the population center of Judah. The resources and resourcefulness of the kingdom, including its technology, are portrayed elegantly through its fleet of *oniot Tarshish*, craft strong enough to withstand a lengthy sea voyage. Access to Eilat passes through the territory of Edom. Thus, Jehoshafat's ability to protect the port and its supply lines testifies to his absolute control of the region.[2]

The passage ends with Jehoshaphat's enigmatic rejection of an offer to team up with Ahab's successor, Ahaziah:

> Then Ahaziah son of Ahab proposed to Jehoshaphat, "Let my servants sail with your servants by sea," but Jehoshaphat would not agree. (22:50)

Why does Jehoshaphat rebuff Ahaziah? What is wrong with his offer? Have relations between the southern and northern kingdoms cooled

---

1. Ezion-Geber is on the coast of the Red Sea; see Deuteronomy 2:8. Some scholars identify it with today's Aqaba, Tel El-Halifa, or Jezirat Farun, an island near Eilat.
2. Based on archaeological evidence, such as the Mesha Stele, we know Ahab wielded similar influence further north, in Moab.

since the death of Ahab? Also curious is the breaking of Jehoshaphat's fleet at Ezion-Geber. Why is this detail relevant? Is there is more to the story? As we shall see, Chronicles supplies the missing information.

CHRONICLES

II Chronicles 17 lists several elements of Jehoshaphat's reign:

17:5	Wealth
17:7–9	Spreading Torah study nationally
17:10–11	Regional power
17:12	Building projects
17:13	Prosperity
17:14–19	A huge, organized army

With all these impressive features, Jehoshaphat's reign recalls that of Solomon (without the latter's sins!). Maybe this parallel explains the king's desire to unify the nation through his alliance with Ahab and later Ahaziah. He sees the country returning to its heyday, so the natural thing to do is to unify. This unity finds its ultimate expression in the marriage of Jehoshaphat's son to Ahab's daughter.[3]

Jehoshafat's battle with neighboring Moab and Edom is described with numerous references to God. He paraphrases Solomon's prayer at the Temple's inauguration; the nation celebrates with *Hallel* and praise to God (II Chr. 20, especially 20:9). The depiction here is idyllic.

Dilemmas of Unity

But all is not perfect in the kingdom of Jehoshaphat. After Jehoshaphat returns from the war (as described in I Kings 22) in which his ally Ahab is killed, the prophet Jehu son of Hanani reprimands him for collaborating with the idolatrous northern kingdom:

---

3. The question of who married whom is complicated; see II Kings 8:18, 26–27 and II Chronicles 18:1–2. The verses do not state clearly whether Jehoram married Ahab's daughter or Jehoshaphat married Omri's daughter. Most commentaries assume that Jehoshaphat allowed his son to marry Ahab's daughter, but *Seder Olam* 17 records that Jehoshaphat married Ahab's sister, Omri's daughter. See Yehuda Kiel, *Da'at Mikra*, *II Kings* (Jerusalem: Mossad Harav Kook, 1989) [Hebrew].

Do you seek to assist the wicked and love those who hate God? (II Chron. 19:2)

Similarly, Elazar son of Dodavah prophesies against Jehoshaphat after he joins with Ahaziah to build a navy:

"Because you have joined with Ahaziah, the Lord will destroy what you have made"; and the ships were wrecked and could not sail to Tarshish. (II Chron. 20:37)

The prophets disparage the kings of Israel harshly and criticize Jehoshaphat's association with them. Yet Jehoshaphat persists in his efforts! In II Kings 3, we find him alongside yet another king of Israel, Jehoram. Given this prophetic censure, is this stubborn attempt at unity misguided?

Clearly, each of the joint ventures falters or fails: The military alliance of Ahab and Jehoshaphat results in defeat and the death of Ahab, the Jehoshaphat-Ahaziah naval alliance never makes it out to sea, and the war in which Jehoshaphat joins with Jehoram ends on a sour note. The Midrash draws the obvious conclusion:

Nittai HaArbeli said: Keep far from a bad neighbor, and **do not associate with an evil person**... (*Avot* 1:7) – As we see with Jehoshaphat, who joined with Ahab, and they went up [in war] together to Ramoth Gilead, rousing God's anger against him. Again he associated with Ahaziah, and they made ships together in Ezion-Geber, and God disrupted their actions.... (*Avot DeRabbi Natan* 9:4)

The prophetic and rabbinic evaluation is clear. Yet I wonder about Jehoshaphat as a model for our fragmented contemporary Jewish world. Is it wrong to forge alliances – thereby generating a sense of national cohesion – if our partner contravenes the Torah? Is it proper to lessen internal friction despite differences in religious orientation? Or were Ahab and his sons so potentially harmful that it was inadvisable in their case? As we shall see in II Kings, the marriage between Jehoshaphat and the house of Omri results in a disastrous descent into idolatry (8:18) and violent political opportunism.[4] There is no doubt that the prophets were alerting the king to genuine problems. Ideologically, however, the question nags us – is this the only legitimate model?[5] When do we overlook religious differences and unite, and when do we act discriminatingly?

Jehoshaphat and Justice

Jehoshaphat's name hints at his commitment to education, law, and *mishpat*, justice. He begins his monarchy with a passion for spreading Torah:

> In the third year of his reign, he sent his officials, Benhail, Obadiah, Zechariah, Nethaneel, and Michaiah, to teach in the cities of Judah; and with them the Levites, Shemaiah, Nethanaiah, Zebadiah, Asahel, Shemiramoth, Jehonathan, Adonijah, Tobijah, and Tobadonijah, the Levites; and with them Elishama and Jehoram, the priests. They taught in Judah, having the book of the law of the Lord with them; and they went throughout all the cities of Judah and taught among the people. (II Chron. 17:7–9)

Furthermore, when he returns from his military campaign with Ahab and is greeted by the prophet, who calls upon him to do *teshuva* – to improve or repair – Jehoshaphat decides to rehabilitate the legal system:

> Jehoshaphat lived in Jerusalem and went out among the people from Beersheba to Mount Ephraim and brought them back to the Lord, the God of their fathers. He appointed judges in the

---

4. See the story of Athaliah, Jezebel's daughter, who kills the entire royal family of Judah (II Kings 8:26, 29; 11:1–16). According to *Midrash Eliyahu Zuta* 3, this tragedy befell Jehoshaphat's family as a result of its association with wicked Ahab and Jezebel.
5. In the past century, confronted by rampant secularization, scholars ranging from Rabbi Abraham I. Kook to the Hazon Ish (Rabbi Avraham Yeshayahu Karelitz) affirmed a readjustment of sanctions against Shabbat desecrators, understanding that these people were far from the traditional heretic or renegade Jew. Is there a difference between a Jew who engages in direct, self-aware, flagrant rebellion against God and those whom we deem victims of circumstance? For further reading, see Jacob J. Schacter, ed., *Tradition and the Non-Traditional Jew* (Northvale, NJ: Jason Aronson, 1992).

land in all the fortified cities of Judah, city by city. He instructed
the judges, "Consider what you are doing, for you judge not for
man but for the Lord, who is with you when you render judgment.
Now let the fear of the Lord be upon you; be very careful what
you do, for the Lord, our God, will have no part in unrighteous-
ness or partiality or the taking of a bribe." And in Jerusalem too,
Jehoshaphat appointed some of the Levites and priests, and some
of the heads of the fathers' households of Israel, for the judgment
of the Lord and to judge disputes…. (19:4–8)

Jehoshaphat's admonition is the basis of an important instruction to
judges:

"Do not fear any man" (Deut. 1:17) – You might say: I am scared
of that man. Perhaps his son will murder me, or he will set my
haystack alight or cut down my orchard? Therefore the Torah
teaches: Do not be afraid of any man, for the law is God's. This
is what Jehoshaphat said: "Consider what you are doing, for you
judge not for man but for the Lord." (*Sifrei, Devarim* 17; *Tosefta,
Sanhedrin* 1:4)

In other words, this king understands that his mission is to spread God's
law. He embarks on a huge undertaking to make justice accessible to
the nation, establishing courts in every locale. He trains and coaches
his judges, fully aware of pitfalls such as intimidation, impartiality, and
bribery, and warning these men that they are answerable to God Himself.
Reading this chapter, one is impressed by Jehoshaphat's God awareness
as he encourages and instructs his judiciary, warning that it is imparting
God's law and that He dwells among His judges.[6]

As noted, Jehoshaphat reflects Solomon in many respects, such
as in his extensive building, regional power, and wealth. But this focus
on justice seems to be Jehoshaphat's greatest parallel with the man
who requested "a listening heart to judge Your people" (1 Kings 3:9).

---

6. See Psalms 82 and Nahmanides on Exodus 24:8, where he deals with the connection
between judges and God.

Solomon's opening story is a difficult courtroom battle; Jehoshaphat establishes an entire network of courts, spreading God's law beyond the confines of Jerusalem. Given his positive responses to the prophets and the fact that, despite his association with Ahab, he resists idolatry, Jehoshaphat stands out as one of the greatest kings of Judah.[7]

---

7. There is some indication of succession struggles between Jehoshaphat's sons at the end of Jehoshaphat's reign; see II Chronicles 21:1-3 and *Daat Mikra* to II Kings 1:17 and 8:16.

In Conclusion

We bring our study of 1 Kings to a close very much in the middle of the story. As noted in our introduction, Kings is a single work, and the division between 1 Kings and 11 is arbitrary and not indigenous to the book. The ending of 1 Kings offers no natural point of closure; the great prophet Elijah remains on the scene, and the dynasty of Ahab still reigns in Samaria. Nevertheless, we will note two themes that develop throughout 1 Kings as an independent unit.

The first is Jewish unity. The story begins with a single kingdom. We have argued that Solomon attempted to strengthen the unity of Israel. However, when social and economic stress heightened, the country fragmented along the familiar fault line of entrenched tribal identities. Following the split, the two kingdoms periodically waged bloody civil wars. Yet in the final chapter of 1 Kings, we witness an alliance between the kingdoms of Israel and Judah, between Ahab and Jehoshaphat, which somewhat unites the divided county. Rabbinic commentary reinforces that prophetic criticism of Jehoshaphat for associating with the sinful house of Omri. Nonetheless, we would be justified in asking when national unity is a worthy goal even at the cost of exposure to problematic agendas and religious cultures.

The second theme relates to the main characters we have encountered in 1 Kings. Most dominant are undoubtedly kings Solomon,

Jeroboam, and Ahab. Each of these personalities is far from simple, torn between loyalty to God and a conflicting attraction.

Solomon's initial years as king reflect his religious purity and earnest pursuit of wisdom. His grand construction of the Temple constitutes both a towering religious achievement and a national milestone. Yet these accomplishments are tainted by his foreign wives, attraction to wealth and luxury, and idolatry. Solomon seems caught between his commitment to God and his universal interests, between humility and excess, failing at the delicate balancing act between his pure allegiance to God and the zeitgeist of imperial grandeur and international engagement.

Jeroboam too is a complex character. Initially designated by prophetic mandate and motivated by social and religious justice, he swiftly becomes haunted by the prospect of losing his national following, leading him to instigate an illicit religious cult. Jeroboam is suspended between the prophet and his own pursuit of political power, between his allegiance to God's law and his self-made sacrificial centers. His commitment becomes entangled by his need to ensure political control.

Ahab similarly believes in the God of Israel, but he also believes that the key to national prosperity and security is his alliance with Phoenicia. Ahab pays a heavy spiritual price, as Israel is overwhelmed by Baal. Elijah depicts the nation as schizophrenic, "wavering between two opinions." Ahab seeks to lead his nation with a dual allegiance, to both God and Baal, but the two are mutually exclusive.

Each of these kings suffers from divided loyalties, finding his religious orientation at variance with his national agenda. Each embodies contradictory objectives, making singular adherence to God's law impossible.

These leaders raise questions for us, as we too find it difficult at times to juggle our Judaism with the competing commitments of life. Whether we are caught between particularism and universalism, or whether life's myriad attractions collide with our religious priorities, these personalities leave us much to think about.

Chronology of Kings of Judah and Israel*

David 1004–965			
Solomon 967–928			
The Kings of Judah (southern kingdom)		The Kings of Israel (northern kingdom)	
Rehoboam	928–911	Jeroboam	928–907
Abijah	911–908	Nadab	907–906
Asa	908–867	Baasha	906–883
Jehoshaphat	870–846	Elah	883–882
Jehoram	851–843	Zimri	882
Ahaziah	843–842	Omri	882–871
Athaliah (queen)	842–836	Ahab	873–852
Joash (Jehoash)	836–798	Ahaziah	852–851
Amaziah	798–769	Jehoram (Joram)	851–842
Azariah (Uzziah)	785–733	Jehu	842–814
Jotham	758–743	Jehoahaz	817–800
Ahaz	743–727	Jehoash (Joash)	800–784
Hezekiah	727–698	Jeroboam II	789–748
Manasseh	698–642	Zechariah	748–747
Amon	641–640	Shallum	747
Josiah	639–609	Menahem	747–737
Jehoahaz	609	Pekahiah	737–735
Jehoiakim	608–598	Pekah	735–733
Jehoiachin	597	Hosea	733–724
Zedekiah	596–586		

---

* Haim Tadmor, ed., *The Biblical Encyclopedia* (Jerusalem: Bialik Institute, 1962), vol. 4, cols. 301–302. All dates are Before the Common Era (BCE).

Haftarot from 1 Kings

Haftara	Torah Portion
1:1–31	Ḥayyei Sara
2:1–12	Vayḥi
3:15–4:1	Miketz
5:36–6:13	Teruma
7:40–50	Vayak'hel
7:51–8:21	Pekudei
8:2–21	second day of Sukkot (outside Israel)
8:54–66	Shemini Atzeret (outside Israel)
18:1–39	Ki Tissa
18:46–19:21	Pineḥas

Study Questions

The following questions are intended to facilitate ḥavruta (paired) study, to clarify the storyline of each chapter and stimulate discussion beyond the raw text. The questions will be best addressed after reading each chapter in its entirety.

CHAPTER 1

1. We find two candidates for the kingship, two coalitions of supporters, and two sites of coronation.
   A. Who are Adonijah's supporters? Who supports Solomon? Are the factions equal? What advantage can each claim? Where is each group?
   B. Note how the text describes a reversal of fortunes: The initially stronger and more organized group loses power and disbands, while the weaker coalition gains power. What is the critical factor in this switchover?
2. How is Adonijah described (1:5–6)? How is Solomon described? (See also 3:7.)
3. Bathsheba speaks of an oath made by David. Have we seen such an oath? See Radak on 1:13.
4. How is Solomon's coronation different from those of Saul (1 Sam. 10) and David (1 Sam. 16)?

CHAPTER 2

1. What are the four parts of David's last testament to Solomon?

2. How old is David when he dies (2:10)?

3. List all the people David mentions (2:5–9). How has each of them behaved toward him? How is Solomon to treat each person? See the following sources:

   Joab – 11 Samuel 3:20–32; 19:9–10

   Barzillai – 11 Samuel 17:27–29; 19:32–40

   Shimei – 11 Samuel 16:5–13; 19:19–24

4. Why, in describing Joab, does David refer to war "in the belt on his thigh and the shoe on his foot" (3:9)?

5. Why is Adonijah's request such a betrayal of the king? See 11 Samuel 16:20–23.

6. "And his kingdom was firmly established" (2:12)/ "And his kingdom was established" (2:46).
   Why is this line restated? Is there any difference in the Hebrew wording?

CHAPTER 3

1. How does the text describe Solomon's marriage to Pharaoh's daughter (3:1)?

2. Why do the people worship God using *bamot* (3:2–3)? See Rashi on Deuteronomy 12:11. Is this worship wrong? See Rashi at the end of 1 Kings 3:3.

3. What does Solomon's request of God tell us about his national priorities?

4. Two women come to Solomon for judgment; the first is called *ha'isha ha'aḥat* (the one woman), while the second is *ha'isha ha'aheret* (the other woman).

   A. Who is telling the truth? Prove it from the text. Do we know at the end of the story which woman was lying?

   B. What does this story tell the people about Solomon? (3:28)

CHAPTER 4

1. Compare the list of Solomon's government with that of David in 11 Samuel 8:16–18 and 20:23–26, and identify the differences between lists.

2. What is the purpose of Solomon's regional districts (4:7)? Is the tribe of Judah included? What does this tell us about Solomon's administration?

CHAPTER 5

1. What geographical markers indicate the extent of Solomon's kingdom? What are we told about the state of the nation?

2. How many horses does Solomon have? Compare 11 Samuel 8:4. Does Solomon require so many horses, such extensive military power? Find his three chariot cities on a map.

3. In how many different spheres is Solomon's wisdom manifest in our chapter? See Rashi on 5:12–13.

4. What is the trade agreement between Hiram and Solomon? What is the destination of all the wood Solomon imports?

5. How does Solomon have enough workers? How long are they away/at home (5:27–28)? Why does he send workers to Lebanon? Didn't Hiram offer his workers (5:23)?

CHAPTER 6–7

Read these chapters and get a sense of the dimensions of the Temple and the materials used in building it.

1. What is the significance of the message in 6:11–13?

2. How do Solomon's *keruvim* (6:23–28) differ from those in Exodus (25:17–22)?

3. In what year of Solomon's reign does the construction of the Temple begin? When is it completed? (6:37–8)

4. What takes thirteen years to build? (17:1)

5. What "halls" are there in Solomon's palace? (7:2–12)

6. What "technology" is described in 7:13–48? (Note the craftsmen [7:13–14] and the mines [7:46].)

7. What are *Yakhin* and *Boaz*, the *yam*, and the *mekhonot*?

CHAPTER 8

1. The first section of this chapter describes the installation of the Ark of the Covenant. Why is this ceremony so critical?
2. What happens once the Ark is installed (8:10–11)? Compare Exodus 40:34–35.
3. If God does not reside in the Temple, then what is its purpose? (8:27–30)
4. What is the role of the non-Jew in Solomon's vision of the Temple? (8:41–43, 60)
5. The Talmud learns from this chapter that we should pray toward Jerusalem. From where do Ḥazal derive this law?
6. At what point in the year does this event take place? (8:3, 65–66)

CHAPTER 9

1. The chapter opens with God's appearing to Solomon; 9:2 refers to the prophecy in chapter 3. Is there a change in tone?
2. What has changed in the trade deal between Solomon and Hiram? Why does Solomon give Hiram land?
3. How is the building tax in chapter 9 different from that in chapter 5? What is the tax used to build? What is the difference between Canaanites and Israelites (9:20–22)?
4. Where does the royal fleet sail? What is the purpose of the voyage? (9:26–28; see also 10:11, 22)

CHAPTER 10

1. With what purpose does the queen of Sheba come to Jerusalem? What impresses her there? Does she attribute Solomon's grandeur to God or Solomon? What does she bring from her land? What does she take home?
2. This chapter describes the kingdom's wealth (10:14–29).
   A. Is the text complimentary of Solomon or critical of him?
   B. How many times is the word *zahav* (gold) used? How many times did it appear in chapter 5?

CHAPTER 11

1. What sins is Solomon guilty of? (11:1–10)
   A. Whose fault is it – his wives or his own? When in his reign do the problems begin?
   B. See the commentaries of Radak and Ralbag, who indicate that Solomon did not actually serve idols. What is the basis of this claim?
2. How does God respond? Why does He state Solomon's punishment and then mitigate it? (11:11–13)
3. Three *satanim* rebel against the king (11:14–28). Describe the biography of each. What trouble do they cause Solomon? Are they a real threat to his kingdom?
4. What is Jeroboam's role in Solomon's government? Why does he oppose Solomon? (11:26–29, 40; see also 9:24).
5. What is the Millo? See commentaries on 9:24.
6. What is the significance of the ripping of the robe (11:30–39)? What is the Hebrew word for "robe" here? How does it relate to Solomon's name? See also another ripped robe in 1 Samuel 15:27–28.

CHAPTER 12

1. At what event does the rebellion actually begin?
2. What do the people request of the king? What does this request tell us about Solomon's era? How does it relate to 11:27?
3. What mistakes does Rehoboam make in relating to the people? What is the cause of these errors?
4. Why does Rehoboam not attack the northern rebels?
5. Jeroboam institutes a new religion for the northern tribes.
   A. What stimulates Jeroboam's new religious practices? List the elements he introduces.
   B. Who are his priests? Why is this important? (See also 13:33.)
   C. Has the kingdom of Jeroboam rejected God?

CHAPTER 13

1. Where does the *ish Elokim* (man of God) come from? Is he a genuine prophet? How do we know?
   Whom does he address? Why does he make his pronouncement at this time and place? What effect might he have had? What restrictions govern his mission? Why?

2. What word is used to describe the breaking of the altar in Bethel? Why is this word significant? (See 11:30–31.)

3. How does Jeroboam react? Does he accept the word of God or try to reject it? Why does he invite this (enemy) prophet home (13:10)?

4. Why must the prophet go home a different way than he came?

5. Who is the elderly prophet (13:11–20)? Is he genuine? How do we know? Why does he lie to lure the *ish Elokim* to return to Bethel with him? See Rashi.

6. What is the effect of this man's death? Does it corroborate the prophecy against Jeroboam or delegitimize it? (13:21–26)

7. Why does the elderly prophet wish to be buried alongside the *ish Elokim* (13:27–32)? See II Kings 23:17–18.

8. How does this incident affect Jeroboam? Why is his "reaction" placed at the end of the chapter (13:33–34) instead of in verse 11?

9. What is the message of this chapter?

CHAPTER 14

1. Why does Jeroboam send his wife to Ahijah? Why must she disguise herself?

2. What does the prophet tell her? What is the sign that the prophecy will come true? What punishment awaits the following people?
   A. Jeroboam
   B. His son
   C. The nation

3. Using the information in this chapter, assess Rehoboam's monarchy:
   A. religiously
   B. internationally (what happened in the fifth year of his reign?)
   C. in its interaction with the northern kingdom

4. See II Chronicles 12 for more details about Rehoboam, and compare and contrast with the account in Kings.

CHAPTERS 15–16

1. Assess Abijam's monarchy:
   A. religiously
   B. in its interaction with the northern kingdom
2. See II Chronicles 13 for more details about Abijah/Abijam and a very different perspective.
3. What can we say about Asa religiously?
4. Asa battles Baasha, king of Israel. What is the conflict about? How does Asa resolve this "international incident"? (See the parallel in II Chronicles 15–17.)
5. List the kings who succeed Jeroboam (15:25–16:28).
   A. How many rebellions are there? What does this tell us about the stability of the northern kingdom? Why is it like this?
   B. Does Israel experience a religious revival, as Judah has under Asa?
6. How does Omri ascend the throne? Who supports his choice as king? What does Omri build?
   Why is he worse than his predecessors?
7. How long is Ahab's reign? Whom does he marry? What is his religious orientation? How is he assessed here? (16:29–33)
8. Why is the story in 16:34 related here? See the commentaries.

CHAPTER 17

1. What statement does Elijah utter at the start of the chapter? Does God command him to say it?
2. The chapter includes three stories about Elijah and his survival during the three years of famine. How do these three stories form a progression?
3. How does Elijah address the woman in Zarephath, and how does he address God?
4. What is the objective of this collection of stories?

CHAPTER 18

1. What does God instruct Elijah in 18:1?
2. Who is Obadiah? What do we hear about him? What does Elijah ask him to do? Why?
3. According to Ahab, who is responsible for the famine? According to Elijah, who is responsible?
4. What accusation does Elijah level at the people? (18:21)
5. How does Elijah choreograph the events on Mount Carmel to maximum effect? How does he induce the people to be increasingly active and vocal in the course of the day? (18:22–40)
6. What is Elijah demonstrating by repairing the broken altar with twelve stones (18:31)? Why is it broken?
7. What does Elijah do to the prophets of Baal? (18:41)
8. What is the objective of the segment of the story in 18:40–45?

CHAPTER 19

1. Identify parallels to Moses in the stories of Elijah.
2. Why does Elijah seek to end his life?
3. Explain the conversation at Mount Horeb. Why does Elijah repeat himself? (19:10, 14)
4. What three tasks does God give Elijah? (19:15–16)
5. Elijah meets Elisha. What is Elisha's background? Is he rich or poor? He returns and makes a feast for his community as Elijah waits for him. What does this scene say about the contrast between the two men?

CHAPTER 20

1. How many kings join Ben-Hadad, king of Aram?
2. Why does Ahab accept his offer the first time but reject it the second time? What has changed?
3. How does Ahab defeat the enemy? Is it a miracle?
4. Note the central role of the prophet throughout this chapter. Where are the Baal prophets? Has Ahab changed?
5. Why does God save Ahab? (20:23, 28)
6. What is the reputation of Jewish kings? (20:31)

7. Why is God angry with Ahab at the end of the chapter? What should he have done? Why?

CHAPTER 21

1. Why does Naboth refuse Ahab's request?
2. How does the king react to this refusal? Does he intend to take things further? What changes the situation?
3. How does Jezebel kill Naboth? Why is the plan so elaborate? Does the king know about it? If not, why is he responsible?
4. Where does Elijah confront Ahab? Why? What is the result of their first exchange? When does Ahab begin to react?
5. Does Ahab repent? Can an evil person be forgiven? See 22:35–38. Is the king punished for his sins?

CHAPTER 22

1. Who is Ahab's ally in this war? Why do they go to war?
2. Who are Ahab's prophets? Why does Jehoshaphat suspect them? Don't they use God's name?
3. Why does the prophet use iron horns? What do they signify?
4. What does Micaiah predict? What qualities does the prophet exhibit in this encounter?
5. What happens to Ahab in the battle? How do we know it is God's doing?
6. Assess Jehoshaphat's reign (22:41–51):
   A. religiously
   B. economically
   C. politically
   D. in its relations with the northern kingdom
7. What is the strange incident described in 22:48–50? See the commentaries.
8. Read the expanded story of Jehoshaphat in II Chronicles 19. How might Jehoshaphat have gotten his name?

Index of Biblical and Rabbinic Sources

General Index

A

Abiathar, 19–20, 32–37, 214
Abishag, 16–19, 23–24, 32–35
Abner
    murder of, 31, 38–44
    and Saul's concubine, 34
Adonijah, 15–22, 32–35
    and Absalom, 18–19, 251n
Ahab, 226–320
    and Ben–Hadad, 273–287,
    and Elijah, 226–7, 231–2, 241, 251–
        252, 256, 259
    faith, 273–274, 276n, 279–230, 319–
        320
    and Jezebel, 220–221, 260–262, 272–
        274, 293–299, 309–310, 320
    murder of Naboth, 289–301, 306–
        309
    name, 281n
    repentance, 304–309
Ahijah, the Shilonite 13, 148, 163, 181–187

altar
    to Baal, 221,
    at Bethel, 171–173
    escape to the altar, sanctuary, 16,
        45–46
    Gibeon, 51–45
    Mt. Carmel, 248–249,268n
    sacrifice on local altars (*bamot*),
        51–53, 162, 168, 195
Amasa, 42
Ark of the Covenant, 27, 36–37, 45n,
    53–54, 83–84, 93, 99
Asa, King, 7, 197–207

B

Baal, 166–167, 174, 220–224, 235, 246–7
    prophets of, 241–251, 259–260, 273–
        274n, 310, 314n
    theology, 223–224
Baasha, 186, 198–199, 203–215
Bathsheba 15, 20–27, 33–35

The fonts used in this book are from the Arno family

Maggid Books
The best of contemporary Jewish thought from
Koren Publishers Jerusalem